AF564694

ACADEMIC ACHIEVEMENT AND ITS INFLUENCING FACTORS

ACADEMIC ACHIEVEMENT AND ITS INFLUENCING FACTORS

By

Dr. D. Sivakumar

Associate Professor in Education
Dr. Sivanthi Aditanar College of Education
Tiruchendur, Tamil Nadu
(India)

DISCOVERY PUBLISHING HOUSE PVT. LTD.
NEW DELHI-110 002

Published by:
Tilak Wasan
DISCOVERY PUBLISHING HOUSE PVT. LTD.
4383/4B, Ansari Road, Darya Ganj
New Delhi-110 002 (India)
Phone : +91-11-23279245, 43596064-65
Fax : +91-11-23253475
E-mail : discoverypublishinghouse@gmail.com
sales@discoverypublishinggroup.com
parul.wasan@gmail.com
web : www.discoverypublishinggroup.com

***First Edition:* 2013**

ISBN: 978-93-5056-232-1

Academic Achievement and Its Influencing Factors

© 2013, Author

All rights reserved. No part of this publication should be reproduced, stored in a retrieval system, or transmitted in any form or by any means: electronic, mechanical, photocopying, recording or otherwise, without the prior written permission of the author and the publisher.

This book has been published in good faith that the material provided by authors is original. Every effort is made to ensure accuracy of material, but the publisher and printer will not be held responsible for any inadvertent error(s). In case of any dispute, all legal matters are to be settled under Delhi jurisdiction only.

Printed at:
Aditi Fine Art Press
Delhi

Dedicated to
My Teachers, Parents,
Friends and
My Wife

Preface

The destiny of India is being shaped in the classroom. In a world based on science and technology, it is education that determines the level and prosperity, welfare and security of the people. According to Radhakrishnan (1956) the aim of education is the development of an integrated personality of the individual. A truly educated person is cultured and fearless and has a scientific attitude. The enlightened citizen is the most valuable asset of a democratic society. Biology forms an important part of the syllabus of life science. It is the compulsory subject for the higher secondary school examination. A biology student is engaged in a human activity that is directed towards seeking new knowledge about living things. A student tries to acquire new concepts of biology through practicing science or passing through the process of biology. India shall need specialists in the fields of medicine, health, agriculture, animal husbandry, etc. The talent in these fields shall come from biology. It is for these reasons that this subject has become so popular in our secondary schools and is taught as a compulsory subject in secondary schools.

Higher secondary school students belong to the adolescent stage of development. Adolescence is a period of concomitant growth. It is the formal operational stage of development (Piaget, 1952). They think in abstract terms, follow the logical propositions and form hypothesis. They can isolate the elements of a problem and systematically explore all possible solutions to problems. It is essentially a period of rapid development and transition and is full of complexities. Academic failure may lead to frustration and poor adjustment. They are emotionally disturbed and develop an unhealthy attitude towards life. The sense of failure complex which in turn may lead to a retreat into non communicative fantasy or overt misbehavior. Maximizing achievement scores is one of the goals of education. A large number of investigators had made efforts to study the determinants of academic achievement. As Carrel (1943) points out "the bond between intelligence and academic achievement appears to be smaller than is usually assumed". According the Weinner (1972) intelligence accounts for only 25% of the observed variance in grades. Hence, it follows that the remaining 75% of the variance is due to non intellectual factors. Taylor (1956) has pointed out the importance of personality factors on achievement.

Environment is such a powerful factor that it influences the development of child consciously or unconsciously or both. One cannot escape its influence at any cost. The environmentalist holds that as the child gradually comes into contact with the physical and social environments, his/her innate tendencies. Lower out and behavior begins to change step by step. In this sense, it is the environment which makes a child musician or artist and not the heredity. Thus according to environmentalist, education is a process based on and conditioned by the environment in which the child is brought up. Students, no doubt, have been blessed with intelligence but the reason, why they do not fare well, in academics, is due to the fact that, they are exposed to a lot of problems and setbacks, related to their families, school, health, finance, environment, sex, religion, social and personal relationship, etc.

Even a good student, who has the potentiality to achieve better, may not be able to achieve as per expectations if he/she fails to do proper management of time, allocation of weight age to various subject preparing notes and individual modes adopted for preparation of different subjects .In other words, habits and practices are relevant factors in determining the achievement of an individual.

Self-esteem tends to be fairly resistant to change once it is established. Individuals who have little self-esteem are afraid to let down their guard. Convinced that they are inadequate, the individuals with very little self-esteem are likely to be maladjusted. Those with good self-esteem have a capacity that will affect their adult live, the capacity to give and receive love. If the higher secondary results are observed, there is very less number of centum scorers in biology. This has been the result for the past ten years of higher secondary examination of Tamil Nadu. In order to have good academic achievement, one should have good study habits, social environment and self esteem.

Higher secondary education plays a very significant role in every individual life since after this education all decisions are made for the future. Students need proper guidance for the management of their time and efforts for better prospects. The study habits individually cultivated by them are likely to determine the level of their success. High self-esteem quickens the work, while low self-esteem slowed down the work leads to low motivation, and inhibits the capacity of human beings to care for themselves, Hence a growing number of people in society no longer have sufficient energy power or means of self reliance (mentally or physically) and have to rely on state provision. So, there is lack of self respect and a lack of respect for others. It leads to discrimination and poverty.

In addition to routine class room academic activities, all faculty students should be encouraged to explore themselves in order to gain self esteem. The teachers, parents and the society should encourage students to entrance their self esteem.

Abdul Kalam A.P.J. had expressed that the youth had to develop aspiration and aspiration leads to achievement. This research, in this regard will help the students to lead a better achievement.

Dr. Pawan Kumar 'Bharti'

Contents

1

Introduction and Conceptual Framework

Introduction

"Moments make minutes, Minutes make Hours,
Hours make days, Days make weeks,
Weeks make months, Months make years, Years make life".

Yet one has every moment of live life. Modern Science has acted as a springboard for the progress of mankind and enables us to conquer time, distance and many more things. It has improved the conditions and quality of life.

Life is experience, Experience is education. Education is enlightenment;
Enlightenment is truth. Truth is wisdom and wisdom is God.

—*Vedic Wisdom*

In the present world of science and technology, the education has to determine the levels of well-being and prosperity of the people. Education is considered to be one of the most powerful agencies in moulding the character and in determining the future of individuals. Education is regarded as the potential instrument of social transformation and an important means of national development. Education is a service commodity, which involves the process of acquisition to attain knowledge, skills and attitudes, which are essential for achieving success in one's life.

Education leads individual from darkness into light and from falsehood to truth. It brings about considerable changes in the individual relating to his/her physical intellectual and spiritual conditions. Education, thus, is concerned with bringing about changes in the three-board domain of the individual, normally cognitive, affective and psychomotor.

Education today has become a powerful tool for the development of the society. Education is considered as an instrument for social changes resulting in industrialization, urbanization and social enlistment. Many people believe that education solves many of the individual and social problems, resulting in individual and social disorganization and disintegration. The main question is whether education can solve the social problems generating from social process. The educators believe that education should also take this added function within its purview.

The modern school is a community centered and teacher is a friend, philosopher and guide. The school is a miniature society or a social constitution, which is entrusted with the responsibility of bringing up the students to participate effectively, efficiently and harmoniously in the community to which they belong. The modern school is not a knowledge shop and the learning experience should not be limited to four walls of the classroom. The school should provide various opportunities to the students for participating in social services, community activities and health campaigns literacy derives and other kinds of public service of educational importance. This will break the barriers between the school and the community and make school life and experiences meaningful lively, realistic and natural. (Mohanty 1991).

Importance of Education

The Kothari Commission (1964-1966) pointed out, "The destiny of India is being shaped in the classroom". It is the education that determines country's level of prosperity, welfare and security of people. Realizing this fact, the Government of India has been spending large sum of money on education; no investment is likely to yield greater returns than investment of human resources of which the most important component is education.

The National Policy on Education (1986) emphasizes the need for a National System of Education to promote its unique Socio-cultural identity and to meet the challenges of times and education for equality. The National system of Education represents common educational structure throughout the country and national curricular frame work with common core components of national significance. Laik (1994) States "The contemporary system of education has become mechanical as it stuffs the young minds with dry information leaving little scope for thinking. The present system of education needs to be revamped and stimulated with a spirit of scientific thinking in teaching and learning process". (Suresh Bhatnagar, 1990)

Education is the process by which people acquire knowledge, skills, habits, values or attitudes. It is a human endeavour and modification of human behaviour and knowledge prepares men and women to serve as true citizens of a country. The country depends very much upon the educational system of that country and it prepares the pupils who become the citizens of tomorrow.

Education is a process of adjustment of the individual to adjust himself/herself to the world of nature, the world of human being and the world of value. It also exercises influence on ones' vocation, home life, friendship, marriage, travel, recreation and hobbies and tells upon his/her personality. There has been a constant quest to determine the basic issues of education. Various philosophers and educators have attempted to define the term "education". 'The scholars from Socrates and Plato to Dewey and Mahatma Gandhi have expressed divergent views'. (Mohanty, 1991).

The primary meaning of education appears to be "bringing up", leading out' or making manifest and explicit the potentialities in a child. That is Education means bringing out of the idea of universal validity which are latent in the minds of man. (Chaube, 1999).

Education should help to discover lasting values so that pupil does not merely cling to formulate or repeat slogans; it should help them to break down their national and social barriers, instead of emphasizing for they bread antagonism between man and man. Thus "Education should awaken the capacity to be self-aware and merely indulge in gratifying. That education is given in five different levels in India such as primary, upper primary, secondary, Higher secondary and tertiary i.e. higher education.

Objectives of Higher Secondary Education

The objectives of secondary Education as proposed by higher secondary Education Commission involve the full and all-round development of every individual's personality. According to Patel committee, the objective of secondary education is "acquisition of the skills and habits of self-training, broad-based general education, develop aesthetic appreciation and creativity through participation in artistic activities". (Quoted by Bhatia, Ahuja, 1993, P. 109).

According to Edmonson et al. (1953), "The duty of the higher secondary school is to provide experiences and information that will lead to the fullest development of students as individuals, both in their adolescent years and in adult life. Before this can be accomplished, those in charge of the institution must determine as accurately as possible the present and probable future needs of students. These needs should be translated into the significant general aims and more toward performance of these functions and attainment of these aims. By encouraging the maximum development of its students, the schools contribute to the welfare and progress of Society through improving the quality of participation in social situations" (P.27).

The Commission on 'Life Adjustment Education' in 1947 by the federal government has laid down the objectives of higher secondary education as successful citizenship, training the young man in day-to-day life requirements, making worthy members of the family, to be able to understand the basic rules of learning, to prepare for a vocation, to be able to make worthy use of leisure, to develop spirit of appreciation of beauty, to understand the significance and method of science to developmental health and physical fitness and good moral and ethical development (Edmonson et, al., 1953, P.39).

Judd et, al., (1942) pointed out that the objective of higher secondary education should be to provide such general education as to equip the students with basic knowledge in all subjects and skills in some fields to enable them to pursue a life of their own, the knowledge and skills for the student to pursue higher academic or technical courses. Thus, higher secondary education should be both terminal and continuing (P.S). Science is one among the different subjects offered at higher secondary level.

Science Education

Sharma R.C. (1991) in his book "Modern Science Teaching" has noted Jawaharlal Nehru's remark that the progress of any nation depends upon scientific knowledge and a population that knows how to apply it in life. This is very true because science and its application have pervaded every sphere of life.

"Education is an integral indispensable part of the scientific enterprise". For example, although every body learned how the nutritional deficiency disease kwashiorkor can be prevented, the problem is not solved as long as large numbers of people are not aware of this knowledge or of how to use it. This is largely an educational task. Similarly, scientist or engineer, who does not educate himself and others, is threatened with obsolescence. Without continuing education, one may find out of the mainstream of the field and floating in a stagnant pool going nowhere.

(a) Emerging Trends in Science Education

(*i*) Establishment of state institution of science education: Separate institutions of science education are being established in a number of countries. These institutes are responsible for curriculum development in science and also for planning and implementing science education in schools.

(*ii*) Development of Indigenous curriculum: There is progressive shift towards development of indigenous science curriculum based on the past experience of the country and suitable to the needs and requirements of the children and the country.

(*iii*) Emphasis on conceptual learning: Although the traditional approach to teaching science as a body of facts is still prevalent, there is a shift in some countries from factual to conceptual understanding of science.

(*iv*) Integrated science: There is a trend towards unified or integrated approach to the organization of content within various branches of science especially at the primary level. In some countries there have been attempts to integrate science with social studies and humanities.

(*v*) Development of de-centralized curriculum: There is a greater realization of the importance of decentralizing the development and implementation of curriculum attempts are being made to decentralize the development of curriculum materials relating to certain topics while retaining a core of other topics development at the central level.

(*vi*) Pupil-centered teaching: There is increasingly greater recognition of providing first hand experience to the pupils and seeking their active involvement in the learning process through discovery and inquiry approach.

(*vii*) Self-learning materials: In addition to the traditional instructional materials new multi – media learning packages are being developed. They include self-learning kits, modules, programmed materials, etc.

(*viii*) Low-cost science materials: Many developing countries have established centers for designing and developing equipment suited to local conditions and using local raw materials. There is an emphasis on developing low cost science materials rather than buying expensive and sophisticated equipment.

(b) Importance of Science in the School Curriculum

One has to live in a scientific civilization whether he/she likes it or not. Science is no longer confined to a few seriously devoted persons. Since living in the present world invariably warrants, to variable degrees, knowledge of scientific facts and laws. Science has now become everyday science for everybody. Teaching of everyday science for everybody has become an unavoidable part of general education. Nobody questions its inclusion as a subject in the school curriculum. It is included in a school's curriculum for the same reasons as any other subject. But in addition, science inculcates certain special values peculiar to it and which no other subject can provide. It is a part of liberal education. But besides satisfying the usual needs for its inclusion as a subject in the curriculum-such as intellectual, cultural, moral, aesthetic, utilitarian as well as vocational values, science learning provides training in science method and also helps to develop a scientific attitude of mind in the learner. The qualities imbibed by the learner through learning science are valuable for a citizen living in the society. The teaching of science in schools in India was conspicuously deplorable still after 1953 when the Secondary Education Commission, popularly known as the Mudaliar Commission (1952-53) recommended teaching of general science as compulsory subject at the secondary school stage.

Science has now become a compulsory subject in the school curriculum because of its multifarious value to the individual as well as the society. Some of the Values are intellectual, utilitarian, vocational, cultural, moral, aesthetic, psychological, training in the scientific method and inculcation of scientific attitude.

(c) What is Biology?

The word "Biology" comes from the Greek word.' Bios' means "life" 'logus' means "science". The word biology is the knowledge of living things. The term biology applies to the two sciences of zoology and botany, the study of animals and plants." biology arose out of man's curiosity about himself and other living things". Some of the major branches of biological science are earth science, biotechnology, biochemistry, molecular biology, genetics, microbiology, bacteriology and marine biology.

(d) Place of Biology in School Curriculum

In primary schools biology forms a part of general science course or it is taught as environmental science or as natural history. Even when biology exists as a separate subject, there is increasing awareness of its relative importance with consequent increase in time allotted to it. More time has to be allotted to biology because it is a time consuming subject. In most of the countries, biology is a compulsory subject at primary school stage and sometimes even upto high school stage. In higher classes, biology is given about 6 periods a week. In school system where biology is available as an elective subject about 80% students opt for it. It is the most popular of the sciences and continues to grow in popularity relative to other subjects in the curriculum. Realizing the need of science Kothari Commission (1964-66) has very rightly remarked in its recommendation as follows:

"We lay great emphasis on making science an important element in school curriculum. We, therefore, recommend that science and mathematics should be taught on a compulsory basis to all pupils as a part of general education during the first ten years of schooling"-(Education Commission-1994-66). It is in this spirit that science incorporating physical as well as biological sciences has been made a compulsory subject in the school curriculum up to ten years of schooling.

(e) Nature and Scope of Biology

A biology student is engaged in a human activity that is directed towards seeking new knowledge about living things. A student tries to acquire new concepts of biology or science. It is easy to recall that biology has emerged a bit late through schools were teaching hygiene and human physiology for a long time which were later on replaced by botany and zoology. At the turn of the last century, the separate courses of botany, zoology and human physiology were unified into a course known as biology.

In last twenty years, the situation has changed drastically. Not only has the content of biology been brought up to date in the schools but the teaching approach has also been changed from taxonomic to inquiry approach. Today it is not sufficient to teach cell or tissue. It needs teaching of DNA and the process, which helps in its replications. Today, biology need not be a simple grouping of phenomena for the same of description, classification and correlation. Biology students are no longer concerned with memorization of facts alone. They are interested in relating facts to the understanding of a given process. A problem-solving attitude prevails among the students.

(f) Major Thrust Areas in Biological Sciences

Some of the major thrust areas in biological sciences at the present juncture may be named as molecular biology, genetic engineering, bio-remediation, bio-medical, metabolic engineering, space biology, bio-diversity, bio-informatics, industrial bio-technology, industrial micro-biology, environmental bio-technology, environmental resource management, gene therapy and genetic counseling, herbal products of pharmeutical value, nutritional quality improvement, industrial bio-chemistry, plants genetics, storage and conservation of food, health care, erosion and pollution control, use of fertilizers, population control and maintenance of ecological balance.

(g) Educational Role of Biology

The relative popularity of biology reflects a changing emphasis in the philosophy of curriculum. In past, more importance was given to the descriptive and taxonomic subject matters in teaching of biology but now-a-days more emphasis is laid on the concept of evolution and the history of life on earth. Since, evolution now is considered more of a law than theory, more emphasis is laid on teaching of mechanism of evolution than that on the details of structure and taxonomy. The outdated and imbalance content has been replaced by modern discoveries in the fields of cell biology, basic genetics, bio engineering and bio technology. Newer areas such as ecology, demography and population genetics give meaning to studies of diversity and evolution. School biology is seen as performing a social role. In some countries, emphasis is on overcoming alcoholism, drug abuse, obesity and other counter productive social needs. It also helps in programmes of family planning, health and nutrition, agricultural policies and the utilization of natural resources.

(h) Biology Education in Indian Schools

In 1964, UNESCO Report on science teaching in secondary schools of India was submitted, which presented a comprehensive report on the teaching of physics, chemistry and biology. It reflected the poor conditions of biology textbooks and laboratories. In the light of the availability of highly technical facilities and every increasing interdependence of biology, chemistry and physics, the UNESCO team gave the following suggestions to improve biology education at the school level.

(*i*) Fundamentals of biology should be compulsory as a part of general education for all irrespective of one's future vocation.

(*ii*) In the syllabus, attention should be paid to the studies of cell, life activity and individual development of organism.

(*iii*) Achievements of modern biology for practical purposes should be emphasized.

(*iv*) Knowledge of biology should stimulate working out of basic sanitary-Hygienic experiences for pupils.

(*v*) Methods in the study of biological sciences should emphasize sufficiently observation and experimentation.

The NCERT has developed biology textbooks that reflect the spirit of Biological Science Curriculum Study (BSCS) project materials and also distributed and published BSCS materials. The biology courses at both the secondary and higher secondary stages are rich in content and include environmental aspect and the biology teacher is prepared both in content and teaching methodology.

(i) Teaching of Biology

The main aim of teaching is to bring about socially desirable behaviour changes in the students and this can only be achieved if the teaching is effective and based on the principles of teaching. The teaching of biology should be an essential part of course in general education. The leaner's should be encouraged to think reason and to draw inferences from what they observe. For proper teaching of this subject schools should possess a small aquarium, a vivarium and garden plants, pot-plants, caged birds, insects and botanical specimens which are quite helpful for the school garden. The teacher should illustrate with experiments and encourage pupils to perform simple experiments themselves. Excursion to the countryside, local garden parks, nursery, museum and the zoo must be encouraged to provide students and opportunity for getting first hand information.

(j) Recent Trends in Teaching of Biology

Life sciences or biology, the study of living things, gets new knowledge added to the existing one by observation, experimentation, collection of data, analysis, interpretation, etc. The goal must help the students lead more meaningful, satisfying and responsible lives, both personally and socially. Modern biologists accept that there are five characteristics of living system, which should be taken as a basis for teaching and learning of biology.

It will be possible to teach biology by providing an opportunity to students to carryout short investigations for themselves and also study methodology of experimental research. Thus, students will be able to learn both concepts and the processes. Relevant literature highlights the following trends in biology education.

(*i*) Biology education should be helpful in preparing students to utilize their knowledge for improving their personal lives.

(*ii*) Biology education should produce informed citizens for copying with the science and technology oriented would deal with the biology related social problems.

(*iii*) Biology education should prepare students for academic pursuits appropriate for their needs.

(*iv*) The content of the biology syllabus should be selected for its utility in improving the quality of the individual and social effectiveness.

(*v*) Biology courses should be more interdisciplinary or multidisciplinary.

(*vi*) A biology teacher should possess all teaching competencies and should have a humanistic outlook.

A study of life sciences is useful in becoming aware of the biosocial problems and to acquire decision-making abilities.

(k) Role of the Biology Teacher

Secondary Education Commission (1953), in its report, says: "We are convinced that the most important factor in the contemplated educational reconstruction is the teacher, his personal qualities, his educational qualifications, his professional training and the place he occupies in the school as well as in the community .The reputation of a school and its influence on the life of the community invariably depend on the kind of teachers working on it."

From the above quotation, the major role can be played by the biology teacher in developing scientific attitudes among his students and that he can do by manipulating various situations that infuse among the pupils certain characteristics of scientific attitudes. In the classroom and laboratory the teacher uses the best knowledge acquisition process. A good biology teacher makes use of instructional material and audio-visual aids and also prepares it. An ideal teacher provides useful instructions to the students. He/she takes part in all the instructional activities and keeps all information of help opportunities and also appraises the students about them.

The teacher selects important principles and facts from the entire syllabus and presents it in front of the students in a collective manner. Using appropriate method, he/she is familiar with the latest technique of evaluation to evaluate his/her students correctly. He/she is fully competent in selecting biological apparatus and making proper use of it. The biology teacher makes his teaching successfully by knowledge acquisition process by obtaining complete knowledge of personal needs, understanding capacity and problems of the students. He/she has to an expert in organizing exhibition, science fair and other activities for the people of school and community. The practical examples given by the teacher leaves an indelible mark on the personality of the students.

In order to cater to the needs of the heterogeneous group a teacher has to adopt several methods and techniques. The knowledge of the psychological traits is helpful to the teachers to know about the needs of the students and to succeed in their teaching process. They should also know that many factors are influenced in the learning process likely

(1) Environment (2) Study habits (3) Self esteem, etc.

Environment

Environment is a general term designating all the subjects, forces and conditions that affect the individual through such stimuli as he/she is able to receive (Halsey, 1962). The learning environment refers to the background of a pupil, which means his home environment and school background.

Environment is a powerful factor, which influences the development of a child. Every child is born in a family at a particular place and time in a specific environment .This environment, either controlled or uncontrolled, exerts its influence upon the growing child in different ways. Influence of the environment on personality can roughly be divided into that at home and school. The elements of both school environment and home environment have a strong and direct impact on the academic achievement of students.

"Be careful the environment you choose for it will shape you; be careful the friends you choose for you will become like them".

According to (Resnick, 1987) environments may be divided in the six kinds

(*i*) Communication environment, where learners participate in the discourse by actively constructing goals, problems, meanings and information.

(*ii*) Information transmission environments, where learners participate by receiving information.

(*iii*) Problem solving environments, where learners work on projects and problems.

(*iv*) Training environments where learners practice exercises to improve specific skills and knowledge.

(*v*) Evaluative performance environments, where learners perform for an audience.

(*vi*) Recitation and testing environments, where learners demonstrate their ability to work

(a) Factors of Learning Environment

All children are not brought up in similar environment and hence the effect of learning on the child differs according to the learning experiences provided in different environments.

A proper and adequate environment is very much essential for the fruitful learning of the child. Especially, the home and the school should provide the necessary stimulus for learning. Environment stands for all those circumstances which are asserting their influences on the individual since birth to death. Learning takes place effectively only when congenial environment is provided for children in class room, school, home and the societies, which are the parts of the child's learning environment.

The learning environment is an important determinant of success in any educational system. In the present investigation, the factors of learning environment considered are divided by internal and external factors.

(i) Internal Factors

Internal factors are also called subjective factors influence in learning. There are six internal factors involved during the learning period.

Age: Age can influence upon the capability of learning, a child can not learn the things what elders can learn and an aged person will have difficulty to learn modern ways of knowledge.

Intelligence: Intelligence effects very much on learning. If subject / individual has maximum level of intelligence he/she can learn more and easily at maximum level.

Attention: Attention is also very important factor which influences on learning. If a person does not pay attention towards how to learn a specific knowledge, skill or experience, he/she can not learn easily but if the individual pays attention the results are vice versa.

Interest: Subject may here intelligence and can also pay attention towards learning. But if he/she does not have interest in how to learn a specific knowledge, skill or experience, his/her level or process of learning would be very slow.

Mental and physical health: Learning also depends upon mental and physical health of the individual or subject. If an individual does not have mental health or physical one, the subject can fulfill the demands of the process of learning due to his/her weak mental and physical capabilities.

Fatigue: If an individual is tired, he/she cannot pay full attention towards learning something.

(ii) External Factors

There are six external factors are involved during the learning period.

Nature of knowledge: If knowledge is interesting in nature, any individual can learn it more efficiently.

Recitation: Recitation is more effective tools of learning. If an individual recite something louder, he/she can learn more effectively.

Meaningfulness: If the material of knowledge is meaningful, the individual will learn it more effectively and easily. Meaningless material neither can be learnt easily nor kept in memory on long term basis.

Exercise of repetition: Single act is learnt in single trial but complex acts require repeated trails. If a material is difficult to learn, it can be learnt through exercises or repeated trails.

By parts learning: If the material is so long it can be divided into small parts, so individual can learn specific knowledge, skill etc more effectively.

Reward and punishment: The presence or absence of reward can affect learning, generally reward is more effective in promoting learning than is punishment, the latter does have some effects on learning, it tends to repress a desired response than to extinguish it.

(iii) Some other factors

Some other factors are directly influencing the learning period. They are home environment, school environment and social environment

(*a*) Home Environment: If refers to the environment existing in home, which includes the atmosphere created by parents, siblings and other family members. Burgers and Lock defined family as a group of persons united by the ties of marriage, blood or adoption, constituting a single house hold interactions and inter communications with each other in their respective social role of husband and wife, mother and father, brother and sisters creating a common culture.

During the last hundred years, great changes have taken place in the family as an educational agency. Multifarious scientific inventions have changed the needs of living of even an ordinary person. As a result, the responsibilities of the family are being gradually reduced. However, there is no other institution except the family to provide emotional and social security to children, so the need to protect family as an institution in the interest of our children.

Home is said to be the first school of the child and home environment is one of the most potential factors which influences a Childs' achievement (Jain, 1965: Tandon, 1978: Jaganathan, 1986) and it develops various abilities in children (Frasser, 1959).Children coming from high home environment achieve better in schools than their counterparts coming from low home environment (Misra, 1960).

Family: Family is the oldest, basic and fundamental unit of human society .It may be regarded as a small social group united by the ties of marriage, blood or adoption (Clare, 1943). The family carries the responsibility for the welfare of its members from cradle to grave (Coleman, 1965) and it serves as a bridge between the child and the world outside. Two children may attend the same school, may come under the influence of the same teachers and the same course of study and yet may differ in their learning readiness and academic achievement may me due to their family. (Harson and Robinson, 1967).

Parents: Parents have been performing the role of the teacher, though the nature of this role has been changing in response to the needs that varies individually from one child to another. Parents education, personality characteristic, emotional and social behavior, mutual affection, love and quarrels, their interest and attitudes and general character etc. (Dave and Dave, 1971: Tiwari, 1981) Parents are responsible for developing disciplined behavior and creative thinking in their child from very early childhood. Parents with sound ethical values will be effective role models for their children. A Child's personality development is determined by the way in which his/her parents especially his/her mother interact with him/her and how he/she perceives these interactions (Winch and Machinnis, 1959) Parents also play a very important role of counselor or guide to their children and most often do an excellent job because they are readily available for guidance.

Educative influence of home: Chronologically and psychologically, home starts the child off into life and its experiences. It is the original and basic source of informal and incidental learning which sale sequentially limits and slants the individuals' quality and rate of progress on different chosen fronts the overall influence of home itself through affection, care and attention which are diffused and displayed in different ways, on an appropriate scale of frequency and intensity.

Home environment refers to the psycho-social environment of family in which the child is brought up. Home provides an excellent opportunity for socialization, by laying the foundation for physical, mental and social health of the child. All families do not have uniform culture and standards of life, so they differ in the ways of meeting the physical, emotional, psychological and mental needs of the children.

Effect of environmental influences start from the pre-natal stage of the child. Hence the homes are the most important ingredients in the process of growth and development. This social institution develops the finest and most vital qualities in cognitive, affective and psychomotor fields in the Childs' formative periods. The foundation of education is laid in the home and the school and teachers simply work on it.

Family means the Child's basic needs for affection and protection. It is on the lap of family, a newly born learns the language of nature and his/her environment. The scholastic achievement of an individual is often attributed to one's scholastic home environment than to innate mental potentialities. The factors like psychological condition of the family, social status, economic status, interpersonal relationship of family members and family discipline are some of the factors, which influence educational attainment.

The home environment teaches many things to the child both consciously and unconsciously i.e. mutual respect, adjustment, tolerance, love for weak, suffering and self-confidence, etc. The home should provide facilities and varieties of stimulating experiences through warm emotions which foster academic achievement of pupils.

(*b*) School Environment: It plays an important role in the development of positive attitudes. School environment should provide feelings of security in every student irrespective of their religion or socio-economic conditions. It should be free from caste, creed or religious feelings. It should provide conducing environment for learning, free from fear, tension and frustration.

The needs of adolescents should be given proper place in the school curriculum. Good libraries, opportunities for the discussion and community service help in the proper development of the mental abilities of the child. Meeting the needs and interests of the pupils is a factor of tremendous importance in education. The main objective of school as a socializing agency is to raise the standard of living of the community.

Next to home, school is the second most important institution in the developmental process of child. Schools should promote the complete development of individuality of a child. It can provide a variety of learning experiences through curricular and co-curricular activities. To widen the horizon of the students' knowledge, methods of teaching like group discussion, assignment, workshops, seminars etc, can be of prime importance. Experiments, excursions, exhibitions visit promote co-operation and we feeling. Sports and games help to develop leadership qualities. Sportsmanship and co-curricular activities like debates, elocution, dramatization develop the skill of expression, arguing and reasoning. All these learning experiences play vital role in the academic achievement of the pupils. The students who undergo a type of passive teaching and learning do not get the real foundation of the subject, due to lack of understanding of the subject.

(*c*) Social Environment: It includes the psycho-sociological influence of the society of which the individual forms a part. Man/women has his/her birth and development in the society and acquires socialization through his/her contact with family members, relatives, neighbors, friends etc. This satisfies physical and psychological needs. The social environment which influences the intellectual development of the child includes the family, friends, classmates, neighbors, teachers and the members of the community and society. The means of mass communication, recreation, religious places, social centers, clubs and libraries can form contributions factors for academic achievement. Learning takes place effectively only when congenial environment is provided for children in classroom, school and home which are a part of their social environment.

The socio-economic status of the family and the academic achievement of the children are related. The type of society in which the family lives and the type of extra-curricular activities that a child gets are all determinants of social growth, which contribute to scholastic achievement. Studies also support that a democratic atmosphere promotes more adjustment and hence achievement.

(b) The role of the Environmental Factors in Human Development

Bronfenbrenner (1979, 1989, and 1994) has proposed an ecological model of human development (Figure 1.1). In this context, the human individual is considered to be at the center of a series of concentric circles. The elements in each circle influence the circles inside it. In this model, a person, initially consisting of his or her biological makeup, is most directly influenced by the *immediate environment*. For most children, this includes the home, family, toys, peers, classrooms and teachers. The immediate environment is influenced by the social and economic context. For example, the home environment will be influenced by the makeup of the neighborhood including such factors as the noise level and the lead content of the soil. The family will be influenced by such factors as whether a parent is able to take a job that permits frequent contact with the child and the degree to which the parent feels oppressed or happy at work. The social and economic context is influenced by the cultural context - the beliefs, values, and guidelines that people in a particular society tend to share.

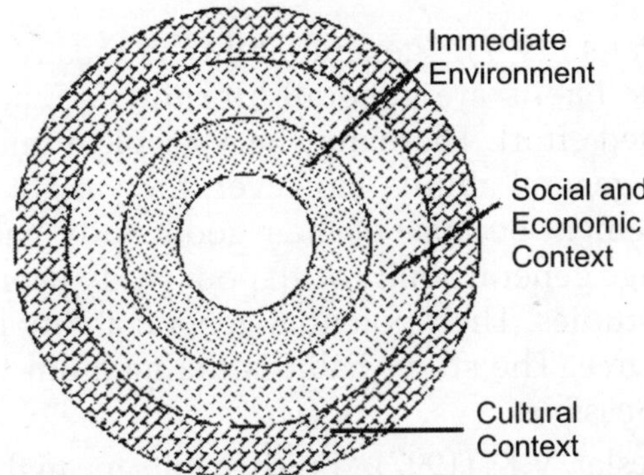

Fig. 1.1: Bronfenbrenner's Ecological Model of Human Development

(c) Relationship between Learning Environment and Academic Achievement

According to Dewey (1926) "Education is a continuous process of experiences and of revising or non-revising experiences. It is the development of all these capacities in the individual which enables him to control his environment and fulfils his possibilities". The forces of environment begin to influence the growth and development of the individual right form the womb of the mother. Educational process of development occurs in physical, social cultural and psychological environment.

A proper and adequate environment is very much necessary for a fruitful learning of the child. Especially, the home and the school should provide the necessary stimulus for learning experience. Skinner (1995) defined school is a special environment where a certain quality of life and certain types of activities and occupations are provided with the object of securing Child's development along desirable lines".

In the school, great emphasis is placed on achievement from the beginning of formal education. It is the prime concern of teachers, educators and psychologists. A number of academic related studies reveal that factors have been identified as predictions of academic achievement. Some of these factors are intelligence, personality, self-concepts, achievement motivation, interest, socio-economic status, methods of teaching and so on. These factors are the contributions of the physical and social environment of the child on the learning environment.

Study Habits

The development of good study habits is the highway to the goals of an individual, whatever they are. A simple, small change in study habits makes a big difference in goal setting and organization of one's life. The success of an individual depends upon his study habits. Education is the manifestation of perfection already existing in man. The tool enabling his manifestation is study habits.

According to Patel (1997), "general ability is mostly concerned with an innate ability while habits are generally formulated, acquired, cultivated and fixed by repeated effort. There may be a sizable number of pupils below the line of average general ability. However, they might get good scores in their school achievement because of their good study habits. Not all pupils having above average general ability with poor study habits may be expected to do better in the studies. Their potential general ability is to be transmitted into a Kinetic resource. The study habit is the medium through which this transformation is possible.

According to Geslat, V.K. (1997), "Study habits mean the ways of studying whether systematically or unsystematically, efficiently or otherwise. Study can be interpreted as planned programmes of subject mastery". According to Ron Fry (2000), "Studying is a skill process. Like any other process, studying has certain characteristics. They are as follows:

(*i*) An individual makes use of an appropriate study skill in various stages of his/her life. Studying is not to study harder, just smarter.

(*ii*) Studying is breaking a complex process into easy-to-follow simple steps.

(*iii*) Studying is more difficult if one is tired, unhealthy and drunk. So, studying needs use of common sense.

(*iv*) A good studying needs one's responsibility for creating his/her own study system.

(*v*) An effective studying is based on the usage of available study time.

(*vi*) Studying prefers 'listening' to seeing to have little problem on getting the necessary knowledge"

(a) Study Habits-a long-term process

Learning how to study is really a long-term process. As one goes on studying, one finds more techniques and methods that offer new information leading one in an interesting and successful direction. So, learning how to study or to develop good study habits is a life long process, and one should be ready to modify one's method of study according to the need of the time.

(b) Formation of Study Habits

On account of poor study Habits, an individual may be doing poorly in school even with reasonable amount of study time. The steps by which good study habits can be formed are given below:

- It is much easier to replace one of our habits than to break it entirely. So, one should not attempt to stop poor study habits, but just to learn the good ones that substitute them.
- Go on practising. There is no way around it. The more we do something, the more ingrained it becomes.
- It is better to seek the help of friends and family to look into one's new practice of a study habit regularly followed. Additional pressure by others is a good motivation.

(c) Study Habits and Content Reading Ability

Each reading skill applied in a content area needs to be taught to students in a systematic, direct fashion.

Table 1.1: Illustration of the Application of Reading Skills in A Study Skills Task

Task	General	Specific Skill
Selecting appropriate texts		Use of title
Locate specific information	Locational Skill	Use of table of Contents
Locate page for Specific information		Use of index
Obtaining general information in text	Comprehension Skill	Determining author's pattern by reading center heads and paragraph heads
Reading for information	Comprehension Skill	Finding main idea
	Comprehension Skill	Differentiating important from unimportant
	Organizing Skill	Outlining
	Organizing Skill	Summarizing

(d) Teaching Techniques

The following strategies can help youngsters to be successful when using a single content text.

- **Directed Reading Activity (DRA):** This teaching strategy should be applied to all content reading, not just basal materials. The use of the elements of readiness (motivation, vocabulary, background, purpose setting), silent reading and review (Comprehension check, meaningful oral reading, direct instruction lesson on a study skill, and transfer activities) will help students successfully read and learn specific content. An example of a Directed Reading Activity for science is shown on pages 4-7 of the first color insert.
- **Advanced Organizer:** This teaching technique involves providing students with a short written summary of a content chapter before the actual silent reading.
- **Structured Overview:** This technique is similar in function to an advanced organizer. A Structured overview presents a chapter's Key ideas and their relationships in a visual format (usually in the shape of a flowchart, hierarchy, spoke, or pie). The Chapter's key vocabulary words are usually included and discussed with youngsters before and after silent reading.
- **Study Guides:** This technique provided students with a set of questions covering each section or page in a chapter to answer while reading. Study guides provide students with purposes for reading. The questions asked should be balanced among literal, interpretative, and critical comprehension levels and in terms of being vocabulary related.

(e) Heading Readiness for Learning

Texas State Board of Education identified essential elements in reading programs to include: (1) discriminating sounds for each letter of the alphabet; (2) discriminating visual shapes, forms, and letters (3) understanding the direction of formal print; (4) following oral directions; (5) telling what a story is about; (6) appreciating repetition, rhyme, rhythm, and alliteration; (7) following simple story line in stories read aloud; (8) supplying missing words in oral context; and (9) recognizing the ordinal and spatial features of print. This list does not include all of the essential elements that are required in reading instruction. However, it is representative of the fact that many of the reading skills which were typically taught at the first-grade level. Ausubel defined readiness as the "adequacy of existing capacity in relation to the demands of a given adequacy of existing capacity in relations to the demands of a given learning task".

(f) Variability in Learning Rates

Prior to focusing on specific readiness factors and diagnostic factors and diagnostic measures, teachers should be aware of the differences that exist among children in regard to their rate of learning to read.

***(i)* Sex differences:** Research data compiled over the past several decades have shown that girls as a group usually experience less difficulty in learning how to read than do boys as a group. A number of explanations have been offered for why girls are generally more successful than boys in early reading achievement. Among the major explanations are maturation differences, the school curriculum and environment, the content of reading materials, and cultural environments.

***(ii)* Maturation differences:** Boys and girls mature at different rates, and some phases of growth have been assumed to be closely related to reading. Since the data are conclusive that girls develop more rapidly than boys, this hypothesis is sometimes seen as the key to the problem under discussion. However the likelihood of this factor alone being the key to sex differences in early reading achievement is questionable.

***(iii)* School curriculum and environment:** Two important variables related to both the school curriculum and the environments are the teacher and his/her behavior patterns. The effect of female teachers on the achievement of boys has been considered as a possible reason for explaining sex differences in reading development. In a recent review of the effect of female teachers on boy's reading achievement, Johnson and Greenbaum categorized their findings into four curriculum and environment areas with the following conclusions:

- Negative treatment—Boys appear to have more types of interaction with both male and female teachers. Female teachers do not exhibit a greater amount of negative treatment to boys.
- Grades—There is little evidence to suggest that female teachers are biased toward giving higher grades to girls.
- Higher achievement—No support was found for the idea that boys achievement is higher when taught by males.
- Alienation—It does not appear, based on the research evidence, that female teachers structure their classrooms in ways that alienate boys.

***(iv)* Content of reading materials:** Some investigations have found that the content of reading materials has a similar appeal to both boys and girls. Further more, story content did not often reflect those things that would appeal only to girls.

***(v)* Cultural environments:** Several recent studies have suggested that cultural factors may play a significant role in producing sex differences in early reading performance. A number of these studies suggest that boys perceive reading as a female activity. This perception could result in a conflict between their role as a student and role as a male. In school, boys are encouraged to be passive and conforming, whereas socially they are encouraged to be active, aggressive, and achieving. Cultural factors may be the most credible factors affecting sex differences in reading. A boy's perception of reading as a female activity could have a negative influence on his/her motivation to read and engagement in reading instruction. The important implication here is that there are variables within the learning environment that, when taken into consideration, could enhance the reading performance of boys. A major concern would be enhancing the appeal of reading to boys rather than reinforcing their conception that reading is for girls only.

(g) Study Habits and Reading Readiness Factors

Numerous factors have been studied in relation to their impact on learning to read. Since reading is a complicated process, it is difficult to establish precise relationships or to completely rule out certain factors as being of no importance. The following discussion will be limited to a few factors that have been either widely studied or accepted, but may not be necessarily valid.

Data from several inquiries have suggested that high intelligence is not an absolute for early reading. During (10) found in her studies of early readers many youngsters who fell within an average range of intelligence (IQs in the range of 90-120). Recent research by Standovich, Cunningham and Freeman pointed out that general intelligence shares a moderate relationship with early reading; however, they noted three relatively independent abilities that are important in predicting early reading progress. These abilities were (1) verbal comprehension ability, (2) phonological awareness (knowledge of spelling-to-sound correspondence), and (3) decoding speed (rapidly recognizing words).

(h) Reading Readiness Tests

A large number of reading readiness tests is available, and they vary in terms of content, format, and purpose. These tests are often used to predict future performance in reading and to diagnose specific strengths and weaknesses. Readiness tests are, as a rule, administered as group tests, though some may contain one or more subtests that must be given individually.

- Associating pictured objects with the spoken word for that object.
- Visual discrimination.
- Sentence comprehension.

(i) Improving Reading Ability

Reading is a complex activity. Many skills are required for its mastery. Most students are poor readers because they do not know how to read in the correct way. Surveys have shown that poor readers are generally poor achievers in school and college. Reading is not merely going through the matter without understanding it.

Reading with understanding means:

1. Locating the main ideas in each para.
2. Listing all the important details in a para and
3. Reading with comprehension.

In order to correctly pick out the main idea and the important details, one should understand the passages.

Speed in reading increases comprehension. It is not difficult to improve one's speed of reading, which can be developed by practicing. The various factors of reading ability are:

1. Good vocabulary
2. Reading a number of words in groups
3. Good speed of writing
4. Good comprehension
5. Independent selection of appropriate material for reading and locating information.

(j) The Parent's Role in Developing Study Habits

Ron Fry (2000) says, "The parent's involvement is absolutely essential to a child's eventual success. A parent, not even for a minute can underestimate the importance of his/her commitment to his/her child's success.' Nancy L. Weishew (1993) points out; "parents can help to improve their children's behavior in school by becoming more involved in their education, monitoring their actions, and helping to increase their achievement, educational expectations and positive self-perceptions'. It is clear that parents have a specific role in developing one's study habits.

(k) The Teacher's Role in Developing Study Habits

The teacher will change the way of one's study. Effective teaching with its four components, knowledge, understanding, application and skill, can definitely elevate one's own study habits. Some teachers encourage the students to memorize and some others emphasize the need for learning by understanding avoiding memorization. Hence, in developing a study habit, it's not only a student who performs, but also a teacher. Teachers are unique in their teaching approach. Accordingly a student adopts a particular approach in a particular class. As is the teacher, so is the student.

The Concept of Self-Esteem

Self-Esteem

The amount of value ascribed to the self in "Self-Esteem". Like the other aspects of the self, this is learned from others and becomes a reflection of how others regard or, more accurately, the value we think others attach to as persons. One's behaviour is likely to reflect the self-esteem, and this, in turn, has a reassuring effect on others. Thus there is "a reciprocal interaction between one's self-esteem and the esteem expressed for one by others".

(a) Meaning of Self-Esteem

When an individual has established a concept of self, then he/she is able to determine or not he/she is satisfied with what he feels about himself. Thus self-esteem can be judged. It will be more appropriate to indicate that all individuals have self-esteem because they have worth, value and high regard, but it may range from high to low in various individuals and in various aspect of the substantive self.

Becker (1971) urges that the dominant motive of man is the need for self esteem. Hayakawa (1963) also suggested that the main purpose of all human activity is to enhance self-esteem. It is the affective portion of the self. It refers to the extend to which one admires or values the self. Different people have different levels of awareness of the self different feelings about themselves as persons.

Self-esteem is the individual's satisfaction with his/her self-concept; positive beliefs of them are termed as positive self-esteem. It is the complex picture of perceived self value. It is the disposition to feel worthy of happiness, respect, friendship, achievement and success defined feelings of self-worth provide the foundation for motivation, mental development and healthy interpersonal relationships. It is usually defined as the personal judgment of worth lying along a dimension with positive and negative ends. It is usually defined in terms of self-attitudes, as which have an emotional and behavioral components.

According to Wells and Marwell (1976) self-esteem refers to the way a person perceives and defines himself/herself is postulated to have an effect upon his/her behaviour, how he/she will relate to other people, what tasks he/she will attempt, what states of tension he/she will experiences and how he/she subsequently will perceive himself/herself.

Self-esteem refers to the extent to which we admire or value of self. Coopersmith and Feldman (1974) have explained the constructs of self-concept and self-esteem; self-concept consists of the beliefs, hypothesis and assumptions that the individuals have about him. On the other hand, self-esteem represents his/her judgment of the concept that he/she has formed through his/her interpretation of the feedback from his/her physical and social experiences. Self-esteem is the persons evaluation of whether his/her self-concept attains his/her standards and value or not, it is a generalized positive and negative attitude towards, himself/herself.

(b) Aspects of Self-Esteem

- **Self-concept:** In the Dictionary of Behavioral Science self-concept is described as, "the individuals appraisal or evaluation of himself."
- **Self-image:** It is the perfect and ideal state which the individual imagines himself to be after identification with an idealized conception of what he should be. (K. Horney,1937)
- **Self-acceptance:** A healthy attitude towards one's worth and limitations consisting of an objective recognition of each quality and an acceptance of each as being part of the Self.
- **Self-insight:** Self-insight means an awareness of one's basic motivation and the effects that these motivations may have on thinking and conduct.
- **Self-knowledge:** Self-knowledge requires an intelligent inventory of personal assets and liabilities. Personal improvement begins with the courage and determination to face the truth about one's self.
- **Self-understanding and self-esteem:** "Ellen is a happy and confident child because she has such a positive self-confident."

The statement like this is heard all the time. Obviously, the term self-concept is used in a particular way in a statement of this sort. These terms one used to refer to children's evaluations of themselves, that is, whether they feel good or bad about themselves. In other words, we are talking about children's Self-Esteem. But a statement like "Arden thinks of himself as a helpful individual" is concerned with people's cognitive conceptions about themselves that is, how they think about themselves. Thus, this discussion is talking here not about self-esteem but about self-understanding.

Healthy self-concept as a sign of mental health: The effect of self-concept on mental health has received a great deal of attention in recent years. Writers in various fields have emphasized that healthy concept of self is a desideratum of mental stability. A distorted concept of self can lead to neurotic formation. Here, in this area of the ideal versus the real self, the virtue of humility and the destructive force of pride can play dominant roles in mental health or ill health. A healthy self-concept leaves ample room for humility and banishes the foolish pride that leads to the development of egotism or neurotic defense mechanisms.

(c) Types of Self-Esteem

People can develop the following types of self-esteem.

(*a*) High self-esteem (Normal): The persons love themselves and accept who they are.

(*b*) Low self-esteem: The persons don't love themselves, don't accept who they are and don't value their qualities.

(c) Inflated self-esteem: The persons love themselves more than others and they exaggerate their qualities.

(d) Characteristics of High Self-Esteemers

High self-esteem has different potentials. Achievement is not the most important thing. Authenticities. The authentic person experiences self-reality by knowing, being, and becoming a credible, responsive person. Authentic people actualize their own unprecedented uniqueness.

- Authentic persons-high-self-esteemers do not dictate their lives to a concept of what they imagine they should be; rather, they are themselves and as such so not use their energy petting on a performance maintaining pretence and manipulating others.
- High self-esteemers can reveal themselves instead of projecting images that please, provoke or entice others. They are aware that there is a difference between being loving and acting knowledgeable.

  High self-steamers need not hide behind a mask. They throw off unrealistic self-images of inferiority or superiority.
- Autonomy does not frighten high self-stemmers. They are able to sustain their autonomy over-increasing periods of time. They may lose ground occasionally and may even fail. In spite of set backs, high self-esteemers maintain a basic self-confidence.
- High self-esteemers are not afraid to do their own thinking and to use their own knowledge. They can separate facts from opinions and don't pretend to have all the answers. They listen to others; evaluate what they say but their own conclusions. Although they can admire and respect other people, they are not totally defined, demolished, bound, or awed by them.
- High self-esteemers do not play "helpless" nor do they play the blaming game. Instead, they assume responsibility for their own lives. They do not give others a false authority over them. High self-esteemers are their own bosses and know it.
- High self-esteemers respond appropriately to the situation. Their responses are related to the message sent and preserve the significance worth, well-being and dignity of the people involved.
- High self-esteemers respond appropriately to the situation. Their responses are related to the message send and preserve the significance worth, well-being and dignity of the people involved.
- High self-esteemers know that for every activity a time is needed.
  - A time to be aggressive and a time to be passive,
  - A time to be together and a time to be alone,
  - A time to work and a time to play,

- A time to cry and a time to laugh,
- A time to confront and a time to withdraw,
- A time to speak and a time to be silent,
- A time to hurry and a time to wait.

- To high self-esteemers time is precious. They don't kill it, but live it here and now. Living in the now does not mean that they foolishly ignore their own past history or fail to prepare for the future. Rather, high self-esteemers know their past; are aware and alive in the present, and look forward to the future.
- High self-esteemers learn to know their feelings and limitations and to be unafraid of them. They are not stopped by their own contradictions and ambivalences. Being authentic, they know when they are angry with them. They can give and receive affection.
- High self-esteemers can be spontaneous. They do not have to respond in predetermined, rigid ways, but can change their plans when the situation calls for it.
- High self-esteemers have a zest for life, enjoying work, play, food, other people, sex and world of nature. Without guilt they enjoy their own accomplishments.

  Although high self-esteemers can freely enjoy themselves, they can also postpone enjoyment; can discipline them in the present to enhance their enjoyment in the future.
- High self-esteemers are not afraid to go after what they want, but they do so in appropriate ways. Self-esteemers do not claim security by controlling others. They do not set themselves up to lose.
- A self-esteemer cares about the world and its people. He/she is not isolated from the general problems of society, but is concerned, compassionate, and committed to improving the quality of life. Even in the face of national and international adversity, a High self-esteemer's self-image is not one of a powerless individual. A high self-esteemer works to make the world a better place.

(e) Characteristics of Low Self-Esteemers

Although people are born to win, they are also born helpless and totally dependent on their environment. High self-esteemers successfully make the transition from total helplessness to independence, and then to interdependence. Low self-esteemers do not. Somewhere along the line they begin to avoid becoming responsible for their own lives.

- Some low self-esteemers speak of themselves as successful but anxious, successful but trapped or successful but unhappy. Others speak off themselves as totally beaten, without purpose, unable to move, half dead, or bored to death. Low self-esteemers may not recognize that, for the most past, they have been building their own cages, digging their own graves, and boring themselves.

- A low self-esteemer seldom lies in the present, but instead destroys the present by focusing on past memories or future expectations. The low self-esteemer who lives in the past dwells on the good old days or on past personal misfortunes. Nostalgically, the low self-esteemer either clings to the way things used to be or bemoans his or her bad luck.
- The low self-esteemer is self-pitying and shifts the responsibility for an unsatisfactory life on to others. Blaming others and excusing oneself are often part of the low self-esteemer's games.
  - A low self-esteemer who lives in the past may lament if only:
  - "If only I had better parents ...."
  - "If only I had been born rich ...."
  - "If only I had been handsome ...."
  - "If only I had a different job ...."

People may in the future dream of some miracle after which they can 'Live happily ever after'. Rather than pursuing their own lives, low self-esteemers wait-wait for the magical rescue. How wonderful life will be when:

- "When the kids grow up ..."
- "When the new job opens ..."
- "When the boss dies ..."
- "When my ship comes in ..."

In contrast to those who live with the delusion of a magical rescue, some low self-esteemers live constantly under the dread of future catastrophe. They conjure up expectation of what if:

- "What if I lose my jobs ..."
- "What if I lose my mind ..."
- "What if something falls on me ..."
- "What if I break my leg ..."
- "What if they don't like me ..."
- "What if I make a mistake ..."

By continually focusing on the future, these low self-esteemers experience anxiety in the present. They are anxious over what they anticipate-either real or imagined-tests, bill paying a love affair, crisis, illness, retirement, the weather, and so forth. Persons involved too much with imaginings let the actual possibilities of the moment pass them by. They occupy their minds with material that is irrelevant to the current situation. Anxiety tunes our current reality. Consequently, these people are unable to see for themselves, hear for themselves, feel for themselves, or taste, touch, or think for themselves.

- Unable to bring the full potential of their senses into their immediate situation. Low self-esteemer's perceptions are incorrect or incomplete. They see themselves and others through a prism like distortion. Their ability to deal effectively with the real world is hampered.
- Low self-esteemers spend much of their time play-acting, pretending, manipulating and perpetuating old rules from childhood. Low self-esteemers invest their energy in maintaining marks, often projecting a phony front. Karen Horney writes, "The fostering of the phony self is always at the expense of the real self, the latter being treated with disdain, at best like a poor relative." To the play acting low self-esteemer performance is more important than reality.
- Low self-esteemers repress their capacities to express spontaneously and appropriately the full range of possible behaviour. They may be unaware of other options for a more productive, self-fulfilling life path.
- Low self-esteemers are afraid to try new things and instead maintain their own status quo.
- Low self-esteemers are repeaters, repeating not only their own mistakes, but often those of their families and culture as well.
- A low self-esteemer has differently giving and receiving affection and does not enter into intimate, honest, direct relationships with others. Instead, a low self-esteemer tries to manipulate them into living up to his or her expectations. Low self-esteemers often live up to the expectations of others.
- People who are low self-esteemers are not using their intellect appropriately, but instead are misusing it to rationalize and intellectualize. When rationalizing, low self-esteemers give excuses to make their actions seem plausible, when intellectualizing they try to show others with verbiage. Consequently, much of their potential remains dormant unrealized and unrecognized. Like the frog-prince in the fairly lake, low self-esteemers are spell bound and live their lives being something.

High versus low self-esteem: When self-esteem is high, one can be confident, feel free to be ourselves and to express. When it is low, he one would to hide himself/herself, expert very little of ourselves. Some of the characteristics of individual with high self-esteem versus low self-esteem are given table 1.2.

Table 1.2: Characteristics of Individual with High Self-esteem Versus Low Self-esteem

High Self-Esteem	Low Self-Esteem
Perceives reality	Avoids reality to avoid anxiety
Relatively undefensive	Defensive
Spontaneous	Reserved
Natural	Plays a Role
Task centered	Self centered
Self-reliant	Dependant
Relationships are intimate	Relationships are Casual
Feeling valuable	Feeling unworthy
Makes growth choices	Makes fear choices
Non-judgmental of others	Critical of others
Wholeness	A feeling of not belonging
Enjoys being alone	Oriented towards approval of others
Acceptance	Strive to be perfect and avoid mistakes.
Experiences without self-consciousness	Consider what others think as most important.

(f) Causes of Low Self-Esteem

Some of the important factors considered to be the causes for low self-esteem are given below :

- *Negative body image:* Feeling inferior in contrast with someone else.
- *Criticism:* A pattern of acceptance from parents and others that makes the child feel unworthy because of criticism.
- *Critical blow-ups:* Negative Self-criticism the child gives him or herself.
- *Chronic comparisons to others:* Makes each child know that he/she is not valued.
- *Demands of perfection:* Perfections are driven by feelings of insecurity, so they compensate by being perfect.
- *Sense of hopelessness:* Negative input from others has destroyed hope.

(g) Sources of High Self-Esteem

Every child needs parents' approval in terms of

1. his/her own sense of personhood
2. his/her proven ability
3. his/her sense of individuality
4. his/her framework of meaningful value.

- Other good examples and about role models.
- Sibling and peer approval.
- Educational achievements.
- Skills, mystery in sports, music, hobbies etc.
- To learn to feed self good strokes.
- To receive God's love and acceptance.
- Career expertise and enjoyments and Root-value transfer.

(h) Gender Role and Self-Esteem

Perhaps as a result of the women's movement over the past twenty-five years young men's and women's concept of masculinity and femininity are changing. Among many young adults, gender-role stereotypes are breaking down, and those whose personalities do not fit the traditional stereotype for either gender show the highest self esteem and most advanced psychological development (Hyde, Krajnik, and Skuldt–Niederberger, 1991). These women and men are androgynous: they are high both in personality traits considered masculine (they are self-reliant, independent, and assertive) and in traits considered feminine (they are affectionate, sympathetic and understanding). Among college students studied by Janet Spence (1979) more than a decade ago, those who were low in both masculine and feminine traits also had low self-esteem. Male students who fit the traditional gender-role stereotype (high in their own genders traits and low in traits ascribed to the gender) tended to be higher in self-esteem than women who fit their traditional gender role. This may explain why many women see themselves as less competent than men. Recent studies have found an increase in the proportion of androgynous students, with women now being twice as likely as men to have androgynous personalities (Hyde, Krajnik, and Skuldt–Niederberger, 1991).

Most young men and women seem comfortable with androgyny. Among one group of young adults, men felt easy about expressing their "feminine" qualities as women did about expressing their "masculine" side (Reedy, 1977). Both genders wanted to see themselves as self confident, intelligent, independent, loving and understanding. This way of thinking about masculinity and femininity widens the possibility for both sexes.

(i) Self Concept Brings Self-Esteem

Whether stable or unstable a person's self concept is a motivating force in his/her behaviour. The individual acts in accordance with how he/she sees himself/herself at the moment. If one feels that he/she is misunderstood or discriminated against, he/she will act like a martyr. If he/she feels that people accept him/her he/she will act in a friendly cooperative way. Much unpredictable behaviour can be traced to unstable slept.

Because self-concept is the dominant element in the personality pattern, it governs the individuals' characteristic reaction to people and situations and determines the quality of his/her behaviour children and adults are governed by the concept of self which they develop and make part of themselves. Thus we have boys and girls who assign to themselves the role of clown, good citizen, manager, shrinking violet little demon, sage, featherhead.

Research studies from several areas of behaviour illustrate how the concept of self, built up in the early years of life and reinforced by later experiences, influences the quality of the person's behaviour and his/her characteristic reactions to people and to situations. Many school children work below their capacities because they have learned at home or from members of the peer group, to think of themselves as 'dumb'. A child whose ability is limited, may work beyond his teacher's expectation if he/she has a favorable self-concept characterized by feelings of competence and self-worth.

Success brings self-esteem: Academic success is highly valued by most adults; the degree of success a student achieves affects his personality via self and social evaluations. Every student becomes aware of how successful or unsuccessful in the area by academic symbols of success, promotion, grades, honours and diplomas and degrees. How significant people in the student's life react to these symbols of success influences how he/she reacts.

At all ages people are judged by now their achievement compare with those of their peers. The person whose achievements in highly valued areas are superior in quantity and quality is favouably judged by the social group. However, whether favourable social judgments will lead to favouable self-evaluation will depend on whether the person's achievements come up to his/her own aspirations.

Aspirations: Aspirations are the ego involved goals persons set for. The more ego involved his/her aspirations are and the more they relate to areas of behaviour that are important to him/her. Most people want to be regarded as successful in areas that are important to others. And what is important to others varies from age to age and from one social group to another. To effectively play its role as a symbol of self, success must be visible. A person may communicate his/her success to others in various ways, some of which are crude and some extremely subtle.

Effect of success: Because of the high prestige associated with success, it is not surprising that the degree of success the social group attributes to a person has a profound influence on self-concept. Further more, the more prestige the group attributes to the area in which the person is successful, the more prestige value his success has and the more favourable the effect on his/her self concept. The more symbols of success a person has and the more visible the symbols are, the more favourable the judgements of others, and in turn, the more favourable the effect on the success in his/her self esteem.

Motivating effects of self esteem: Much research has been based on the assumption that people are motivated to behave in ways that maintain and enhance their self-image. Moreover, people will distort their perceptions of others behavior toward themselves so as to preserve this self-image. Thus, as noted in the discussion of attribution process, the people discredit information that they have done poorly on a task by attributing their failure to their lack of effort, to bad luck, or to the fact that the task would be impossible for any one to do well. In fact, they are motivated actively to seek information that helps to maintain their self-esteem: if they score low on an intelligence test, they may seek information that questions the validity of the test in preference to information that suggests the test results are accurate. The tendency to disparage people who evaluate unfavorably, predicted by balance theory, and may also be viewed as a means of preserving self-esteem by discrediting the source of the evaluation: the teacher who failed is incompetent: the person who left for another lover is not worth having. The reasons for this motivational effect are fairly clear. In the extreme, the failure to preserve the self-esteem can have devastating consequences for the mental health, such as serve depression

The discussion, here, provides only a few examples of the ways in which the "self" enters into the processing of information, as

1. A source of information
2. A basis for comparison, or
3. A motivating factor that affects reactions to information and behavioral decisions.

The role of self is also critical with respect to the effect of other persons on ones behaviour the issue to which the people now shall turn.

(j) Measuring Self-Esteem

Ideally the most appropriate way of assessing self-esteem levels of a child or class is to get to know them well over a period of time. However this is not always possible if dealing with a new (unknown) class or a difficult individual child, when speed of assessment, is of the essence. If the teacher does not wish to engage in complex assessment methods, a few simple techniques can be uses such as:

- Interviews-where by a skilled teacher (such as a counselor, head of year or pastoral care teacher) encourage the child to discuss their self-concept. Interaction with the child can be both helpful and inhibiting dependent upon the previous relationship between teacher and pupil. The drawing up by the teacher of a list of standard question responses, in advance, can be of great advantage in the approach.

- A Teacher Check List - this is filled in by the teacher based on observations, of the pupil's behaviour.

For example:

Does Pupil make self-disparaging remarks?
Is pupil boastful?
Is pupil hesitant and timid in new situations?
Does the pupil make excuses to avoid situations which may be stressful?
Is pupil continually asking for help and/or reassurance?
Is pupil continually asking if they are liked or popular?
Does pupil hang back and remain on the fringe of a group?
Is pupil apathetic in a learning situation?
Does pupil daydream a lot?
Does pupil avoid work even though risking teacher's displeasure?
Does pupil tend to blame others for their own failures?
Is pupil reluctant to assume responsibilities?

Even if all these questions are answered affirmatively, the feelings of low self-esteem are merely being *inferred*, not *observed directly*. There is also a set average (or Mean) value, as to what a child with average self-esteem should score, leading to inaccuracy in results.

- A Child Check List - basically a list of similar questions to the Teacher Check List, however this is for self-completion by the child. A list of personal attributes, such as;

  * Outgoing or Not Outgoing,
  * Friendly or Unfriendly,
  * Helpful or Unhelpful,
  * Good Worker or Poor Worker, etc.

  These are examined by the child, who ticks those they feel apply to them. The completed list is studied by the teacher and based upon the results and their own personal knowledge of the child, a judgment is made. This approach has the added advantage of providing material for discussion later with the child or children, as to why they perceive themselves that way.

- Free Response Method-the child is asked to write an essay about themselves, and to list attributes which they believe to be personal characteristics. This can also take the for of twenty or more questions about the child, beginning with "I am ...." For children with learning difficulties, this additional structure can be very helpful. The completed essay/list is then analysed by the teacher, as per the Child Check List (as above), giving points for later discussion.

- Q-Sort-this involves the sorting into different piles by the child, of a series of card. Each card contains a statement about the self (e.g. I am always happy). The first ordering is ranked in priority of how the child sees itself, and the second ordering is how the child would like to be. There are over 22 different set of these cards on the market, however Bulter and Haigh's (1954) 100 card set, is the most frequently used and is fairly accurate. Although time consuming to set-up, the effort is repaid by the involvement and interest levels.
- Psychometric Tests - Some psychometric tests are sufficiently user-friendly to be considered for use in the mainstream classroom. Included here are the LAWSEQ "Primary School" Version (Lawrence, 1982) and the LAWSEQ "High School" Version (1983) which measure global self-esteem in a speedy and simple manner.

(k) Self-Esteem and Evaluation

Although people customarily speak of self-esteem as a single entity, global-esteem-our-esteem also includes many compartmentalized or situation. Specific aspects which vary according to circumstances. Nevertheless, all of us some of the time and sizable minority most of the time suffer from low self-esteem. Because self-esteem resides largely within yourself, ultimately you have the power to change it. As **Seneca,** the ancient philosopher said, 'what you think of yourself is much more important than what others think of you.'

(l) Development of Self-Esteem

The development of self-esteem is important because it may play a mediating role in assisting an individual to adjust to environmental demands and to develop socially appropriate behaviors and self-regulations (Higgins, 1991). Positive self-affects may also foster development and mastery of various competencies, whereas negative self-conscious emotions may provoke behaviors that inhibit the individual's pursuit of life goals. A positive view of self will affect the feelings, behaviors, and thoughts of an individual child. The resulting sense of self-efficacy may assist the child in working through difficult times and applying the self regulation necessary for personal growth.

(m) The Importance of Self-Esteem

Even though self-esteem has been studied for more than 100 years, specialists and educators continue to debate its precise nature and development. Nevertheless, they generally agree that parents and other adults who are important to children play a major role in laying a solid foundation for a child's development. Good self-esteem is important because it helps your students to hold their head high and feel proud of their accomplishments and abilities. It gives them the courage to try new challenges and the power to believe in themselves. It allows them to respect themselves-even when they make mistakes. And when they respect themselves, adults and other friends usually respect them, too. Having good self-esteem is also the ticket to make good choices about their mind and body. If they think they're important, they'll be less likely to follow the crowd if their friends are doing something dumb or dangerous. If they have good self-esteem, they know that they are smart enough to make their own decisions. Success in school, getting along in a family or with peers all depend on self-confidence. Without it, children's talents may be developed as they may be afraid to take risks or be creative. Research shows that a positive self-concept is more important to academic success than a high IQ score. Children will have greater self-esteem if they feel a sense of ownership and responsibility for their experiences.

(n) Self-Esteem and Academic Achievement

An integrated self concept acts as a motivational force in maintaining mental health and influencing the learning situations. A positive relationship has been found between self esteem and intelligence and self esteem and scholastic achievement irrespective of the subjects belonging to either of the sexes, to forward or backward communities, to urban or rural communities, although the degree of intelligence or achievement may vary from person to person. There is a perfect relationship between high scholastic achievements and a positive self-concept, while the low ones have got a negative self-concept. Marsh (1992) said that the relationship of self-esteem to school achievement is very specific. General self-esteem and non-academic aspects of self-esteem are not related to academic work; general academic achievement measures are related moderately to academic success specific measures of subject-related self-esteem are highly related to success in that content area.

Using linear discriminate analysis. Byrne (1990) showed that academic self esteem was more effective than academic achievement in differentiating between low-track and high-track students. (Hamachek, 1995) also asserts that self-esteem and school achievement are related. The major issue is the direction of the relationship: does self esteem produce achievement or does achievement produce self-esteem. George and Berliner (1992) state "the evidence is accumulating, however, to indicate that level of school success, particularly over many years, predicts level regard of self and one's own ability (Bridgeman and Shipman 1978; Kifer, 1975); whereas level of self-esteem does not predict level of school achievement, the implication is that teachers need to concentrate on the academic success and failures of their students. It is the student's history of success and failure that gives them the information with which to assess themselves" (p - 159)

If academic achievement leads to increased self-esteem, but self-esteem is a better predictor of being a low-track or high-track student, it would appear that there is some intervening variable. James (1890) states that the intervening variable is personal expectation. His formula is self-esteem = success + pretensions.

That is increasing self-esteem results when success is improved it relatives to expectations and self-esteem: success = pretensions + self-esteem.

Academic Achievement

Achievement refers to the knowledge attained or skill development in school subjects usually designated by test scores or by marks assigned by the teachers or by both. According to (carter V. Good, 1973), achievement means accomplishment or proficiency or performance in a given skill or body of knowledge, help in declaring the examine successful or unsuccessful choosing the students for various professional and academic courses and selecting the candidates for different jobs. (p.6)

Suppose you have a choice of three video games to play. One game is easy, you know you can get a high score on it. but so could any one else. The second game is more difficult, you are not sure how well you would do. The third is so difficult that you are sure you would lose quickly, as most people do. Which do you choose. Most people prefer the difficult but not impossible game, especially people with a strong need for achievement (Alkinson & Birth 1978)

When people receive feedback on their performance, such as "You got 82% correct on the first test", those with a strong need for achievement usually increase their efforts, no matter what the results were. Apparently, they interpret almost any feedback as meaning that they have room for improvement and need to try harder. People with a lord need for achievement or a high fear of failure react to feedback by decreasing their efforts. The feedback either tell them that they are achieving their modest goals, or that they are failing and may as well quit (Matsui, Okada and Kakuyama, 1982).

Evaluation of learning outcomes of the students by measuring their academic achievement, the appropriateness of the methods of imparting knowledge may be judged. In the present socio economic and cultural context, academic achievement is of paramount importance and the schools place great emphasis on it. At all school levels there exist enormous differences in the academic attainment of students ranging from high to low. Progress in future to a great extent depends upon the academic attainment of the students. It has to be pointed out that though several attempts have been made to study the impact of non-intellectual factor on achievement in general, no concrete attempt has been made to study how much variance in achievement in biology is accounted for environmental factors, study habits and self esteem. The present study is aimed at finding out the influence of environmental factors, study habits and self esteem on academic achievement in biology.

Organization of the Dissertation

The dissertation has been organized in five chapters.

- The first chapter presents a systematic introduction of the study, its significance and way of approach to the problem.
- The second chapter deals with the abstracts of Review of related literature regarding the study done abroad and in India, which presents a vivid picture about the state of art of the study.
- The third chapter deals with the methodology of the study comprising a description of statistical techniques used for the study, tools, sample, data collection and scoring.
- The fourth chapter deals with the analysis and Interpretation part of the collected data.
- The fifth chapter comprises the Summary of the study, Findings, pertinent recommendations and suggestions for further study.

Conclusion

The first chapter deals with the significance of the problem. The review of related literature and research studies related with the present investigation are included in the next chapter.

2

Review of Related Literature

Introduction

An essential aspect of a research project is the review of related literature. Though the search for related material is time consuming, it is a fruitful phase of any research programme. For any worthwhile study in any field of knowledge, the research worker needs an adequate familiarity with the work which has already been done in the area of his/her choice. The review of the literature is an exacting task, calling for a deep insight and clear perspective of the overall fields. According to Mouly (1964), "Review of related literature is a crucial step which invariably minimizes the risk of dead ends, rejected topics, rejected studies, wasted effort, trial and error activity oriented towards approaches already discarded by previous investigators and-even more important-erroneous findings based on a faulty research design".

Man has the unique advantage of not having to "Begin now in every generation, but can take advantage of the knowledge, which has accumulated through the centuries. This fact is of even greater importance in research. The knowledge gained by previous research leads not only to greater understanding of the problem but also provides comparative data the basis of which the investigators evaluate and interpret new research. In order to benefit from previous research, a survey of previous studies in the field becomes imperative.

According to (Best, 1995), "effective research must be based on past knowledge. This step helps to eliminate the duplication of what has been done already and provides useful hypotheses and helpful suggestions for significant investigation".

The review of the literature promotes a greater understanding of the problem and its crucial aspects and ensures the avoidance of unnecessary duplication. In the light of the earlier research done, the problem was better understood and better viewed in different perspective.

In the following pages, the studies conducted related to the present study have been discussed.

Studies on Environmental Factors and Academic Achievement in India

Molia and Manganlal (2000) did a study on "A comparative study on Home environment of rural and urban students of secondary school". The objectives were (1) to study the home environment of the class VIII students of the schools. (2) to compare the home environment of rural with urban students of the secondary schools; and (3) to study the language stimulation, physical environment, encouragement of social maturity, variety of stimulation and maternal attitude and disciplining on home environment of rural and urban students. The sample consisted of 300 boys selected from class VIII (150 rural and 150 urban) of secondary schools of Rajkot district. Mohite Home Environment Inventory (MHEI) by Mohite P. was administered for data collection. The data were analysed by 't' test. Findings were (1) Urban students were found to be superior on home environment than the rural students. (2) The urban students were also found superior on language stimulation, physical environment and encouragement of social maturity than the rural students, but in variety of stimulation and maternal attitude and disciplining the differences were not found significant between the two.

Navang (2000) did "A comparative study of the socio-economic and home factors affecting the academic achievement of boys and girls in the rural and urban areas." The objectives were (*i*) to study the effect of socio-economic status on the academic achievement of boys and girls in city, town and village areas, (*ii*) to study the relationship between the number of siblings and academic achievement. (*iii*) to study the relationship between home work and academic achievement. The study employed survey method. The tools used were (*i*) The socio-economic status scale, (*ii*) The exposure to mass media scale, (*iii*) An interview schedule. The statistics used were (*i*) Standard deviation (*ii*) Mean (iii) "t" test (*iv*) Product movement correlation. The major findings were (*i*) Socio-economic status did not affect academic achievement. (*ii*) The number of siblings seemed to affect performance. (*iii*) Regularity in doing home work helped achievement.

Patel and Minakshi (2000) did a study entitled "Perceived family environment: A study in relation to economic status of family." The objective is to attempt to explore the impact of economic level of various dimensions of family environment. The sample consisted of 526 adolescents both girls and boys aged 13-16 years belonging to different socio-economic strata drawn from nine high schools of Rajkot city using stratified random sampling technique. Tools like personal data sheet and Hindi adaptation of family environment scale developed by Moos (1974) and adapted and standardized in Hindi by Joshi and Vyas (1996) were used for data collection. The collected data were analysed using't' test. (1) It was found that economic level of the family was an important factor influencing the nature of various dimensions of family environment. (2) Families having low income were found to be less cohesive, allowed less expression of feeling, had more conflicts, permitted less independence, was less organized and exercised more control in comparison to the families having average and high income.

Jaga, Basanitha and Mukhonadhyaya (2001) conducted a study on the "Effect of Environment factors on Achievement of Rural students." The objectives were (i) to study the effect of home and school environment on gender differences and achievement differences of rural students: and (ii) to study interrelationship among home environment, school environment and academic achievement of rural school students. The result showed that academic achievement of secondary school students was significantly related to their home environment, but the school environment was not significantly related to each other, Boys and girls were different in home environment and school environment. High achieving boys and girls enjoyed good home and school environment; high and low achievers differed significantly in their school environment.

Pant (2002) did a study entitled "Understanding talent in science classroom: An exploratory study." The purpose was to study the attitude of the talented students in science towards their subject. The population consisted of 205 students from classes IX and X of two reputed public schools. Out of which only fourteen students were selected as talented in science on the basis of criterion test. Five inventors were used to focus student's attitude towards science and other aspects. The findings revealed that the identified talented students possessed positive attitude towards science. Although these students reflected a very favourable attitude towards science, most of them did not want to become a scientist.

Apartha and Malathi Latha (2003) studied the relationship between schools discipline, student behaviour and student achievement. The objective was to understand the relationship among school discipline, student behaviour and student achievement. Tool employed was multilevel analysis on data from the national education longitudinal study; 1988. Result shows that stringent discipline has some beneficial effects when it is perceived as moderate mean to improve minor misbehaviour.

Branda Carol, Adams and Cumming Ham (2003) conducted a study on the relationship between school culture and student achievement. The objective was to conduct a study on the relationship between school culture and student achievement Sample were taken from 61 elementary schools. Tool employed was survey instrument to 102 elementary schools. Results showed that there was a relationship between the overall culture of collegiality and the self-efficacy of the elementary school in this study and the reading achievement of students in those schools.

Edward (2003) conducted a study on the effect of family structure, family income and home environment on graduation rates of special education students in three urban high schools. The objective of the study was to determine whether the present methods being used to teach the specific learning disabled students will enable them to graduate with the standard high school diploma and prepare them for some form of post high school education. The finding is that parents of the ESE children regardless of socio economic status aware of the interest in their child's success

Mary Joise and Arockiasamy (2003) did a study. The study has been conducted on a sample of 450 first generation learners studying higher secondary course in Kanyakumari district. An attempt has been made to find the level of educational aspiration against a few selected psychological factors and home factors of first generation learners. A comparison of these factors between first generation learners and subsequent generation learners has also been made. Educational aspiration of first generation learners is found to be very high. Significant relationship between the educational aspiration and psychological factors such as self concept, independence, frustration and anxiety as well as home factors of first generation learners with reference to certain background variables has been established.

Venita Singh (2003) conducted a study on "Achievement motivation and parental background as the determinants of students' academic achievement." The study was to determine the achievement motivation and parental background as the determinants of students' academic achievement. The study was to find out the relationship between students' academic achievement and their achievement motivation. The sample consisted of 100 students of class 10th from 4 English medium schools of Abonar and Malour (Punjab) and achievement value and Anxiety inventory for achievement motivation by P. Mehta (1989) was used as a tool.

The findings of the study were i. Academic achievement and achievement motivations are positively correlated. ii. Children of both parents working group have better academic achievement. iii. There is no difference in the achievement motivation of children due to parents working. iv. Academic achievement of students is not affected by parents education. v. Parents education does not affect achievement motivation of students.

Arati, Ratna and Prabha (2004) studied the influence of family environment on emotional competence of adolescents. The main objectives are (1) to study the family environment (2) to study the emotional competence of the adolescents (3) to study the relationship between family environment and emotional competence of the adolescents. The sample is consisting of 120 adolescents including equal number of 13-16 years studying in different high schools of twin cities Hyderabad and Secunderabad. The Family Environment Scale developed by Bhatia and Chadola (Adaption of Moos scale, 1974), and Emotional Competence Scale developed by Sharma and Bharadwaj (1995) were used for data collection. Findings revealed that in family environment dimensions, majority of the adolescents perceived average cohesion, expressiveness, conflict, acceptance and caring active recreational orientation organization and control except independence. In family environment in general two-third of the adolescents perceived average, 16.60% perceived low and 18.34 perceived high about their family environment.

Chin and angels (2004) studied the pupils' classroom environment perception attitudes and achievement in science at the Upper Primary Level. The study examined the relationship between pupils' perception of their science classroom environment and their achievement and attitude in science. The findings revealed the existence of positive association between the nature primary science class environment and pupils attitudinal and achievement outcomes. Girls held more favourable perception than boys.

Goel (2004) studied the effect of gender in home and environment on Educational aspiration. The main objectives were to study the relationship between certain factors related to the homes of pupils and levels of their educational aspirations and also whether there was a significant gender difference in the levels of education aspirations,. The sample of the study comprised of 100 students (50 boys and 50 girls) of intermediate classes, ranging the age of 16-20 years. K. S Mishra's Home Environment Inventory (HEI) and V.P.Sharma's Educational Aspiration Scale (EAS) were used. The results revealed that girls had a much higher educational aspiration than boys. Boys feel more rejected with the autocratic atmosphere at home in comparison with girls who experience more nurture than boys.

Vijya Avinashilingam and Upayana Singh (2004) conducted a study on Identification of Factors Influencing the Student's Academic Performance. This study attempted to find an answer to the variation between students who perform well and who don't. The present study was conducted to find out the factors influencing the students academic performance, It was found that classroom factors, environmental factors, hostel factors, developmental factors, extracurricular factors and library factors are the factors motivating students academic performance.

Webster and Bertha (2004) conducted a study on the Effects of Adolescents Classroom Perceptions on Motivation and Achievement in the Classroom. The research examined whether there existed any interaction between classroom perception and gender. Students' perception is influenced by a variety of factors like student's abilities, self-efficacy, intrinsic goals, learning strategies, interests and also the qualities of teachers. A quasi-experimental design was used to study the multiple variables of classroom perception. Results indicated no sex differences in motivation and classroom perception

Amruth Kumar (2005) studied emotional balance of secondary school students in relation to their home environment. Objectives are to estimate the relationship between Home Environment and Emotional Balance of secondary school children for the total sample and for the relevant sub samples and to test whether the correlations obtained for the comparable sub samples differ significantly. A representative sample of 180 secondary school children was selected randomly for the present study. The investigator constructed two tools for the present study. Home Environment Rating scale and emotional Balance Inventory for secondary school students were used for data collection. The results showed that (1) the relationship between home environment and emotional balance was positive and significant (2) This relation was not influenced by sex, locale and parental occupation of the students

Mehra and Mondal (2005) conducted a study on "Effects of Peer Tutoring on Learning Outcomes of High School Science Students". The objectives are (1) to determine the effect of peer tutoring and traditional instruction of learning outcomes, viz achievement in science of students with high and low intelligence. (2) to compare learning outcomes in science of high and low intelligence groups of students. (3) to study the learning outcome of students in science at knowledge and comprehension category of objectives. (4) to study the interaction effects of the instructional treatments intelligence. A sample of 108 students (54 high intelligence and 54 low intelligence) was randomly selected. This study employed a pre test/post test control group with one experimental group design. The 2 × 2 × 2 factorial design and ANOVA were employed for analyzing the data. The Findings were peer tutoring exhibited better gain in achievement in science compared to those taught through traditional instruction. It was found two important aspects. The study cites thirty one references.

Jeba Sheela and Arockiasamy (2006) the present study aims at finding out the differences in the perceived level of school environment and academic achievement by higher secondary students in matric and non-matric schools. A sample of 1100 higher secondary students has been selected for the study. The findings of the study clearly indicate significant differences in the perceived school environment and academic achievement between matric and non-matric higher secondary students. Significant relationship also has been observed between perceived school environment and academic achievement of non-matric students.

John Louis Manoharan and Christie doss (2007) attempted to find the relationship between home environment and adjustment of higher secondary students. The study aims at finding out the relationship between home environment and adjustment of higher secondary students. The sample of 305 students consisted of 169 boys and 136 girls. Data were collected using appropriate tools and analyzed by't' test and Karl Pearson product moment correlation. The results indicate that there is a significant relationship between home environment and adjustment.

Meers and Prathapan (2008) did a study, 'Classroom learning Environment and self esteem as correlates of Achievement in social studies'. The objectives are: (1) to study the main effect of classroom learning environment and self-esteem on achievement in social studies for the total sample and sub samples. (2) to study the interaction effects of classroom learning environment and self esteem on achievement in social studies for the total sample and sub samples. The study was conducted with the sample of 600 students from 16 schools of Thrissur districts in Kerala, the tools used are Scale of classroom learning environment (Usha and Suchitra, 2002), Self esteem inventory (Usha and suchitra, 2002) and Achievement Test in social studies (Meer and prabhitha, 2007). Statistical techniques used are Two-way analysis of variance with 3×3 factorial design. The achievement in social studies varies with regards to difference in their classroom learning environment, the achievement in social studies varies with regard to difference in their self esteem, the achievement in social studies of boys varies with regard to difference in their classroom learning environment, the achievement in social studies of boys varies with regard to difference in their self esteem and the interaction effect due to classroom learning environment and self esteem on achievement in social studies for boys is not significant.

Selvaraj Gnanaguru and Suresh Kumar (2008) found the relationship between home environment and attitude towards teaching. The present study aims to find out the relationship between underachievers' home environment and their attitude towards teaching. For this purpose a sample of 892 B.Ed students was randomly selected from Cuddalore and Nagappattinam Districts of Tamil Nadu State. The researchers identified the underachievers by regression equation method. In the sample 252 were identified as underachievers. The study reveals that the underachievers have satisfactory home environment and unfavourable attitude towards teaching. There is no significant relationship found between the underachievers' home environment and their attitude towards teaching. Male and female students differ significantly in their home environment and attitude towards teaching but not in their achievement score and intelligence score.

Amutha Ranjini and Sivakumar (2008) found out the relationship between classroom environment and academic achievement in biology of XI standard students in Thoothukudi educational district .The sample of 235 students consisted 130 boys and 105 girls .Data were collected using appropriate tools and analyzed by two- tailed "t" test and Pearson product moment correlation .The results indicate that there is a significant relation between classroom environment and achievement.

Subramanian and Sivakumar (2009) found the impact of environment factors on academic achievement of higher secondary biology students in Tirunelveli district. The aim of the present study was to find out the relationship between environmental factor and academic achievement of higher secondary students. The sample consisted 325 higher secondary students of whom162 were male and 163 were female. The data were collected using appropriate tool and analysed by 't' test and product moment correlation. The results indicated that there was significant relationship between environmental factors and academic achievement of higher secondary students.

Studies on Environmental Factors and Academic Achievement Abroad

Tonglet Jenifer Philips (2000) did a study "Influences on math homework completion and achievement attitudes towards teacher-related factors student motivational factors, and environment-related factors in fifth and eighth graders." The present study examined fifth and eight grade students math related attitudes and perceptions which potentially influenced the frequency of math homework completion students attitudes and perceptions were divided into three major categories. Teacher-Related components (encouraging teacher and evaluative teacher) Students-Related components (Mastery orientation) consisted of an incremental view of ability, student learning orientation, and utility value: Ego orientation consisted of an entity view of ability, student performance orientation, and anxiety: the third factor was self-efficacy and environment-Related components (time spend on math home work, homework environment, and time spent in competing activities). A questionnaire was developed specifically for this study and completed to 83 fifth graders and 106 eighth graders in the greater New Orleans area. The results indicated that when students completed more homework assignments, they earned higher grades, particularly if they adopted an ego orientation. Both encouraging teachers and evaluative teachers fostered mastery, orientation in the students and positive feelings of self-efficacy. Students who indicated adopting a mastery orientation reported awareness of increased time needed to do math homework and a homework environment conducive to studying.

Acosta Esther (2001) did a study "The relationship between school climate, academic self concept and academic achievement." To examine the relationship among school climate, academic self concept and academic achievement, the tool used was students self report of their last recorded grades. The findings of the study provided support for the concept the school climate and academic self-concept influence students perceptions of themselves as learners as well as their academic achievement.

Jewell and Jeremy Dean (2001) did a study "The family environment of conduct disordered children and adolescents with depressed parents". It is hypothesized that the depressed family environment and erratic discipline style of families with depressed parents will be related to externalizing behaviours in their children. This study examined family environment variables that were related to depressive symptoms in parents of youth with conduct disorder. Participants came from a larger study of adolescents who were receiving treatment at a residential treatment facility. Also youth from these families endorsed an ambivalent or chaotic family style, while endorsing items from both the authoritarian and Laissez-Faire family styles with the findings from this study, it was hoped that the treatment of parent depression, as well as externalizing behaviour disorders in their children, were better informed.

Rashid and Fontina Louise (2001) found the influence of home literacy environment on reading achievement in children with reading disabilities. The relation between parent and child home literacy activities and the child's academic outcomes were investigated with a sample of 65 children with reading disabilities. The potential role of parental beliefs about education was also examined as was the relation between home literacy environment and improvement in reading during a reading intervention. To provide support for the findings, the relation between child home literacy environment and academic achievement was cross validated with a sample of children from Canada. The results indicated that child home literacy activities were not significantly related to any of the academic outcomes while parent home literacy activities were a significant predictor of the child's passage comprehension and spelling scores. There was not a significant relation between parental beliefs and home literacy environment, and the home literacy environment did not predict reading improvement during an intervention. Surprisingly, child home literacy activities were a significant predictor of arithmetic scores for the Canadian sample.

Robinson-Health and Deborach (2001) compared African-American achieving and underachieving students". The focus of this investigation was to determine if urban, low socioeconomic status, African-American students who were classified as academic achievers demonstrated higher levels of achievement motivation than students from a similar background who were classified as academic underachievers. Gender and grade levels were explored to determine their impact on the students reported levels of achievement motivation as measured by Schultz's Achievement Motivation Inventory (AMI). The study's 277 participants were elementary-school students (intermediate grade levels 5-6, upper grade levels 7-8), from one large urban, inner city, low-income community. This study revealed that urban, low-socio economic status, African-American students classified as academic achievers attained significantly higher total AMI scores than students who were not classified as academic achievers. Female students attained significantly higher total AMI scores compared to male students. However, gender interacted with grade levels. Intermediate females, whereas in the upper grades, there was no significant difference between male and female students on total AMI scores. Intermediate female students scored significantly higher on total AMI scores than upper grade female students. There was no significant difference between male students in the grade levels. The finding of this investigation illustrates that intra-group similarities and differences on achievement motivation exist in low income, inner-city African-American elementary-school students and are linked to academic achievement. Further research is needed to fully understand this phenomenon.

Roderiques and Adrienne Blunt (2001) did a study "A comparison of ability-achievement discrepancy models for identifying learning disabilities." Three ability-achievement discrepancy methods for identifying learning disabilities were compared. The first methods used simple standard score difference calculation; the second method a regression equation; and the third, a variation of the second, took the standard error of estimate into account. These three methods were examined using varying significance criteria, producing five individual models: the simple difference models (IA and IB) used 16 and 23-point discrepancy criteria, respectively; the basic regression models (2A and 2B) used 16 and 23 points; and the regression variation model (3) used a 95% confidence level. The five models were applied to 145 student's IQ (Wechsler Intelligence Scale for children-Third Edition) and achievement. (Woodcock-Johnson Achievement Tests-Revised) scores; all students had been referred for psycho-educational testing. Mean diagnostic proportions produced by each model yielded no significant distinction between simple difference and basic regression methods; however, within methods, models using less stringent. Criteria identified significantly more students ($p<.05$). Of the students identified by Model 1A, 17% were declassified by model 1B; 24% of those identified by 2A were declassified by Model 1B; 24% of those identified by 2A were declassified by 2B. Model 3 functioned much like model 2B. Student's classification across models was dependent on their age and ability level. These findings suggest that the criterion chosen for significance has more impact on eligibility outcomes than the discrepancy method.

Cakiroglu, Jale, Telli and Sibel (2003) did a study entitled "Turkish High school student's perceptions of learning environment in biology classroom and their attitudes toward biology". The purpose of this study was to examine student's perceptions of learning environment in biology classrooms and to investigate relationships between learning and students attitudes toward biology. A total of 399 from nine and tenth grade students participated in the study. Data were collected utilizing an adapted version of the WIHIC instruct and biology attitude scale. Data analyses indicated that Turkish high school students generally had positive perceptions of biology class room environment and there was a positive perception of biology classroom association between the nature of the biology classroom environment with respect to teacher support, involvement, task orientation, equity and the students' attitudes to ward biology. In addition, result of the study revealed that there were significant differences in the perceptions of biology learning environment by gender.

Skinner and Amy Danielle (2003) perceived autonomy support in alternative academic environments: Implications for the academically delinquent study. The purpose of this study was to examine the relationship between perception of autonomy support in alternative educational environments and its impact on study motivation and goal commitment, as well as the relationship between perceived autonomy support and academic outcomes. Data were analyzed using correlation analysis, ANCOVA and stepwise multiple regression analysis. The findings provide evidence that the self-determination theory is a viable tool in predicting the academic outcomes of an academically delinquent population. Results also support the claim that perception of the alternative school climate plays a determining factor in the academic success of students remaining in the alternative environment, as well as those who have returned to their mainstream school setting.

Sueh-Fang, Chuarag and Yeong-Jing cheng (2003) did "a study on attitudes toward biology and learning environment of the seventh grade students". The purpose of this study was to investigate the relationships between student's attitude toward biology and classroom learning environment of the seventh grade students in Taipei area. The tools used were Attitudes toward Biology Scale (ATBS), what is happening this class (WIHIC) and learning out questionnaire. Statistical techniques were used to analyze the data. The findings showed that there was no significant change in attitude toward biology of the students at the end of the first semester. However, the subjects exhibited negative changes in attitude towards biology after the end of second semester. It is due to the increasing differently of the content of the biology text bode volume II. Associations between attitudes toward biology and perceptions of learning environment were significant. Further more, the findings also showed that significant correlations existed between attitude towards biology and variables related to students interest in learning biology and teacher's instructional management and teaching strategies.

Chen, Jennfier and Jun-Li (2004) did a study "Academic support form parents, teachers, and peers Relation to Hong Kong adolescent's academic behaviour and achievement." Research has substantiated that parents, teachers, and peers are important sources of academic support to students' achievement. The participants were 270 students (range 13-15 years, range

14-20 years) from three grade levels (forms 3-5, equivalent to grades 9-11 in the vs) in a Hong Kong secondary school. Date were collected using a self-report questionnaire, including a demographic profile and four scales assessing students perceptions of the availability of (1) parental support, (2) teacher support, (3) peer support and (4) their own academic behaviour. Academic achievement was measured by self-reported grades in Math, English and Chinese. Findings of this research are interpreted with respect to four main areas: (*i*) Socio-cultural values, (*ii*) relationship dynamics with parents, teachers and peers (*iii*) gender socialization and bias; and (*iv*) development influences suggestions for enhancing, home-school partnerships are discussed recommendations for improving pedagogical practices and parental involvement by considering gender as well as developmental differences of students is also provided.

Hill and Jennifer Lynne (2004) found the impact of learning styles and high school learning environment on student's decisions regarding higher education. The purpose of the study was to identify the learning styles of students at non traditional college and then examine whether the match or mismatch between their learning styles and their high school learning environment influenced their decisions regarding higher education. It was also hoped that the results of the study would indicate whether or not students with non-traditional learning styles select non-traditional higher education because of their impression that the learning environment will be different than their traditional high school learning environment and whether students with non-traditional learning styles and preferences would attend non-traditional colleges, but not traditions colleges.

Birdwell and Angela Denise (2005) found students' achievement in relation to poor factors in a district experiment hyper growth. This study included data collected from 1,400 student subjects, 193 teachers and 10 principals. Additionally the models were designed to examine relationships among qualities of individual trajectories and covariates. The growth models were analysed with the software program plus, a statistical package designed to deal with structural equation modeling. The finding of this research reflected a correlation between the covariates of mobility teacher experience and certification and principal experience. A significant correlation was found between fine-independent covariate of ethnicity. In the math model the covariates were found to be significantly related to the latest factors. Ethnicity was significantly related to the intercept in the negative direction indicating that non-Caucasian children scored on average 27-38 points lower than Caucasians children.

Laibach and Colleen (2006) found the relationship between social support and academic achievement in registered nursing education students. The population of this study was limited to 200 culturally diverse first and third semester nursing students. This study used a survey with 33 questions in a Likert scale that measure the students' attitude towards the importance and actual existence of social support in 5 dimensions. This study revealed that there were to relationships between each of the social support dimensions and students grade point average. In addition, there was a significant difference of actual nursing peer support for white students above non-white students. There was no significant difference for white and non-white nursing students on the dimensions of intimacy, social integration, social affirmation, faculty support, and grade point average. When nursing students whose grade point average was 3.0 and above or below 3.0 for 20 or more semesters were compared, their attitudes were not significantly different on the five dimensions of social support.

Zuhdi and Mohammad (2006) found the political and social influences on religious school: A historical perspective on Indonesian Islamic school curricula. As the most populous Muslim country in the world, Indonesia has a unique experience in dealing with Islamic education, a system that was established years before the country's independence. This dissertation focuses on the development of Indonesian Islamic schools in facing the challenges of modernization and globalization, with special reference to their challenging curricula. Using the social constructionist perspective as an approach, this study examines the significance of political and social changes to the development of Islamic schools curricula throughout the century's history. This study finds evidences of a reciprocal relationship between the changing curricula of Indonesian Islamic schools and the changing social and political circumstances.

Anderson-Jeffrey (2007) found "Effect of perceived success for children with individual education programs (IEP) in reading and persistence and comparison with peers". Reading ability is central to academic success, vocational success, and every day functioning. Yet there is a significant percentage of the population that strongly with reading. Problems attaining reading skills in early schooling affect not only initial academic success, but perception of self, perseverance in difficult tasks, and the degree to which the student seas him or herself affecting his or her external world. Analysis of variance was used to assess the differences between the high and low perceived success groups with the IEP and the non IEP groups. Results showed significantly higher persistence in IEP children with high perceived success compared to those with low perceived success. These results level support for the need to provide opportunities for non readier success for children who struggle with reading.

Davis and Joy (2007) did "An exploration of the impact of family on the achievement of African American gifted learners originating from low-income environments". The purpose of this study was to determine what, if any, impact families have on the academic achievement of African American gifted learners from low income environments. This study was designed to explore family and student perceptions of a complex set of variables related to families and home environments. Study participants were junior and senior level high school students and their parents. The most pronounced findings were the role of the mother as nurturer and encourager; the emphasis within the house holds on positive achievement orientation, and certain family traditions which taken together form a cohesive, supportive family environment, even in the midst of challenging life circumstances. Provide the educational practice include improving professional development for educators' family and parent educational programes and enhancing guidance and counseling programes for African American and other culturally diverse gifted learners.

Harris and Arthur (2007) did a study "Analysis of teacher, curricular, parental, and support influence on study achievement in an urban district". The main focus of this study is on the analysis of teacher, curriculum, parental and support influences on student achievement in an urban school district. The achievement levels of groups of students by race, gender and special services were analyzed. The findings indicate that although all groups of students made progress in all areas. The achievement gaps among them still persisted. For The findings showed that 30% gap separate white and Black students, while 35% between Asian and Hispanic student. The level of students' performance in terms of the percentage passing the high school assessment exams, graduating, and dropping out of school was analyzed in relation to the percentage of certified teachers.

Phelps and Kenyatta Danielle (2007) conducted a study "Partners, parents, and peers effects on African American youths school achievement". Thus using data from the Toledo Adolescent Research study, the researcher asked whether romantic relationships variables influence school grades and school engagement. In addition, are these relationships conditional or race? Finally do separate models examining the influence of romantic relationships on the dependent variables produce different results for African Americans and Anglos. The major findings from this study suggest that partners school grades, perceptions of partners as caring and trusting as certify and trusties, partners' academic orientation, and sex with the partner predict school grades and school engagement. However, sex with the partner predict school engagement for African Americans; whereas partner, grades, partners academic orientation, sex with partner, and the perception of the partner as caring and trusting predict school engagement for Anglos.

Smith Kath Leen (2007) fount the impact of district and school climate on students achievement. This was a quantitative correlation study that examine the possible relationships between district climate, school climate and students' achievement of the 2007 standards of learning assessments for grades 3,4, and 5 English (reading, research and literature) and mathematics in 25 low-and 44 high poverty elementary schools in 36 Verginia districts. A Pearson g was used to determine the relationship between the constructs and was computed procedure compared the means for school climate and district climate in low and high-poverty schools and the means for mean scale scores on SOL assessments in low-and high poverty schools. Significant relationships were found between district climate and school climate and between constructs of district climate and school climate in all schools and in high poverty schools. No significant relationships were found between district climate and students achievement however, relationships were found between school climate and student achievement and the constructs of school climate and student achievement.

Mihaly and Kata (2007) prepared "Essays on peer effects" This study considers the relationship between peer and individual student interaction. The central finding is that self reported friends play a crucial role in individual behaviours, a role that is more significant than other students in their school. Also, using the network of friendships within a school it is possible to construct new peer effect measures and account for endogenous peer group formation. It is however important to distinguish these measures from an observed individual characteristic that may also influence behaviour peer.

Francis, Adesoji, Segun and Olatunbosun (2008) did a study "student, teacher and school environment factors as determinants of achievement in senior secondary school chemistry in Oyo state, Nigeria". The study constructed and tested an eight-variable model for providing a causal explanation of achievement of secondary school students in chemistry in terms of student variables - attitude to learning chemistry, background knowledge in Integrated Science, teacher variables - attitude chemistry teaching, attendance at chemistry workshop and school environment related variables-class size, laboratory adequacy and school location. The study adopted an ex-post facto research type the population was made up of 621 senior secondary III chemistry students and 27 Senior Secondary III chemistry teachers in Oyo State, Nigeria. Four sets of instruments were used; These were chemistry Achievement Tests (SACS), Teacher Attitude Towards Chemistry Teaching Scale (TATCTS) and Laboratory Adequacy Inventory (LAI). The results revealed that 7.20% of the total effect on achievement in chemistry was accounted for by all the seven predictor variables when taken together. It was also revealed that only four variables -school location(X1) laboratory adequacy (X3), teachers' attitude towards chemistry teaching(X5) and teachers' attendance at chemistry workshop(X4) had direct causal influence and also made significant contributions to the prediction of achievement in chemistry (X8) (the criterion variable).

Studies on Study Habit and Academic Achievement in India

Kumaran and kamala (2001) conducted research ;which deals with the study habit of the variables such as study habits, study involvement, science interest and scientific attitude on the successful and unsuccessful learning of science subjects by higher secondary students. The sample consisted of 319 students drawn from six different types of higher secondary schools in the city of Chennai. Four standardized tools were used to measure the variables. The achievement scores in the science subject on the basis of which the students in the sample were classified as successful and unsuccessful learners were collected from the school records. The data were subjected to statistical analysis such as descriptive differential the discriminate.

Patel (2002) made an investigation into the "Study Habits of the Adivasi students of secondary schools of Panchamahals Districts in relation to some psycho-socio variables". Objectives of the study were (1) to construct and standardize an inventory to measure study Habits of the Adivasi students of secondary schools. (2) to study the study habits of the Adivasi students in relation to area, sex, I.Q., vocational aspirations and socio economics status. (3) to investigate the interaction effects of selected psycho-socio variables on study habits of the Adivasi students of secondary schools. The Methodology to study was descriptive in nature. Survey method was employed. 1035 Adivasi Schedule Tribes students of IX standard from the semi-government secondary schools of Panchmahals district were selected randomly. The tools used for measuring the variables were Desai-Bhatt's Group intelligence Test, Vocational Aspiration measurement by Dr. A.K. Shrivastav, scale of Socio-Economic Status by Patel and a Study Habits Inventory constructed and standardized by the investigator. For data analysis, Critical Ratio and Analysis of Variance were used as statistical technique. The findings are that (i) there is significant effect of Area, I.Q., and interaction between Area and IQ on study Habits. (ii) there is significant effect of area on the Adivasi Students' study habits whereas there is no effect of vocational aspiration and interaction between area and vocational aspiration on study habits of Adivasi student. (iii) there is significant independent effect of area and socio-economic status on the study habits of adivasi students where as there is no significant effect of interaction between area and socio-economic status on the study habits Adivasi students. (iv) there is significant effect of Sex, I.Q, and interaction between sex and IQ on the study habits of Adivasi students.

Thakkar (2003) conducted "A Study of Academic Achievement, Adjustment and Study Habits of Rural and Urban Students". The objectives of study were: (1) to find out the academic achievement of rural and urban students. (2) to compare the study habits of rural and urban students with their academic achievement. (3) to know the relationship between adjustment and academic achievement of rural and rural students. (4) and to compare the effect of therapeutic training on the students of both the segments of society. The present study was experimental type. The sample comprised of 200 students from rural and urban locality of standard IX were selected by using simple random sampling technique. To all members of the group, 16 sessions of one hour were given as therapeutic training consisted of imparting the knowledge of good study habit. Tools used were Adjustment Inventory by M.N. Palsana, Study Habits Inventory by M.N. Palsana and Academic Achievement scores on the basis of their two unit tests, semester/terminals and final examinations. Correlation and t-test techniques were used for data analysis. The findings of study were: (1) With regard to adjustment, in the areas of home and family, personal and emotional and total adjustment, there is positive significant difference between rural and urban students. However, in the areas of social and educational adjustment this difference is not significant. (2) There is no significant correlation between academic achievement and study habit among rural and urban locality. (3) There is no significant correlation between academic achievement and adjustment habit among rural and urban locality. (4) There is no significant correlation between study habits and adjustment among rural and urban locality.

Digumati Bhaskara Rao and Sema Surya Prakas Rao (2004) conducted a study on "Study habits of secondary school students". The main objectives of the study were to study the study habits of Secondary Srhool students and to compare the study habits of boys and girls, private and government school students and students of residence and non-residence schools. The sample consisting of 200 secondary school students was selected by stratified sampling. The finding of the study was: the secondary school students are possessing high study habits. It is the duty of the teacher to make the students excel in academic achievement, as the secondary school students possess high study habits. The students of government and private secondary schools possess high study habits without any significant difference. The students of residential and non-residential secondary schools possess high study habits without any significant difference between them. The teachers should guide the students in developing good study habits. The parents should provide the necessary facilities to the students to complement their plan of action in their studies. The students should also develop right study habits to achieve academic achievement.

Guravaiah (2004) conducted a study on "Study Habits of Residential and Non-Residential Pupils of X Class in relation to certain Psycho-Sociological Factors". The objectives of the study were: (1) to identify the differences in the study habits of residential and non-residential pupils of X class. (2) to study the influence of self-concept, personality factors and academic achievement on the study habits of residential and non-residential pupils of X class. (3) and to examine the impact of certain personal and socio-demographic factors on the study habits of residential and non-residential pupils. The sample consisted of 730 residential and 570 non-residential pupils studying X class in the state of Andhra Pradesh. The findings of the study were: (1) Residence and region have significant influence on the study habits of X class pupils. (2) Gender does not have significant influence on the study habits. (3) The main effects, namely, locality, caste, self-acceptance, HSPQ factor-C (emotionally less stable vs. emotionally stable), HSPQ factor-Q4 (relaxed vs. tense) have significant influence on the study habits of residential and non-residential pupils.

Rajani (2004) conducted a study on "Study Habit of Intermediate Students in Relation to Certain Psycho-Sociological Factors". The objectives of the study were: (1) To identify the influence of academic achievement of students on their study habits. (2) To study the influence of personal and socio-demographic variables on study habits. (3) To develop multiple regression equations in order to predict the study habits score of intermediate students with the help of different sets of independent variables. The sample consisted of 1200-second year intermediate students of the state of Andhra Pradesh. The 2 x 2 x 3 factorial design was used with two divisions of gender, two divisions of locality and three divisions of region. It was a survey and presage-product study. The tools used for the study were: Study Habits Inventory (SHI) constructed by the investigator; High School Personality Questionnaire (HSPQ) Form-A by Cattell adapted in Telugu by the investigator; Self-concept Scale (SCS) by Mukt Rani Rastogi adapted in Telugu by the investigator; Socio-Economic Scale (SES) developed by the investigator, and intermediate public examination marks taken from college records. The inferential statistical techniques used were t-test, F-test and Regression Analysis. The findings of the study were: (2) Most of the self-concept areas show significant influence on study habits of the students. (2) All the academic achievement scores have significant influence on study habits of the students. (3) Caste, native place, father's educational qualifications, mother's educational qualifications, father's occupation, total children of parents, and annual income of the family have significant influence on study habits of the students.

Sirohi (2004) conducted a study on a study of under-achievement in relation to study habits and attitude: Main objectives of this study were to study under-achievement in students in relation to their study habits and attitudes. The study was carried out on a sample of 1,000 students of elementary grade of 10 composite schools of south district of Delhi. The tools used were (a) General mental ability test by Jalota (b) Teachers made achievement test (c) Test of Study Habits and Attitude by Mathur. The findings of the study were all under-achiever indicated deficiency in study habits. 98.7% of the under-achievers tend to possess unfavourable attitude towards teachers and needed guidance. 97.5% had poor concentration. 92.5% of them indicated deficiency in school and hence environment. 96.2% lacked proper attitude towards examination. 72.8% faced mental conflicts. 72.8% were low in self-confidence. 70.3% had problems related to home assignments. 24.6% indicated deficiency in attitude towards education.

Vinecta Sirohi May (2004) conducted a study on "Under achievement in relation of a study habits and attitudes". The main objective of the study was to study under achievement in relation to study habits and attitudes.

The sample consisted 1000 students of elementary grade of composite schools of south district of Delhi. The finding of the study was: the present study has implication for guidance and preparing a remedial implication for under achievers. We find that in schools the teaching learning process is catering to the needs of only the average students where special groups like creative, slow learners, first generation learners, and under achievers are neglected. There is an urgent need to look into the needs of those special groups. Individual and group counseling may also help in improving the general achievement. Group guidance procedure can be used to improve study habits and study skills.

Arockiadoss (2005) studied the Study Habits and Academic Performance of the college students. The study was carried out to find out the level of study habits prevalent among the college students, the influence of personal and institutional background on study habits and the correlation between study habits and academic performance of college students. A stratified sample of 925 undergraduate final year students were selected from 25 arts and science colleges affiliated to Madurai Kamaraj University in TamilNadu. A study habits inventory was used for the study. The statistical techniques employed for the analysis were ANOVA and t-test. The major findings are, (1) Majority of the students are having only average level of study habits. (2) Women and art students have better study habits. (3) Private college and women's college students are having better study habits. (4) The academic performance of the college students are influenced by study habits.

Misra (2005) conducted "A Study of Factors Related to Achievement in Physics with special reference to Secondary School Students in the City of Lucknow. The objectives of study were: (1) to construct an achievement test in physics to assess achievement in physics. (2) to study the relationship of achievement in physics with some demographic factors, like, sex, age, caste, birth-order, and family type. (3) to study the association of achievement in physics with some social-psychological factors including socio-economic status, intelligence, scientific aptitude, achievement-motivation, attitude towards the subject physics and study habits. (4) to assess the relative contribution of social and psychological factors to explain the variance of achievement in physics. The findings of study were: (1) Sex plays an important role in achievement in physics. Boys are found to score significantly higher than girls. (2) Mean value of achievement in physics is higher (maximum) in caste category-1 followed by caste category-2 and caste category-3. (3) The relationship between caste category-1 and caste category-2 and caste category-1 and caste category-3 is significant, while it is not significant in case of caste category-2 and caste category-3. (4) Birth-order does not play any role in achievement in physics.

Jagannath and Dange (2007) made a study into "Study habits and Achievement in Physics of Students of Class XII". The objectives of the study were: (1) To find out the difference between boys and girls in their study habits, (2) To find out the difference between government and private students in their study habits, (3) To find out the difference between boys and girls in their achievement in Physics. (4) To find out the relationship between study habits and achievement in physics of XII standard students. *The Major Findings are (1)* there is no significant difference between boys and girls in their study habits. (2) there is significant difference between boys and girls in their achievement in Physics. (3) there is a relationship between study and achievement in Physics.

Amirthagowri and Sivakumar (2009) The Study which aimed at study habits and academic achievement of post graduate students. For the present study investigator randomly selected 100 post graduate students from Govindammal Aditanar College Tiruchendur. Data were collected using appropriate tools and analyzed by two- tailed "t" test. The results indicate that there is a significant relation between study habits and academic achievement.

Nalini and Ganesha Bhatta (2009) found Study habit and students' achievement in relation to some influencing factors .This study aimed at finding the relationship between study habits and students' achievement in relation to socioeconomic status, learning environment, school adjustment and intelligence. The investigator found significant relationship between study habits and these influencing factors.

Susai Rajendran et al (2009) did a study 'Are study habits gender biased'? study is habit something that is acquired through repetitions. It is semi – mechanical and automatic. Cultivation of proper study habits is the sole aim of education. In the present work the study habits of high school's student in Dindigul area, Tamil Nadu, with respect to home environment, reading , note taking , planning of subject, habit of concentration, general habits and attitudes, preparation for examination and school environment, have been investigated . A standardized tool was used for these purpose students.

Studies on Study Habits and Academic Achievement Abroad

Ehrlish Mark Edward (2000) conducted a study on the "Tran Theoretical model of change. Application to college students study habits". The study examined the relationship between stages of change and the variables. Students in undergraduate educational psychology classes were supervised twice during a semester to assess their level of studying stage of change, use of process of change and self-efficacy for changing their study habits. Cross-sectioned methods were used to test specific production regarding the relationship between stage of change and each Tran theoretical variable for each round of data collection. Result indicated that most of the relationship found in between stage of change and specific Tran theoretical variable applied to college students' study habits.

Medo and Mary Anne (2000) conducted a study on "The Status of high school students learning strategies what students do when they read to acquire knowledge". The study investigated in learning strategies used by high school juniors when they study social studies. The sample included 230 juniors enrolled in social studies classes in three schools and were identified by school, gender and reading achievement. The results showed that between 50% and 91% of students said that they 'always' or sometime use 30 of the 36 strategies listed on the self-report, and used 9 those strategies suggest the students consider task demands and select strategies accordingly. Private school students were reported spending more time on studying and use more strategies than suburban and urban school students. Private school students were more likely to report using deep-processing strategies than urban and suburban students. While urban students were more likely than suburban students to report using surface level strategies. Good and average readers were mentioned using more strategies than poor readers. But poor readers were reported spending more time in studying than good and average readers. Average readers looked more like poor readers in terms of using surface-level strategies. Female students were mentioned using more strategies and spending more time in studying than male students and female students were more than male students in using a variety of sound strategies.

Roberston Nichole (2000) conducted a study on "Differences in eleventh grade students' perception of the condition affecting students' aspiration is Mississippi". The major objective was to find out the relationship between students' perception of the condition affecting student aspiration in Mississippi public high school. The sample included 357 U.S History students from 17 public high schools in Mississippi. Data for his study were computed from responses to survey instrument, student speak, education of variance tests, t-test and one factorial analysis of variance test. The major finding was that the conditions affecting student aspiration were belonging, sense of accomplishment, leadership and responsibility and school environment.

Berg, Charles and Lick Paulette (2001) conducted a study on "literacy and emotions data analysis from the dude large project". The study focused on the relationship between emotions and literacy achievement. It began with a mention of the theoretical contributions, which backed up the study in the Dude large project survey (4th Graders). Data had been reduced in two ways by factor and by cluster analysis. Result indicated a strong relationship between both parameters. It concluded with prospects for further research and conclusion drawn concerning both the theory of reading and practical consequences for the every day work in schools.

Nneji (2002) found the study habits of Nigerian university students. The purpose of this study was to investigate the study habits of university students in Nigeria. The sample consisted of 441 education students chosen from four federally owned universities in Nigeria. Descriptive analysis of data showed that students put some reasonable length of time into reading; some students used. Memorization technique; majority of the students depended on their course handouts or lecture notes as the main sources of information and read mostly for the purpose of passing examinations or tests. They read to absorb information as given by their lecturers and not necessarily to search for new or additional information. It was concluded that although university students in Nigeria read mostly for the purpose of passing examinations and they do not seem to pursue their studies correctly and thoroughly, they were found to be diligent. Some recommendations were made as to how to make university education in Nigeria more beneficial.

Garavalia, Linda, Ray and Marilyn (2003) found the 'Distinctions among Subgroups of Developmental Students: Differences in Task Value, Self-Regulated Learning, and Grade Expectations'. The study showed that only low-achieving and low-aptitude students differed significantly from their peers, indicating that subgroups might have a greater need for remediation in basic study strategies.

Chen et.al. (2005) did a study 'Are learning styles relevant to virtual reality?' This study aimed to investigate the effects of a virtual reality (VR) – based leaning environment on leaners with different leaning styles. The findings of the aptitude – b – treatment interaction study have shown that learners benefited most form the VR (guided exploration) mode irrespective of their learning styles. This showed that the VR – based environmental offered.

Abid Hussain Ch (2006) found the "Effect of Guidance Services on Study Attitudes, Study Habits and Academic Achievement of Secondary School Students". The substantive aim of the study was to examine the effect of guidance services on students' study attitudes, study habits and academic achievement. An experimental study was devised for the purpose. A guidance programme for secondary school students was developed by the researcher. An experiment was conducted to explore the effectiveness of guidance services in terms of improvement in students' study attitudes, study habits and academic achievement. Ten null hypotheses were tested to explore the effect of guidance services on students' study habits, study attitudes and academic achievement in five subjects. All the hypotheses were tested at 0.05 level of significance. The results of the study indicated that the guidance services had significant effect on the students' study attitude, study habits and academic achievement

Camahalan Faye Marsha (2006) did a study on "Effects of Self-Regulated Learning on Mathematics Achievement of selected Southeast Asian Children". This research was based on the conceptual framework that students' low mathematics achievement in school is related to their poor study habits. The main result supported self-regulated learning theory that states that when students are given opportunities to self-regulate and explicitly taught of self-regulated learning strategies, academic achievement is more likely to be positively affected. The study confirmed that students as active agents of their behaviors could be trained to be responsible learners and thus acquired the goal of life-long education which is learning not just "what" to learn but more importantly "how" to learn.

Loyens et.al. (2007) conducted a study on "The Impact of Students' Conceptions of Constructivist Assumptions on Academic Achievement and Drop-out". This study investigated the impact of students' conceptions of constructivist learning activities on academic achievement and drop-out. Although constructivism represents an influential view of learning, studies investigating how students conceptualize this perspective have not been conducted before. A structural equation modeling approach was adopted to test different models relating students' conceptions to their achievement in the university setting. Results suggested an indirect relationship between conceptions and achievement, mediated by actual learning activities. What students believe about the role of knowledge construction in learning predicted the actual learning activities they undertook, how important they considered inability to learn and motivation for learning predicts their study time.

Vandell et.al. (2007) found the outcomes linked to high-quality after school Programs: Longitudinal Findings from the Study of Promising After school Programs. This study was by researchers at the University of California, Irvine, the University of Wisconsin-Madison and Policy Studies Associates, Inc. found that regular participation in high-quality after school programs is linked to significant gains in standardized test scores and work habits as well as reductions in behavior problems among disadvantaged students. These gains helped to avoid the negative impact of a lack of supervision after school. The two-year study followed almost 3,000 low-income, ethnically diverse elementary and middle school students from eight states in six major metropolitan centers and six smaller urban and rural locations. About half of the young people attended high quality after school programs at their schools or in their communities.

Watters, Dianne, Watters and James (2007) did a study "Approaches to Learning by Students in the Biological Sciences: Implications for Teaching". This study is an investigation of the epistemological beliefs and study habits of students undertaking first-year courses in Biological Chemistry and Biochemistry. In particular, the researchers were interested in the relationship between students' epistemological beliefs about learning and knowledge, approaches to learning, and achievement. The study adopted a mixed-methods approach in which quantitative and qualitative data have provided complementary insights into the beliefs and approaches adopted by these students. The findings indicated that most students tend to adopt beliefs that knowledge and learning involves the accumulation of information and the capacity to reproduce on demand in examinations. Approaches to learning reflected these beliefs and were dominated by rote learning and preference for assessment by examination. Few students adopted strategies that emphasize the relationship of concepts to those already learnt or to applications relevant to biological science. Implications of this study were for reform of university teaching practices as well as secondary practices are discussed.

Yumusak et.al. (2007) did a study "Turkish High School Students' Biology Achievement in Relation to Academic Self-Regulation". This study aimed at investigating the contribution of motivational beliefs, cognitive and meta-cognitive strategy use to Turkish high school students' achievement in biology. In order to investigate the specified purpose of the study, 519 tenth-grade students were administered with the Motivated Strategies for Learning Questionnaire (Pintrich, Smith, Garcia, & McKeachie, 1991) and a Biology Achievement Test developed by the researchers. Results of multiple linear regression analyses showed that extrinsic goal orientation, task value, rehearsal strategy use, organization strategy use, management of time and study environment, and peer learning contributed significantly to the prediction of achievement scores.

Flowers, Tiffany, Flowers and Lamont (2008) found the "Factors Affecting Urban African American High School Students' Achievement in Reading". Data analyzed from the Educational Longitudinal Study of 2002 indicated that the reading achievement of urban African American high school students was positively influenced by the amount of hours spent doing homework and by parents' expectations of their child's future educational attainment. Implications for practice and research were provided.

Kim, ChanMin, Keller and John (2008) did a study on "Effects of Motivational and Volitional Email Messages (MVEM) with Personal Messages on Undergraduate Students' Motivation, Study Habits and Achievement". This study investigated what kind of supportive information can be effective in improving the situation where there were severe motivational challenges. Motivational and volitional email messages (MVEM) were constructed based on an integrated model of four theories and methods, which are Keller's ARCS model, Kuhl's action control theory, Gollwitzer's Rubicon model of motivation and volition, and Visser & Keller's strategy of motivational messages, and distributed with personal messages created based on audience analysis to a large undergraduate class. In order to examine the effects of the messages on motivation for the course, study habits (study time), and achievement (test grade), MVEM were sent to 30 students (Personal Message Group: PMG) with personal messages and to 71 students (Non-Personal Message Group: Non PMG) without personal messages. Results indicated that PMG showed a higher level of motivation, especially in regard to confidence, than Non PMG. Also, the mean test grade of PMG increased so that the initial difference of the test grade between the two groups significantly decreased. Although there was no difference between the two groups in study habits, the findings suggest that personal messages addressing specific individual problems raise the positive effects of MVEM constructed based on the integrated model. Future research directions are discussed.

Studies on Self -Esteem and Academic Achievement in India

Kalyani alias Usha Raman and Amalraj (2002) conducted a study on "Effect of self-esteem and classroom culture on the academic achievement". The sample of 250 students in the higher secondary schools of Manur blocks Tirunelveli District. The purpose of the study was to find out whether there is a relationship among class room culture, self-esteem and academic achievement. The study revealed that there was a significant correlation between self-esteem of school students and their academic achievement with reference to all the students' boys, girls, urban and rural schools, co-education schools, government aided management schools and self financed matriculation schools. The study revealed that there was significant correlation between classroom culture and self-esteem with reference to government schools and government aided schools whereas there was no significant correlation between classroom culture and academic achievement of students.

Agarwal and Raj (2004) conducted a study on relation between self-esteem and school performance - A Behaviour Modification Approach was followed to study the relationship between self-esteem and school performance among children and also analyze the effectiveness of psychological intervention in enhancing self-esteem and the effect of enhanced self-esteem on school performance. The study was conducted in two parts, i. e. Part-A and Part-B. For Part-A, a sample of 505 children in the age range of 8 - 14 years were selected from schools of Agra. Taking Part-A as a baseline 130 children with low self-esteem were given psychological treatment. Pre- and Post-test design was used. Self-esteem Inventory (Coopersmith, 1975) and School Performance Scores of the children in tests and examinations in schools were used to measure self-esteem and school performance respectively. Data were treated with product moment of co-efficient correlation and 't' test. It was concluded that higher the self-esteem higher the school performance. Children given psychological intervention proved to be better in their school performance.

Ponni, Santhi and Palanisamy (2007) did a study aim with the to find out the level of self-esteem and its domains (competency, global self-esteem, moral and self-control, social-esteem, family and body and physical appearance) of various professional course student with respect to gender and location and differences between and within the students of engineering, medicine, management and computer applications. It has been found that the level of self-esteem of the professional students is high (74.9%). Further, it was observed that there was a significant difference in the level of self-esteem between rural (71.4%) and urban (75.9%) students, whereas there was no significant difference in the level of Self-esteem between male and female students expect family domain (84.2% female 88.6%). It was also found that there was no significant difference between and within the students of various professional courses.

Amirt Rai and Annaraja (2008) had attempted to find out the self-esteem and level of aspiration of high school students in Sri Lankan Refuge Campus. The sample consisted of 100 high school students of Sri Lankan Refuge Campus in Dindigal and Tirunelveli Districts and the investigators adopted the survey method. The finding revealed that there was no significant relationship between Self-esteem and level of aspiration of high school students. However, there was significant difference between rural and urban high school students in their level of aspiration.

Babu and Sameer (2008) conducted a study "Self-Esteem and Emotional Intelligence among B.Ed Trainees of Tsunami Affected Coastal Belt". Through this study the author investigated the relationship between self-esteem and emotional intelligence among B. Ed trainees of Tsunami affected coastal belt of Alappey district of Kerala, India. Stream of study, martial status and age based comparisons were made among the B. Ed trainees. 92 B. Ed trainees were the participants in the study. It was found that they had a good level of self-esteem and emotional intelligence. While the variables were correlated, it was found a substantial correlation in all the groups except science stream students. The correlation coefficient between self-esteem and emotional intelligence of science stream students was high. Both in self-esteem and emotional intelligence, it was found no significant difference among the students based on stream of study, martial status and age, except in the comparison of them in their self-esteem based on age.

Priyadharshini and Velayudhan (2008) did the study focusing on pro-social behavior and self-esteem of hostel students and day scholars (N=120, Hostellers 60 and Day scholars 60). These students were studying in the various departments of Bharathiar University, Coimbatore. The mean, standard Deviation and ANOVA were used to determine the significant difference among university students in their pro-social behavior and self-esteem. Altruism, courtesy and sportsmanship were found to be more among the hostellers whereas there was no significant difference found among the students in their self-esteem.

Surila Agarwala, Meenakshi Verma and Satya Singh (2008) had undertaken the study to compare the self-esteem of orphan and non-orphan children and to study the effectiveness of behavior intervention in enhancing self-esteem. The study was conducted in two parts. In part 'A', Self-esteem of orphan and non orphan children was compared and in part 'B', the effectiveness of behavior intervention in enhancing self-esteem of children was studied. In part 'A', matched group design was used for the study. The sample of the study comprised two groups of children, group I comprised 50 orphan children and group II comprised 50 non-orphan children. The result showed significant difference in the self-esteem of orphan and non-orphan children. In part 'B', pre and post design was used. The sample of this part of the study comprised two groups of children: group I comprised to orphans and group II comprised to non-orphan children, having low self-esteem. The result showed effectiveness of behavior intervention in enhancing self-esteem of both orphan and non-orphan children.

Thilagavathi (2008) conducted "A Study on Academic Achievement of Adolescents in Relation to their Self-Esteem". This study revealed that the academic achievement of first year higher secondary students was average. Students of high, average and low achievement group significantly differed among themselves in respect to their self-esteem scores. Girls seemed to have comparatively higher self-esteem than boys. Students belonging to private school had a higher self-esteem than those of government schools. Urban school students had higher self-esteem than rural students. Academic achievement and self-esteem were found to be positively and significantly related.

Vasanthi Vinoliya and Sivakumar (2009) fount that Influence of self-esteem on academic achievement of higher secondary students in Thoothukudi District. In the present study, the investigators attempted to find out the self-esteem and Academic achievement of higher secondary school students. The sample consisted of 300 in the Thoothukudi Districts and the investigator adopted the survey method. The findings revealed that there was significant relationship between self-esteem and academic achievement of higher secondary students.

Studies on Self -Esteem and Academic Achievement Abroad

Caldwell and Roslyn Marie (2000) did a study "Family versus peer involvement: the role of self-esteem, sex and cognitive style as predictors of delinquency among high-risk adolescents". Using a sample of 168 high-risk adolescents who were on probation with the juvenile justice system, this study examined the hypotheses that family versus peer involvement would moderate an adolescent's level of self-esteem and that both family versus peer involvement and self-esteem would moderate level of delinquency. The results revealed that an adolescent's level of family involvement was positively associated with their level of self-esteem. Second, an adolescent's level of family involvement was negatively related to severity of delinquent behavior. Third, an adolescent's level of self-esteem was negatively correlated with severity of delinquency. Also, an adolescent's cognitive style was found to be positively correlated with the level of delinquency. Results also showed no significant relationships between an adolescent's level of peer involvement to self-esteem and to level of delinquency.

Chu and Yu-Wei (2000) found the relationship between domain-specific self-concepts and global self-esteem among adolescents in Taiwan. The purpose of this study was to investigate the relationships between domain-specific self-concepts and global self-esteem among adolescents in Taiwan. The research sample included 591 ninth, tenth and eleventh grade students (i-e) (316 boys and 275 girls) enrolled in 2 Junior high schools and 4 senior high schools in Taipei, Taiwan. The interview results indicated that students' self-perceptions built good relationships with peers, parents, and teachers due to good academic performance. In addition students from high and low track schools demonstrated that the traditional entrance examination in Taiwan was a fair but stressful test. These findings might be helpful, for educators, school counselors, and re-searchers to emphasize the relationships between domain-specific self-concept and global self-esteem. Recommendations were provided for future studies, which would be important in developing instruments for assessing specific domains of self-concept as well as enhancing self-esteem programs in Taiwan.

Joanne and Williams (2000) conducted a study on self-esteem and physical development in early adolescence to find out the relationship between self-esteem, pubertal timing and body image. Data were derived from the Health Behaviour in School Children: WHO Cross-National Survey, specifically the Scottish survey. This study showed among 11-year-olds, early maturation and lower ratings of body image (body size and perceived appearance) were associated with lower reported levels of self-esteem. There also was evidence that body image mediated the relation of pubertal timing on self-esteem for this age group. Among 13-year-olds, reports of body size concerns and poorer perceived appearance were predictive of lower ratings of self-esteem, as was late maturation. In this case, there was no evidence of mediation. Results lent support to the contention that pubertal timing influences body image and self-esteem.

Von Essen et.al. (2000) conducted a study on self-esteem, depression and anxiety among Swedish children and adolescents on and off cancer treatment to find out self-esteem, depression and anxiety of Swedish children and adolescents on and off cancer treatment. The self-report measures "I Think I Am" (ITIA), the Children's Depression Inventory (CDI) and the Revised Children's Manifest Anxiety Scale (RCMAS) were used. Data were compared with data previously obtained by others for healthy Swedish children. Children and adolescents on treatment showed levels of self-esteem, depression and anxiety comparable to those of healthy children. However, children and adolescents off treatment reported higher depression and anxiety levels and lower psychological well-being and physical self-esteem than have been reported for healthy Swedish children. Seven children (14%) reported a high level of depression, six of whom were off treatment. The findings suggested that the period after treatment termination was characterized by a higher risk of psychosocial problems than was the actual treatment period.

Bergstrome and Scott Eric (2001) found the "importance of academic achievement in determining the self-esteem of students in rural British Columbia. An empirical examination of students in grades 6, 8, 10 and 12". Data were collected from 263 students in grades 6, 8, 10 and 12 in a small district in South Western Canada. The first part of this study explored the relationship between student self-esteem, and gender. The co-opersmith self-esteem inventory was to measure self-esteem on four scales. As a result of multiple regression analysis it was found that the R^2 values were very low in all cases (ranging from 0.20 to 0.36) which indicated that the factors studied were poor indicators of self-esteem and that there was a great deal unexplained variation associated with the data. GPA, level of involvement, grade and GPA, grade were significant at 0.05 level of significance. Gender was not a significant factor in this study. It appeared that self-esteem was linearly related to GPA, with the intercept depending on the grade, level of level of involvement, and gender as the slope depending on the grade. The relationship between GPA and self-esteem was strongest at grade 6. Self-esteem was found to be strongest for students who were heavily involved in school-related on extra-curricular activities. Eleven survey questions regarding the school experience were analyzed using logistical regression analysis, which showed that the importance of getting good grades and participating in school activities varied according to grade and gender. Academic achievement was most important to grade 6 students, good grades were more important to girls, than boys, and the association between getting good grades and self-esteem was strongest at grade 6.

Malinsky and Marg Ann (2001) matched learning styles of teacher and student, A study of is relationship to achievement and self-esteem. The purpose of this study was to explore the relationship of method teacher/ student learning styles to the achievement and self-esteem of students. Using an ex post facts research design 126 fifth and sixth grade students, and six teachers of two public elementary schools of the Jefferson Parish School system in Louisiana were administered with learning style Inventory (ISI), and teachers were given an adult version, the productively Environmental Preference Survey (PEPS). A significant MANOVA F was obtained. Therefore a post-hoc analysis of variance (ANOVA) at the 0.05 level of significance was done on each dependent variable. F ratios indicated significant differences among the mean scores of the matched and mismatched groups for the dependent variables of general self-esteem, social self-esteem, home/parents self-esteem, and school self-esteem. There was no significant difference, however, between the mean scores of the matched and mismatched groups for the dependent variable of achievement grade.

Aives-Martins et.al. (2002) conducted a study on self-esteem and academic achievement among adolescents to analyze what strategies are pursued in order to protect self-esteem when it was threatened by a negative self-evaluation of school competence. Tools used included Harter's Self-Perception Profile for Adolescents, together with a Scale of Attitudes towards School. The results showed that there were significant differences between the self-esteem enjoyed by successful and unsuccessful students in the seventh grade; such differences disappeared in the eight and ninth grades. They also revealed success-related differences in domain-specific self-evaluation. It was also found that students with low levels of academic achievement attributed less importance to school-related areas and revealed less favorable attitudes towards school.

Brug and Peary (2002) found the ethnic identity and its association with self-esteem among Surinamese adolescents in the motherlands. The study examined the relationship between ethnic identity and self-esteem among 94 Surinamese adolescents in the Motherlands. This research expanded the work of Parham and Helms (1985) and Phinney and Chavira (1992) by examining an ethnic population outside the United States. The investigation had as its fours to determine if ethnic identity was a salient concept for the Surinamese youth and to determine whether ethnic identity was related to self-esteem. Additionally, the study examined the association between an integration mode (Berry 1989) and self-esteem. The findings from this work indicated that ethnic identity and self-esteem had a positive relationship; however, the results did not support the notion that different modes of integration are in any way associated with different levels of self-esteem.

Moore and Malena Katrina (2002) found the relationship between learner-Centeredness and Self-Esteem in two middle schools. The purpose of this study was to examine the relationship between learner-centeredness as perceived by students and self-esteem of students in two middle schools, a charter school and a non-charter public school. Self-esteem was measured through the coppersmith self-esteem inventory administered in October and again in January. Student's perceptions of Learner-Centeredness team inventory administered in October and again in January. The results of this study suggested that a learning environment that was perceived as being more highly learner-centered and approaches the nurturing of self-esteem systemically would result in higher self-esteem scores.

Perez-Rivera and Betty (2003) did a study "Body shape attitudes, eating attitudes, self-esteem and social support among diverse urban adolescents". The purpose of this cross-sectional survey study was to determine body shape attitudes, eating attitudes, self-esteem, and satisfaction with the number and quality of social supports available in diverse urban adolescents to determine if these factors could predict the risk for developing eating disorders in a convenience sample of 236[males (n=65) and females (n=171)] ages 12-16. As Adolescents Matured, BSQ scores increased, also increasing the level of risk as BSQ was found to be the most sufficient prediction of risk for developing eating disorders, Significant correlations were also found between BSQ and EAT(r=0.664, PC 0.001). BSQ, grade, and EAT were found to be most significant, providing important clues to issues to address for future preventive programs. Stepwise multiple regression analyses, with a post HOC Bomferroni adjustment, found that race, gender and other study variables were not significant. The overall prevalence, gender and other study shape dissatisfaction, negative eating attitudes, low self-esteem, and dissatisfactions with social supports was low in this study.

Yunker and Jonel Jones (2003) found the relationship between self-esteem and traditional of career choice among eighth-grade girls. This study of eighth grade girls was designed to address the relationship between the level of self-esteem and the gender traditionality of their levels and ideal career choices. One hundred and twenty nine participants were recruited from two junior high schools in the greater Cincinnati area participants completed the Rosenberg self-esteem inventory as well as questions asking each girl for her likely career choice and her ideal career choice. In a t-test of Equality of means for careers the girls expected to enter, the average self-esteem scores for girls choosing traditional careers was not significantly lower than for girls choosing non-traditional careers. In a t-test of equality of means for ideal choices, average self-esteem scores for girls with non-traditional choice were also not significantly different from the average self-esteem scores for girls with traditional ideal choices. Quantitative analysis did not support the hypothesis that there was a statistically significant positive correlation between self-esteem and career choice among middle school girls.

Clash and Clarice (2004) found the characteristics of rural poverty and female high school athletes: A case study of grade point averages, self-esteem levels, and leadership abilities. The study analyzed and evaluated through case study the characteristics of living in rural poverty in conjunction with grade point averages, self-esteem leadership tendencies, and sexual behaviors and attitudes. The aims of the study were to identify (a) the female athletes' leadership tendencies (b) the female athletes' self-concept levels and (c) the ways female athlete's grade point averages in comparison to other ethnic groups. Based on the leadership ability test results, the study concluded that Hispanic females did not possess the ambition and drive to become future leaders in society but that the Native American, African-American, and Caucasian females needed additional mentors in this area since this group scored lower than any other group. The self-esteem instrument indicated that girls in this community possessed medium to low levels of self-esteem.

Additionally the sexual attitudes survey indicated that at least half of the respondents in the sample would continue having sex. Finally, the research found that Caucasian girls were not performing satisfactorily in academic achievement.

Higher and Donna Louise (2004) Context, moral orientation, and self-esteem impacting the moral development of college students. The purpose of this study was to compare moral orientation and a measure of self-esteem with the degree of consideration given to certain contextual elements of the moral dilemmas presented. Demographic differences (sex / race / ethnicity, and class standing) among respondents were also examined related to the degree of consideration given to certain contextual elements of the moral dilemmas presented. The overall care score was significantly related to peers scale and institutional values scale. The self-care score was significantly related to the relationship and peer scales' the self-justice score was significantly related to the institutional value scale. All other comparisons did not reach a level of statistical significant.

Byrd and Ronald (2005) found the relationship between self-esteem, self-concept and aggression in Black, Latino, and white middle school males. This study collected and analyzed data for a group suburban middle school boys, ages 11 to 14 to ascertain their feelings of aggression, their self-concepts and the relationships between these feelings and the following were also tested age, race, and ethnic group. The piers-Harris self-concept scale (Ellen piers, 1984) and the Aggression Questionnaire Buss and Warren, 2000) were used to collect the data. A total of 95 boys were involved. Race and ethnic groups included black, white and Hispanic. Analysis of variance and Chi-square analyses were used to test for homogeneity of the sample according to race and age. No significant difference was found for either variable. The 0.05 level of significance was applied as a criterion for F and Chi-square values. Applications of analysis of variance and Chi-square also indicated that the responses of the sample were not significantly different from the responses of boys in the norm groups for the instruments. Application of a Pearson product moment correlation analysis to test for relationships between feelings of aggression and self-concept yielded a most important negative relationship (r=54) i.e when self-concepts of subjects went down, feelings of aggression went up. The researcher concluded that higher grade point averages were not related to lower body-fat, high self-esteem, and high levels of physical activity. However, the more physical activity that was performed by the students, the lower the student's percent body-fat. Females tended to be more over weight and participated less in physical activity. Further research is needed to understand why females do not participate in physical activity.

Irandokht Asadi Sadeghi Azar and Promila Vasudeva (2006) did a study self-efficacy and self-esteem was selected to evaluation the effect of employment on women in this study. The samples consisted of 250 married employed and 250 married unemployed women in the age range of 24-41 years, with educational qualification of 10+2 and above and having at least one school going child. Stratified convenience sampling technique was used for the selection of the sample. The General Self-Efficacy Scale (GSE) and the Coopersmith Self-Esteem Inventory (CSEI) were chosen for collection of data. The results; showed that the professionally employed women were found to be significantly higher on self-efficacy and self-esteem than unemployed and non-professionally employed women. Non-professionally employed and unemployed women did not differ significantly on self-efficacy and self-esteem. It was conclude that the Status and level of works was important factor for creation of the positive consequences of work in women.

Jacobson and Steven Dean (2006) perceived parental nurturance and self-esteem across American and Japanese University Students. The purpose of the current study was to examine the relationship between perceived parental nurturance and self-esteem between two culturally diverse populations, to determine how the trends we find in Western Societies, such as the United States, relate to those found in Eastern such as Japan. Participants for the present study were 121 students form a large Midwestern University: 70 (58.7%) Undergraduate students from US born population and 51 (41.3%) international Undergraduate students from a Japanese born population. The study design utilized the Rosenberg Self-Esteem Scale (RSES) and the Parental Nurturance Scale (PNS) to compare the two samples, and the Marlowe-Crowne Social Desire ability Scale (SDS) was used to control for participants' socially desirable response patterns. A 2 by 2 between groups analysis of covariance was conducted to compare the relationship between parental nurturance and self-esteem in two different groups of college students (US group and Japanese group). After adjusting for the social desirability scores, there was no significant interaction effect between country and parental nurturance on self-esteem $F(1,116) = 1.42$, $P = 0.24$. Results also indicated that social desirability scores were more closely correlated with parental nurturance scores for the US group than they were for the Japanese group.

Bucur and David (2007) did a study "defining the self: Locus of evaluation, self-esteem, and personality". The purpose of the present study was to develop and validate the Locus of Evaluation Inventory (LEI), and examine the relationships among locus of evaluation, self-esteem, and measures of personality. The sample size of 47 was not adequate to detect a large effect at the 0.05 level for this type of study (cohen, 1992); There were no significant differences between the two groups for any comparison. Specifically, younger 7th and 8th grades reported the same level of self-esteem, perceptions of family cohesiveness, and level of extra curricular activities as relatively older 7th and 8th graders. Additionally, the academic achievement of the relatively younger groups was 25-items LEI. These results are discussed in terms of the broad implications that locus of evaluation and the LEI may have on conceptualizing, assessing, and facilitating psychological functioning.

Knightley, Wendy, Whitelock and Dcnise (2007) conducted a study on assessing the self-esteem of female undergraduate students to explore the impact on the sense of self and self-esteem of a group of female first-year undergraduates. The tools used included "Self-esteem inventory", a variation on Q Methodology, an "Ideal-self inventory" and a semi-structured interview. The results indicated that participants' self-esteem increased over the duration of the study, as recorded on all four measures. It was suggested that the most appropriate way of uncovering and understanding mediators of self-esteem might be through a mixed-method approach.

Shabazz and Khallid (2007) found the effects of environment and age on locus of control, self efficiency, and self-esteem of military and non-military student's academic achievement. The college drop-out rate for African-Americans, since the 1980s, has risen 63 percent. Due to the negative outcomes associated with the underachievement of the African-American male, researchers began to explore the theoretical proposition from Bandura's (1986). The study results revealed that environment and age have a significant effect on locus of control and self-esteem, but not self-efficacy. The overall result was that while there was a statistically significant predictive relationship of the impact of locus of control, self-esteem and self-efficacy on academic achievement that the relationship was not practically significant as it accounted for only 7% of variance found. In the final analysis, this research neither fully confirms nor disconfirms Bandura's Theory of social learning that there was a definitive impact of environment and age on the three constructs. Rather, this study's results revealed a more variegated and nuanced understanding of conditions under which the theory holds true, or not.

Smith and Gregory (2007) conducted a survey on parenting effects on self-efficacy and self-esteem in late adolescence and how those factors impact adjustment to college. Approximately three months before starting college, 203 high school seniors completed a questionnaire consisting of the General Self-Efficacy Scale, the Rosenberg Self-Esteem Scale, and the Parental Authority Questionnaire (PAQ) assessing their parents' parenting styles. It was found that authoritarian parents had students with lower self-esteem and self-efficacy, while authoritative parents had students with higher self-esteem and self-efficacy. There was no relationship between permissiveness in parents and the students' levels of self-esteem or self-efficacy. Students higher in self-esteem and self-efficacy experienced less homesickness and showed better emotional and behavioural adjustment to college. Conversely, students lower in self-esteem and self-efficacy experienced more homesickness and had a more difficult adjustment to college.

Murphy and Kevin (2007) found the relationship between emotional intelligence and satisfaction with life after controlling for self-esteem, depression and locus of control among community college students. This study investigated the relationship between Emotional Intelligence (EI) and Satisfaction with Life (SWL) among community college students. A convenience sample of 200 Central Florida Community College students completed the instruments.(1) MSCEIT (Mayer, Salovey and Caruso Emotional Intelligence Test, 2002) to assess EI. (2) RSES (Rosenberg Self-Esteem Scale, 1965) to assess self-esteem. (#) BDI-11 (Beck Depression Inventory, 11) Beck, steer and Brown (1997) to assess depression (4) I-E Scale (Internal-External Locus of control Scale) Rotter (1996) to assess locus of control. (5) SWLS (Satisfaction With Life Scale) Diener, Emmons, Larsen, and Griffin (1985) to assess overall (global) Satisfaction With Life. Givariate correlations between the known predictor variables (self-esteem, depression, and locus of control) and the dependent measure (SWL) are in agreement (size and direction) with prior research. However, correlation analysis suggested no correlation between EI as well as all four components of EI with SWI or the known predictor variables. These findings agreed with prior research reporting correlations between EI and components of EI with SWL. A series of five hierarchical regression analyses was conducted to investigate whether EI or any of the four components of EI contributes in the prediction of SWL after accounting for known prediction (self-esteem, depression and locus of control). The results of all five hierarchical regression analysis suggested EI as well as the components of EI do not account for additional variance in SWL among community college students. Therefore, results of the study suggested EI was not an important predictor of SWL among community college students.

Westermann and Lawren Delong (2007) did a study "The social support and Self-Esteem of victims of relational bullying". The present study investigated the perceived social support and self-esteem of third-through sixth-grade students (N=264) who were victims of relational bullying. Correlations among social support and self-esteem scores indicated significant relationships among social support and Self-Esteem for female victims of relational bullying but not males. Finally, total social support moderated the relationship among total (relational and direct) bullying and low self-esteem, but support from individual sources did not moderate the negative impact of relational bullying on specific facets of self-esteem.

Bishop and Josephine Lydia (2008) did a comparative analysis of self-esteem, school involvement in seventh and eighth graders dependent upon their relative age. Although the relatively young represent approximately 50% of a given class room, there was very little research on their mental health, and thus they represented an understudied population. Being relatively young put children at a higher risk for experiencing short-and long-term negative consequences including lower scores on self-esteem measures throughout their academic career. (Thompson et. al. 2004) and a higher rate of suicide (Thompson et. al., 1999). This study sought to add to this literature by looking at between group differences on measures of cognitive, affective and behavioral outcomes for this understudied and vulnerable group. The research participants were 47 middle school 7th and 8th graders from an affluent long Island, NY Suburban Community. The findings were not in line with other research it is important to understand that these children should be considered to be an "at risk" group for cognitive, affective and behavioral difficulties.

Armstrong, Shelley, Oomen and Early Jody (2009) compared collegiate athletes and non athletes to see whether there were significant differences in the perceived levels of social connectedness, self-esteem and depression and it as interaction among the variables. Results revealed that athletes had significantly greater levels of self esteem and social connectedness as well as significantly lower levels of depression, than did non athletes.

Distefana, Christine Moti and Robert (2009) examined the multi group invariance of global self esteem and method effects associated with negatively worded items on the RSE between males and females. Findings suggested that, whereas method effects existed on the RSE scale for both male and females. The method effects associated with negatively worded items did not influence the measurement invariance and mean differences global self esteem scores between the sexes.

Erickson Sarah, Hahn Smith Anne and Smith Jane Eellen (2009) investigated how weight ethnicity body esteem, body dissatisfaction and disordered eating attitudes or behaviours contribute to global and dimensional self-esteem in pre-adolescent girls. It was find out that a complex relationship emerged between weight and body esteem when predicting self-esteem among girls with low moderate body esteem, heavier girls had higher self-esteem than lower weight girls.

Oguz Duran, Nagihan and Tezer Esin (2009) investigated the differences among Turkish first year university students regarding overall wellness and four of its dimensions in terms of self-esteem levels and gender. The findings indicated that students who have higher self-esteem reported higher scores on all the four dimensions of wellness and females reported higher levels of relational wellness and physical wellness than males.

Szymanski, Dawn, Gupta and Arpana (2009) examined the relations between multiple internalized oppressions and African American Sexual minority person's self-esteem and psychological distress. The findings indicated that self-esteem partially mediated the relationship between internalized heterosexism and psychological distress.

An Overview of Research Reviewed

An overview of the research reviewed in this chapter reveals the following.

1. Studies on environmental factors and academic achievement in India

Home environment Molia Manganlal.S (2000), home factor and achievement Navang R.H (2000), family environment Patel and Minakshi (2000), environmental factors Jaga.M, Basantia, and Mukhopadhyaya (2001), understanding in science classroom Pant. M (2002), a school discipline, student behavior and achievement Apartha and malathi latha (2003), school culture and student achievement Branda Carol Adams and Cumming Ham (2003), home environment Edward (2003), home environment on educational aspiration P. Mary Joise and Arockiasamy.S (2003), achievement motivation and academic achievement Venita Singh (2003), family environment on emotional competence of adolescents Arati, Ratna and Prapha (2004), adolescents classroom environment and achievement Chin T.Y and angels F.L. (2004), effect of gender, home and environment on educational aspiration Goel S.P (2004), academic performance Vijya Avinashilingam N.A. and Upayana Singh (2004), classroom perceptions on motivation and achievement Webster, Bertha (2004), home environment Amruth G.Kumar (2005), effect of peer tutoring on learning outcome Mehra.V and Mondal H.R. (2005), school environment Jeba Sheela and Arockiasamy.S, (2006), home environment and adjustment John Louis Manoharan and Christie doss.I (2007), class room learning environment and self esteem (2008), home environment and their teaching Selvaraj Gnanaguru,.A, and Suresh Kumar.M (2008), classroom environment and academic achievement Amutharanjini sivakumar.D (2008), Impact of environmental factors on Academic achievement Subramaninan S. and Sivakumar.D (2009).

2. Studies on environmental factors and academic achievement abroad

Achievement and environmental related factors Tonglet Jenifer Philips (2000), relationship between school climate, academic self concept and academic achievement Acosta Esther (2001), family environment of disorder children Jewell and Dean (2001), home literacy environment on reading achievement Rashid, Fontina Louise (2001), a comparison of affrication – americation achieving and underachieving students Robinson-Health and Deborach .C (2001), comparison of ability achievement discrepancy models for identifying learning disabilities Roderiques and Adrienne Blunt (2001), learning environment in biology classroom and their attitudes towards biology Cakiroglu, Jale Telli and sibel (2003), learning environment and achievement Misra, K.S (2003), academic environment Skinner and Amy Danielle (2003), a study on attitudes toward biology and learning environment Sueh-Fang Chuarag and Yeong-Jing cheng (2003), academic behavior and achievement Chen, Jennfier and Jun-Li (2004), learning styles and learning environment Hill and Jennifer Lynne (2004), student achievement in relation to poor factors in a experiment hyper growth Birdwell and Angela Denise (2005), social support and academic achievement Laibach and Colleen (2006), a historical perspective on Indonesian Islamic school curricula Zuhdi and Mohammad (2006), effect of perceived success for children with individual education programs in reading and persistence and comparison with peers Anderson-Jeffrey M. (2007), impact of family on the achievement Davis and Joy L. (2007), analysis of teacher, curricular, parental and support influence on study achievement in an urban district, Harris and Arthur (2007), partners, parents and peers effect on school achievement Phelps and Kenyatta Danielle (2007), school climate on achievement Smith Kath Leen M.,(2007), essay on peer effect Mihaly and Kata (2007), asian americation adolescents achievement Terry, Alison. J (2007), school environmental factors and achievement Francis .A, Adesoji, Segun and Olatunbosun .M (2008).

3. Studies on Study habits and academic achievement in India

Study habit, study involvement, science interest and scientific attitude Kumaran and Kamala (2001), study habits in relation to some psycho-socio variables, *Patel .Z. (2002,) academic achievement, adjustment and study habit* Thakkar. P.D. (2003), study habits *Digumati Bhaskara Rao and Sema Surya Prakas Rao. A (2004),* "study habits of residential and non-residential pupils Guravaiah. K (2004), study habits in relation to psycho-sociological factors Rajani. M. (2004), under achievement in relation to study habits and attitude Sirohi .V (2004), under achievement in relation of a study habits and attitudes, *Vinecta Sirohi May (2004),* study habits and academic performance Arockiadoss.S (2005), study factors related to achievement Misra S.S. (2005), study habits and achievement *Jagannath K. Dange (2007),* study habits and achievement K.Amirthagowri, D.Sivakumar (2009), study habits and achievement Nalini and Ganesha Bhatta (2009), Are study habits gender biased? Susai Rajendran et al (2009).

4. Studies on Study habits and academic achievement abroad

Tran theoretical model of change,application to study habits Ehrlish mark Edward (2000), learning strategies Medo and Mary Anne (2000), student perception and aspiration Roberston Nichole (2000), emotions and literacy achievement Berg, Charles and Lick Paulette (2001), study habit Nneji .M (2002), differences in task value, self-regulated learning and grade expectations Garavalia, Linda; Ray and Marilyn (2003), Are leaning styles relevant to virtual reality? Chen et al (2005), study attitudes, study habit and achievement Abid Hussain Ch (2006), effects of self regulated learning on mathematics achievement Camahalan, Faye Marsha.G (2006), learning style under two web-based study conditions, Johnson and Genevieve Marie (2007), the impact of students conceptions of constructivist assumptions on academic achievement Loyens et al (2007), barrier courses and persistence Suresh and Radhika (2007), outcomes linked to high quality after school programs Vandell et al (2007), approaches to learning implication for teaching Watters, Dianne .J Watters, and James .J (2007), academic achievement in relation to academic self regulation Yumusak et al (2007), achievement in reading Flowers, Tiffany .A, Flowers and Lamont .A (2008), motivation, study habit and achievement Kim, ChanMin, Keller and John .M (2008).

5. Studies on self esteem and academic achievement in India

Classroom culture, self-esteem and academic achievement, Kalyani alias Usha Raman.T and Amalraj.A (2002), self-esteem and school performance, Agarwal. S and Raj. P (2004), self-esteem and its domains Ponni.V,Santhi.S, Palanisamy.C (2007), self- esteem and level of aspiration Amirt Rai and Annaraja.P (2008), self-esteem and emotional intelligence Babu . M, Sameer (2008), pro social behaviour and self-esteem Priyadharshini S.K, Velayudhan.A (2008), self-esteem of orphan and non orphan Surila Agarwala, Meenakshi Verma and Satya Singh (2008), academic achievement of adolescents in relation to their self-esteem Thilagavathi .T(2008), self-esteem and academic achievement Vasanthy Vinoliya A.D, Sivakumar.D (2009).

6. Studies on self-esteem and academic achievement abroad

Self-esteem and cognitive style Caldwell and Roslyn Marie (2000), self concept and global self esteem Chu and Yu-Wei (2000), self-esteem, pubertal timing and body image, Joanne and Williams. M (2000), self- esteem, depression and anxiety Von Essen et al (2000), achievement in determining the self-esteem Bestrome and Scott Eric (2001), achievement and self-esteem Malinsky and Marg Ann (2001), self-esteem and academic achievement AIves-Martins.M.et al (2002), Ethnic identity and its association with self-esteem Brug and Peary (2002), learner-centeredness and self-esteem Moore and Malena Katrina (2002), Body shape attitudes, eating attitudes, self-esteem and social support Perez-Rivera and Betty, (2003), self-esteem and traditional of career choice Yunker and Jonel Jones (2003), a case study of grade point averages, self- esteem, and leadership abilities Clash and Clarice (2004), context,moral orientation and self-esteem Higher and Donna Louise (2004), self-esteem, self concept and aggression Byrd, Ronald (2005), self efficacy and self-esteem Irandokht Asadi Sadeghi Azar and Promila Vasudeva(2006), perceived parental nurturance and self-esteem Jacobson and Steven Dean (2006), locus of evaluation, self-esteem and personality Bucur and David .R (2007), sense of self and self-esteem, Knightley, Wendy .M Whitelock and Dcnise .M (2007), environment and age on locus of control, self efficacy, self-esteem and academic achievement, Shabazz and Khallid (2007), self efficacy and self-esteem, Smith and Gregory J. (2007), emotional intelligence and satisfaction with life after controlling for self esteem Murphy and Kevin .T (2007), social support and self- esteem Westermann and Lawren Delong (2007), self-esteem and school involvement, Bishop and Josephine Lydia (2008), levels of social connectedness, self-esteem and depression Armstrong,

Shelley, Oomen and Early Jody (2009), global self-esteem Distefana, Christine Moti and Robert . W (2009), global and dimensional self-esteem Erickson Sarah J, Hahn Smith Anne and Smith Jane Eellen (2009), self-esteem levels and gender Oguz Duran, Nagihan and Tezer Esin (2009), self-esteem and psychological distress Szymanski, Dawn, Gupta .M and Arpana (2009).

Conclusion

A close analogy of the review related that majority of the studies were conducted in different states in India. A few studies were conducted in Tamil Nadu .The present study goes further on layout of biology in higher secondary schools in Tamil Nadu. The present study fills the gap left by other studies by analyzing environmental factors, study habit, self esteem and academic achievement of biology on the basis of number of variables, such as sex, classes studying, locality of institution, nativity of the learner, nature of school, type of management, medium of instruction, fathers' education, fathers' occupation, fathers' income mothers' education, mothers' income, mothers' occupation, status of the family of school and strength of the students in eleventh and twelfth standard biology. This investigation makes an attempt to analysis the process of learning biology in higher secondary schools in Kanyakumari, Tirunelveli and Thoothukudi district of Tamil Nadu. The ensuing chapter deals with design of the study

3

Design of the Study

Introduction

Research methodology is a compound of two words research and methodology indicating the mode of doing research .According to John W.Best (1999) research is defined as the systematic and objective analysis and recording of controlled observations that may lead to the development of generalization, principles of theories, resulting in prediction and possible ultimate control of events.

Methodology describes in detail the activities of the research measuring instruments to be used, individuals participating in the research, sample and data analysis. Different methods are used in research studies. According to Best and Khan (1995), "research is a systematic activity that is directed towards discovery of an organized body of knowledge".

The present chapter in this regard discusses how the research is systematically organized in the present study.

Statement of the Problem

The present study started as *"Influence of Environmental Factors, Study Habits and Self Esteem on Academic Achievement of Higher Secondary Biology Students".*

(a) Definitions and operational definitions

(i) Environmental Factors

Environment refers to those factors in the life span of the individual from conception to death as opposed to genetic and congenital factors. These include factors like size of family and social class. (Dictionary of Education, 2008).

In psychology the term by 'environment' refers to the influences belonging to different categories which affect the growth process of the individual, making what he/she is. The present study uses the term environment in an active sense. Mere presence of physical objects does not in itself constitute an environment unless these objects become stimuli for the individual. The external environment consists of the sum total of the stimuli which he/she receives from birth to death. He is always stimulated by environmental factors.

(ii) Study Habits

The term study habits means the skills, strategies and rules, method applied to the process of learning. The student who has acquired good study habits has developed a behavior, which enables him or her to sit down and begin working on his or her assignments with a maximum concentration. According to the investigator, it refers to the skills and methods acquired by the learner. Study habits can be studied in terms of home environment, reading and note taking, planning of the subjects, habits of concentration, habits and attitudes and school environment.

(iii) Self-Esteem

Self-esteem refers to an individual's assessment of his/her own personal worth. It is the judgment about one's worth compared with others. People's evaluations of themselves were derived by comparing their ideal and real selves. The evaluative dimension of the self-concept, is to do with how worthwhile and confident a person feels about him or herself. The global evaluate dimension of the self. (Dictionary of Education, 2009). As the notion of 'who I am' solidities during child-hood and adolescence. So, too does the judgment of 'how worthy I am'. The personal judgment of worthiness, the individuals good opinion of himself or herself is referred to as self esteem in this study.

(iv) Achievement

"Achievement is proficiency of performance in a given skill or body of knowledge" (Dictionary of Education, 1954)

Academic achievement is a measure of knowledge gained in formal education usually indicated by test scores, grade, point, average and degrees. (Encyclopedia Dictionary of Psychology and Education, 2005).

For achievement, the investigator took the half yearly marks in respective school obtained by the higher secondary biology students in 11th standard.

(v) Higher Secondary Biology Students

By higher secondary students the Investigator means the students doing standards XI and XII in higher secondary schools is Tamil Nadu state. The students who have studied biology subject in XI and XII is higher secondary biology students.

Need and Importance of the Study

The destiny of India is being shaped in the classroom. In a world based on science and technology, it is education that determines the level and prosperity, welfare and security of the people. According to Radhakrishnan (1956) the aim of education is the development of an integrated personality of the individual. A truly educated person is cultured and fearless and has a scientific attitude. The enlightened citizen is the most valuable asset of a democratic society. Biology forms an important part of the syllabus of life science. It is the compulsory subject for the higher secondary school examination. A biology student is engaged in a human activity that is directed towards seeking new knowledge about living things. A student tries to acquire new concepts of biology through practicing science or passing through the process of biology. India shall need specialists in the fields of medicine, health, agriculture, animal husbandry, etc. The talent in these fields shall come from biology. It is for these reasons that this subject has become so popular in our secondary schools and is taught as a compulsory subject in secondary schools. Bearing in mind the investigator selected higher secondary biology students.

Higher secondary school students belong to the adolescent stage of development. Adolescence is a period of concomitant growth. It is the formal operational stage of development (Piaget, 1952).They think in abstract terms, follow the logical propositions and form hypothesis. They can isolate the elements of a problem and systematically explore all possible solutions to problems. It is essentially a period of rapid development and transition and is full of complexities. Academic failure may lead to frustration and poor adjustment. They are emotionally disturbed and develop an unhealthy attitude towards life. The sense of failure complex which in turn may lead to a retreat into non communicative fantasy or overt misbehavior. Maximizing achievement scores is one of the goals of education. A large number of investigators had made efforts to study the determinants of academic achievement. As Carrel (1943) points out "the bond between intelligence and academic achievement appears to be smaller than is usually assumed". According the Weinner (1972) intelligence accounts for only 25% of the observed variance in grades. Hence, it follows that the remaining 75% of the variance is due to non intellectual factors. Taylor (1956) has pointed out the importance of personality factors on achievement.

Environment is such a powerful factor that it influences the development of child consciously or unconsciously or both. One cannot escape its influence at any cost. The environmentalist holds that as the child gradually comes into contact with the physical and social environments, his/her innate tendencies. Lower out and behavior begins to change step by step. In this sense, it is the environment which makes a child musician or artist and not the heredity. Thus according to environmentalist, education is a process based on and conditioned by the environment in which the child is brought up. Students, no doubt, have been blessed with intelligence but the reason, why they do not fare well, in academics, is due to the fact that, they are exposed to a lot of problems and setbacks, related to their families, school, health, finance, environment, sex, religion, social and personal relationship, etc .

Even a good student, who has the potentiality to achieve better, may not be able to achieve as per expectations if he/she fails to do proper management of time, allocation of weightage to various subject preparing notes and individual modes adopted for preparation of different subjects .In other words, habits and practices are relevant factors in determining the achievement of an individual.

Self-esteem tends to be fairly resistant to change once it is established. Individuals who have little self-esteem are afraid to let down their guard. Convinced that they are inadequate, the individuals with very little self-esteem are likely to be maladjusted. Those with good self-esteem have a capacity that will affect their adult live, the capacity to give and receive love. If the higher secondary results are observed, there is very less number of centum scorers in biology. This has been the result for the past ten years of higher secondary examination of Tamil Nadu. In order to have good academic achievement, one should have good study habits, social environment and self esteem. Hence the problem is selected as *"Influence of Environmental Factors, Study Habits and Self-Esteem on Academic Achievement of Higher Secondary Biology Students".*

Objectives

Section-I

1. To find out the level of Environmental factors and its dimensions of higher secondary biology students with reference to background variables such as sex, standard, locality of the school, nativity of the student, nature of school, type of management, medium of institution and status of the family.
2. To find out the level of Study habits and its dimensions of higher secondary biology students with reference to background variables such as sex, standard, locality of the school, nativity of the student, nature of school, type of management, medium of institution and status of the family.
3. To find out the level of Self-esteem and its dimensions of higher secondary biology students with reference to background variables such as sex, standard, locality of the school, nativity of the student, nature of school, type of management, medium of institution and status of the family.

4. To find out the level of Academic achievement of higher secondary biology students with reference to background variables such as sex, standard, locality of the school, nativity of the student, nature of school, type of management, medium of institution and status of the family.

Section-II

5. To find out the significant difference ,if any, on certain Environmental factors of biology students with reference to background variables such as sex, standard, locality of the school, nativity of the student, medium of institution and status of the family.
6. To find out the significant difference, if any, in Study habits and its dimensions of higher secondary biology students with reference to background variables such as sex, standard, locality of the school, nativity of the student, medium of institution and status of the family
7. To find out the significant difference, if any, in Self-esteem and its dimensions of higher secondary biology students with reference to background variables such as sex, standard, locality of the school, nativity of the student, medium of institution and status of the family.
8. To find out the significant difference, if any, Academic achievement of higher secondary biology students with reference to background variables such as sex, standard, locality of the school, nativity of the student, medium of institution and status of the family.

Section-III

9. To find out the significant difference, if any, among different nature of school students, type of management in Environmental factors.
10. To find out the significant difference, if any, among different nature of school students, type of management in Study habits.
11. To find out the significant difference, if any, among different nature of school students, type of management in Self-esteem.
12. To find out the significant difference, if any, among different nature of school students, type of management in Academic achievement.

Section- IV

13. To find out the significant association, if any, between Environmental factors and certain democratic variables of biology students at higher secondary level such as education of father, occupation of father, income of father, education of mother, occupation of mother, income of mother.
14. To find out the significant association if any between Study habits and certain democratic variables of biology students at higher secondary level such as Education of father, occupation of father, income of father, education of mother, occupation of mother, income of mother.

15. To find out the significant association, if any, between Self-esteem and certain democratic variables of biology students at higher secondary level such as Education of father, occupation of father, income of father, education of mother, occupation of mother, income of mother.
16. To find out the significant association, if any, between Academic achievement and certain democratic variables of biology students at higher secondary level such as Education of father, occupation of father, income of father, education of mother, occupation of mother, income of mother.

Section-V

17. To find out the significant relationship, if any, between Environmental factors and Academic achievement of biology students at higher secondary level with reference to background variable such as sex, standard, locality of the school, nativity of the student, nature of school, type of management, medium of institution and status of the family.
18. To find out the significant relationship, if any, between Study habit and Academic achievement of biology student at higher secondary level with reference to background variable such as sex, standard, locality of the school, nativity of the student, nature of school, type of management, medium of institution and status of the family.
19. To find out the significant relationship, if any, between Self esteem and Academic achievement of biology student at higher secondary level with reference to background variable such as sex, standard, locality of the school, nativity of the student, nature of school, type of management, medium of institution and status of the family.

Hypotheses

Section-I

1. There is no significant difference in Environmental factors and its dimensions of higher secondary biology students with reference to sex.
2. There is no significant difference in Environmental factors and its dimensions of higher secondary biology students with reference to standard.
3. There is no significant difference in Environmental factors and its dimensions of higher secondary biology students with reference to locality of the school.
4. There is no significant difference in Environmental factors and its dimensions of higher secondary biology students with reference to nativity of the student.

5. There is no significant difference in Environmental factors and its dimensions of higher secondary biology students with reference to medium of institution.
6. There is no significant difference in Environmental factors and its dimensions of higher secondary biology students with reference to status of the family.
7. There is no significant difference in Study habits and its dimensions of higher secondary biology students with reference to sex.
8. There is no significant difference in Study habits and its dimensions of higher secondary biology students with reference to standard.
9. There is no significant difference in Study habits and its dimensions of higher secondary biology students with reference to locality of the school.
10. There is no significant difference in Study habits and its dimensions of higher secondary biology students with reference to nativity of the student.
11. There is no significant difference in Study habits and its dimensions of higher secondary biology students with reference to medium of the institution.
12. There is no significant difference in Study habits and its dimensions of higher secondary biology students with reference to status of the family.
13. There is no significant difference in Self-esteem and its dimensions of higher secondary biology students with reference to sex.
14. There is no significant difference in Self-esteem and its dimensions of higher secondary biology students with reference to standard.
15. There is no significant difference in Self-esteem and its dimensions of higher secondary biology students with reference to locality of the school.
16. There is no significant difference in Self-esteem and its dimensions of higher secondary biology students with reference to nativity of the student.
17. There is no significant difference in Self-esteem and its dimensions of higher secondary biology students with reference to medium of the institution.
18. There is no significant difference in Self-esteem and its dimensions of higher secondary biology students with reference to status of the family.
19. There is no significant difference in Academic achievement of higher secondary students in biology with reference to sex, standard, locality of the school, nativity of the student, medium of the institution, status of the family.

Section-II

1. There is no significant difference among boys, girls and coeducation school students in their Environmental factors.
2. There is no significant difference among boys, girls and coeducation school students in their Study habits.
3. There is no significant difference among boys, girls and coeducation school students in their Self-esteem.
4. There is no significant difference among boys, girls and coeducation school students in their Academic achievement.
5. There is no significant difference among government, aided and self financing school students in their Environmental factors.
6. There is no significant difference among government, aided and self financing school students in their Study habits.
7. There is no significant difference among government, aided and self financing school students in their Self esteem.
8. There is no significant difference among government, aided and self financing school students in their Academic achievement.

Section-III

1. There is no significant association between fathers' education and the Environmental factors of their children.
2. There is no significant association between fathers' education and the Study habits of their children.
3. There is no significant association between fathers' education and the Self esteem of their children.
4. There is no significant association between fathers' education and the Academic achievement of their children.
5. There is no significant association between fathers' occupation and the Environmental factors of their children.
6. There is no significant association between fathers' occupation and the Study habits of their children.
7. There is no significant association between fathers' occupation and the Self-esteem of their children.
8. There is no significant association between fathers' occupation and the Academic achievement of their children.
9. There is no significant association between fathers' income and the Environmental factors of their children.
10. There is no significant association between fathers' income and the Study habits of their children.
11. There is no significant association between fathers' income and the Self- esteem of their children.

12. There is no significant association between fathers' income and the Academic achievement of their children.
13. There is no significant association between mothers' education and the Environmental factors of their children.
14. There is no significant association between mothers' education and the Study habits of their children.
15. There is no significant association between mothers' education and the Self-esteem of their children.
16. There is no significant association between mothers' education and the Academic achievement of their children.
17. There is no significant association between mothers' occupation and the Environmental factors of their children.
18. There is no significant association between mothers' occupation and the Study habit of their children.
19. There is no significant association between mothers' occupation and the Self-esteem of their children.
20. There is no significant association between mothers' occupation and the Academic achievement of their children.
21. There is no significant association between mothers' income and the Environmental factors of their children.
22. There is no significant association between mothers' income and the Study habits of the children.
23. There is no significant association between mothers' income and the Self- esteem of their children.
24. There is no significant association between mothers' income and the Academic achievement of their children.

Section-IV

1. There is no significant relationship between Environmental factors and Academic achievement of higher secondary biology students with reference to background variables.
2. There is no significant relationship between Home environment and Academic achievement of higher secondary biology students with reference to background variables.
3. There is no significant relationship between School environment and Academic achievement of higher secondary biology students with reference to background variables.
4. There is no significant relationship between of Social environment and Academic achievement of higher secondary biology students with reference to background variables.

5. There is no significant relationship between Study habits and Academic achievement of higher secondary biology students with reference to background variables.
6. There is no significant relationship between Self-esteem and Academic achievement of higher secondary biology students with reference to background variables.

Research Methods

Research methods are very important in a research process. Method is a style of conducting a research work, which is determined by the nature of the problem. Webster defined methodology as "the science of method or arrangement." Methodology is the procedure or techniques, adopted in a research study. It has great importance in any kind of research.

Research cannot carryout its function without a suitable method. The selection of a method for research will depend upon the nature of the problem. As stated by Louis Choen and Lawrence Manion (1989), 'By methods, we mean, that range of approaches used in educational research to gather data which are to be used as a basis for interference and interpretation for explanation and prediction'.

There are basically five kinds of research methods in the field of educational research. They are,

1. Historical method
2. Survey method
3. Experimental method
4. The case study method
5. The Genetic method

In any specific study, it is more common to apply any one of the above methods.

Methods used for the Present Study

After reviewing the characteristics of the different methods of educational research, the investigator decided to use stratified random sampling for the present study. The aim of the present study is to find out the influence of environment factors, study habits and self-esteem on academic achievement among higher secondary biology students. It is the study of the present phenomena and the characteristics of the whole population. Hence the survey method is the most suitable method for the present study.

William Wiersma (1986) said "survey research deals with incidence, distribution and relationship of educational, psychological and sociological variables" (p.15).

Survey studies provide three type of information:

(*a*) What exists by studying and analyzing the important aspects of the present situation (*b*) What is wanted by classifying the goals and objectives possibly through a study of the conditions existing elsewhere or what experts consider to be desirable.

(*c*) How to get these through discovering the possible means of achieving the goals on the basis of the experience of others or the options of expert.

Tool Construction for the Present Study

Data are required to carry out any type of educational research because answer to these research problems is sought on the basis of empirical data. Data can be collected using readily available tools of those which are modified or developed by the investigator. The investigator has to take important decisions regarding the selection of appropriate tools for data collection. Many types of tools are available and each type has its own characteristics and each should be considered for its appropriateness for collecting certain kind of data on a selected research problem.

Usually in survey method, interview schedule, questionnaire, scale, test inventory and observation schedule are used. As the questionnaire can be easily administered and also the time and the effort consumed are less than interviews, the questionnaire is widely used. So in the present study, the investigator used a questionnaire for collecting data.

Various tools related to the factors of the present study have been surveyed by the investigator. A careful study of these tools is done and after a through discussion with the guide and the experts in the field of educational research he decided to select the following tools.

1. Environmental Factors Inventory (EFI)
2. Study Habits Inventory (SHI)
3. Self-Esteem Inventory (SEI)
4. Academic Achievement

1. Environmental Factors Inventory

(i) Home environment

The home itself is a socio economic unit, a type but it has its own cultural set-up and norms of behavior. The home environment definitely influences the study habit of the student. The importance of good study habit depends upon the responsibility of the parents and study settings and behaviors at home (Maloney, Raymont, 1987). According to the investigator; it refers to the conducive atmosphere provided in the home for the study of their children.

(ii) School environment

School is an institution representing organized social effort at perpetuating, maintaining and modifying, as per the need of the time. Students enter school with some background characteristics like cognitive ability, motivation, study behavior, attitudes, social origin and achievement values that influence their performance school should provide a conducing atmosphere to form their character and make them learn systematically.

(iii) Social environment:

It refers to interpersonal orientation for a happy and meaningful existence of students. In this highly competitive world they have to freely mingle with others.

The students who maintain healthy relationship with others learn better. The students, who keep themselves aloof, feel timid to get their doubts clarified. The students who exceed in making inter-personal relationship become excellent in their academic pursuit. Hence in the learning process should be good at making and maintaining interpersonal relationship. It includes emotional support, positive cognitive stimulation, attention and social comparison.

Description of the Draft Tool

A research tool plays a major role in any worthwhile research as it is the sole factor in determining the sound data and in arriving at a perfect conclusion for about the problem. In the present investigation in order to measure the environmental factors among higher secondary biology students the investigator has used the open type questionnaire. The researcher referred various books, magazines, websites and journals pertaining to environmental factors to have clarity of concepts. The investigator had discussed with educational experts and collected information and ideas about the content for the development of the tool. The environmental factor has many dimensions but the investigator had selected only three dimensions' is given below.

Table 3.1: Classification of Dimensions in The Draft Tool

Sl.No.	Dimensions	No. of items	Range of scores
1.	Home environment	35	35–175
2.	School environment	35	35–175
3.	Social environment	30	30–150

The respondents were instructed to choose their degree of agreement to the statement by putting a tick mark (√) against the space provided. The score may vary from 5-1 all items are positive statements.

Pilot Study

A preliminary try out of the tools was arranged to find out the weakness and workability of the items. For this purpose the tools were given to 100 eleventh standard students randomly covering high, average and low achievers in four schools. During this pilot study, the difficulties in responding the items and a rough estimate of the time-limit for responding the items were noted. This step helped the investigator modify certain items, which were vague and questionable.

Table 3.2: List of Schools for Pilot Study

Sl.No.	Name of the School	Type of School	No. of Students
1.	Margochis Boys Higher Secondary School, Nazareth	Boys	20
2.	St.Thams Matric Higher Secondary School, Thoothukudi	Co-Education	30
3.	Subbaiyah Vidhyalaya Higher Secondary School, Thoothukudi	Co-Education	30
4.	K.G.S Girls Higher Secondary School, Srivaikundam	Girls	20

Establishing Validity

Validity is the process of examining the accuracy of a specific prediction of inference made from a test score (cronbach, 1971). Validity, refers to the appropriateness of the interpretation of the results of a test or evaluation informed for a given group of individuals and not to the instrument itself (Gronlund and Linn, 1990). It is known that every test is constructed with a purpose that is to provide measures of a defined variable truthfully. Then it is said to be valid. Validity can be of different types. The following validation analyses have been employed in the present investigation

(*a*) Content validity (*b*) Item validity

Content Validity

Validity is the quality of a test or tool that enables it to measure what it is supposed to measure (Best, 1993). Content validity relates to the degree to which a test samples the content area which is to be measured. The draft tool was given to teacher educators and experts for their comments and suggestions. Some items were reformulated and refined on the basis of the suggestions given by them. *The original tool prepared by the investigator were given to the following experts.1. Dr.A.Amalraj, Research guide, St. Xavier's college of education, Palayamkottai. 2. Dr.N.Arunachalam, Director/Associate professor in education, Department Life Long Learning/Education, Alagappa University, Karaikudi. 3. Dr.A. Ponnambala Thiyagarajan, Formal principal, Dr.Sivanthi Aditanar College of Education Tiruchendur. 4. Prof. Dr.Minnel kodi, Annamalai University,Chidambaram.* To estimate the worth of the items, the investigator with the help of the guide and on the basis of the suggestions given by the experts, modified certain items and made them appropriate. Thus, the content validity of the tool was established.

Items Validity

For finding the truthfulness of test items and inter-connectedness of different items in the same tool, item validity was calculated as it is very essential for selecting items to the final tool. From the responses obtained from 100 students on the draft tool, the sum of scores on each dimension of value scale was calculated. Then 'r' is calculated by correlating the individual item score and the corresponding component score. The correlation coefficient at 5% level of significance is 0.4 to 0.9 (Best, 1989), so the item having 'r' value between 0.4 and 0.9 are selected.

For further improvement and refinement of the scale, the tool was administered again to the sample. The scale was scored accordingly't' value was calculated by identifying the high "low group. The total number of sample is taken as N which is multiplied by 0.27 and rounded off the result to the nearest whole number. This number is called 'n' (Stanely, 1978). By applying this simple method, the investigator identified the top 27% and the bottom 27% in other words the high and the low group. The't' value for each item was computed. At 5% level of significance the table value is 1.96 have been retained. The final tool consists of 65 items (The detail is in the Table 3.3.)

Table 3.3: Environmental Factors inventory

Item No.	t value	r value	Item No.	t value	r value
1	2	3	4	5	6
1	2.48	0.50	34	2.72	0.38
2	3.15	0.36	35*	0.86	0.33
3	2.83	0.38	36	2.10	0.40
4*	2.45	0.23	37	3.15	0.42
5	5.12	0.59	38*	0.45	0.11
6	3.95	0.36	39*	0.45	0.07
7	1.96	0.55	40	2.48	0.54
8*	3.19	0.11	41	2.83	0.60
9	2.72	0.37	42*	1.83	0.20
10	3.15	0.41	43	4.78	0.48
11*	0.83	-0.12	44	2.50	0.46
12	2.83	0.49	45*	0.49	0.10
13*	2.45	0.33	46*	0.00	0.03
14	2.48	0.42	47	4.16	0.51
15	2.16	0.39	48	2.10	0.47
16*	3.36	0.23	49	2.16	0.50
17	3.27	0.36	50*	2.30	0.26

1	2	3	4	5	6
18	2.48	0.39	51*	0.61	0.27
19*	0.83	0.16	52	2.50	0.65
20	6.53	0.59	53	4.78	0.47
21*	2.08	0.21	54*	0.45	0.41
22	3.19	0.52	55	3.15	0.39
23	3.19	0.47	56	2.48	0.44
24*	1.97	0.27	57	2.48	0.48
25	3.95	0.36	58*	2.30	0.17
26	3.19	0.50	59	3.27	0.42
27*	0.37	0.11	60	3.84	0.56
28*	1.99	0.24	61	2.53	0.43
29	2.45	0.59	62*	0.86	0.27
30	2.83	0.38	63*	2.10	0.10
31	2.16	0.45	64	2.16	0.43
32	2.48	0.47	65	3.15	0.41
33*	1.99	0.24	66*	0.45	0.41
67*	2.30	0.17	85*	0.20	0.40
68	2.16	0.61	86	2.72	0.50
69	3.41	0.36	87	3.15	0.58
70	2.01	0.61	88*	1.97	0.25
71	2.03	0.36	89	3.15	0.58
72*	0.58	0.10	90	2.48	0.73
73	2.18	0.57	91*	1.00	0.30
74	2.11	0.56	92	2.03	0.46
75*	0.86	0.27	93	2.16	0.57
76*	2.10	0.10	94	2.29	0.48
77	2.10	0.57	95	3.39	0.47
78*	1.45	0.58	96*	0.45	0.59
79	2.03	0.65	97*	0.80	0.02
80	2.83	0.42	98	3.84	0.61
81*	0.93	0.47	99	2.18	0.46
82	2.16	0.57	100	2.48	0.36
83	2.53	0.43			
84	2.53	0.47			

Note: Deleted item are marked with asterisks

Reliability

Reliability is the degree of accuracy and consistency. The prepared tool was subjected to test-retest method .The tool was administered to a set of 100 students of XI standard. Again the same tool was administered to the same set of students after an interval of two week. The responses of the respondents were scored and the correlation co-efficient was found to be 0.85for the two sets of scores .Thus the reliability of the tool was established.

Item Selection

Thus the final form of the environmental factor scale consists of 65 items. The classification of the items in the final form of the scale is given in table. The final form of the tool is given appendix-I

Table 3.4: Details of The Environmental Factors Inventory Final Form

Sl.No.	Dimensions	No. of items	Range of scores
1.	Home environment	20	20-100
2.	School environment	23	23-115
3.	Social environment	22	22-110

Tool No: 2 Study Habits Inventory

Preparation of the Draft Tool

Study Habits inventory scale was prepared and validated by D.Sivakumar and A.Amalraj. The statement that are included in the Study habits Inventory fall into the following seven areas.

1. **Studies at home:** refers to the proper facilities and good home environment for study and the habits of having time schedule for study and preparation of the course content.
2. **Reading and note taking:** refers to the habit of taking notes while studying at home, during the teaching in the class, clearing doubts with the teachers and solving difficulties while reading.
3. **Planning of the subject:** refers to giving special attention and priority to the lessons which are difficult for the students and allotting time while studying.
4. **Habit of concentration**: refers to giving special attention while studying and listening without being subjected to distribution for long periods of time.
5. **Preparation for examination:** refers to the methods of preparation such as studying regularly or preparing before examination, studying only important question etc.
6. **General habit and attitude**: refers to the general habits of reading such as memorizing, reading aloud, reading while sitting, walking or reading on bed, discussing with peers recalling and revising, etc.

7. **Studies at school:** refers to the activities of the students during the class, in the library and in leisure with students and teachers.

The tool consisted of seven dimensions; the dimension as well as the number of items in each dimension to be answered on a five point scale is given below

Table 3.5: Classification of Dimensions in The Draft Tool

Sl.No.	Dimensions	Items
1.	Studies at home	1-17
2.	Reading and note taking	18-38
3.	Planning of the subjects	39-54
4.	Habits of concentration	55-70
5.	Preparation for examination	71-92
6.	General habits and attitude	93-106
7.	Studies at school	107-120

The respondents were instructed to choose their degree of agreement to the statement by putting a tick (√) against the spaces provided. The scores may vary from 5 to 1 for positive statement and reverse for negative statement. Bong and Moredith (1974) apply remarked five point scale however are often

Table 3.6: Description of The Item in The Study Habit Inventory

Nature of the items	Item number	No of item
Negative items	4, 8, 10, 12, 14, 16, 18, 22, 25, 29, 33, 37, 38, 40, 43, 50, 51, 58, 62, 67, 70, 73, 79	23
Positive items	1, 2, 3, 5, 6, 7, 9, 11, 13, 15, 17, 19, 20, 21, 23, 24, 26, 27, 28, 30, 31, 32, 34, 35, 36, 39, 41, 42, 44, 45, 46, 47, 48, 49, 52, 53, 54, 55, 56, 57, 59, 60, 61, 63, 64, 65, 66, 68, 69, 71, 72, 74, 75, 76, 77, 78, 80.	57
Negative items	4, 8, 10, 12, 14, 16, 18, 22, 25, 29, 33, 37, 38, 40, 43, 50, 51, 58, 62, 67, 70, 73, 79	23
	Total	80

Table 3.7: Scoring of The Items in The Study Habit Inventory

Response	Positive items	Negative items
Always	5	1
Often	4	2
Some times	3	3
Rare	2	4
Never	1	5

used in educational research and can be employed effectively in assessing behaviour. Hence the present study uses a five point self rating scale for measuring the study habits.

Table 3.8: List of Schools for Pilot Study

Sl.No.	Name of the School	Type of School	No. of Students
1.	Margochis Boys Higher Secondary School Nazareth	Boys	20
2.	ST.Thomas Matric Higher Secondary School Thoothukudi	Co-Education	30
3.	Subbaiyah Vidhyalaya Higher Secondary School Thoothukudi	Co-Education	30
4.	K.G.S Girls Higher Secondary School Srivaikundam	Girls	20

Validation of the Tool

John W.Best and James. V. Kahn (2000) remarks, validity is that quality of a data gathering instrument or procedure that enables it to measure (p.208). The following validation analyses have been employed in the present investigation

(*a*) Content validity (*b*) Item validity

(a) Content Validity

Content validity is the extents to which the situations include by the test are representative of the group of situations that the test is supposed to sample. The original tools prepared by the investigator were given to the following professors: *1. Dr.A.Amalraj, Research guide, St. Xavier's College of Education, Palayamkottai. 2. Dr.N.Arunachalam, Director/Associate professor in education, Department of Life Long Learning, Alagappa University, Karaikudi. 3. Dr. A. Ponnambala Thiyagarajan, Formal principal, Dr.Sivanthi Aditanar College of Education Tiruchendur. 4. Prof. Dr.Minnel kodi, Annamalai University, Chidambaram.* To estimate the worth of the items. The investigator with the help of the guide and on the basis of the suggestions given by the experts, modified certain items and made them appropriate. Thus, the content validity of the tool was established.

(b) Item Validity

Validity for the truthfulness of test item and the interconnectedness of different items in the same tool item validity was calculated as it is very essential for selecting items to the final tool. From the responses obtained from 100 students on the draft tool, the sum of scores on each dimension of study habit inventory calculated. Then 'r' is calculated by correlating the individual item score and the corresponding component score. The correlation coefficient at 5% level of significance is 0.4 to 0.9 (Best, 1989), so the item having 'r' value between 0.4 and 0.9 are selected (Table3.9). For further improvement the test was again administered to the sample and 't' values calculated .Item having 't' value 2.06 have been retained. The final tool consists of 80 items. The details are given in Table 3.9.

Table 3.9: Study Habits Inventory

Item No	t value	r value	Item No	t value	r value
1	2	3	4	5	6
1	2.05	0.51	32	2.05	0.58
2	2.06	0.52	33*	2.16	0.10
3*	2.05	0.25	34*	2.16	0.19
4	2.05	0.39	35	2.06	0.50
5	2.06	0.52	36	2.05	0.51
6	2.05	0.49	37*	2.05	0.32
7*	2.05	0.21	38	2.06	0.51
8	2.06	0.51	39	2.05	0.49
9	2.05	0.56	40	2.06	0.60
10*	2.06	0.24	41*	2.05	0.33
11	2.05	0.50	42	2.06	0.57
12	2.06	0.48	43	2.06	0.43
13*	2.05	0.21	44*	2.05	0.27
14*	2.02	0.18	45	2.06	0.56
15	2.06	0.48	46	2.06	0.51
16	2.06	0.50	47*	2.05	0.27
17	2.06	0.56	48*	2.05	0.33
18	2.06	0.48	49	2.06	0.45
19	2.06	0.59	50	2.06	0.47
20*	2.05	0.23	51*	2.06	0.31
21*	2.05	0.10	52*	2.05	0.31
22	2.06	0.56	53	2.05	0.45
23	2.05	0.60	54	2.05	0.48
24*	2.06	0.27	55*	2.06	0.20
25*	2.05	0.28	56*	2.16	0.30
26	2.06	0.48	57*	2.06	0.20
27	2.05	0.53	58	2.05	0.54
28*	2.06	0.31	59	2.06	0.45

1	2	3	4	5	6
29	2.05	0.65	60	2.06	0.47
30	2.06	0.57	61	2.05	0.45
31	2.06	0.48	62	2.06	0.48
32	2.05	0.46	92	2.05	0.61
33*	2.06	0.31	93	2.05	0.62
34*	2.05	0.27	94*	2.06	0.30
35	2.06	0.48	95	2.06	0.76
36	2.06	0.52	96	2.05	0.58
37	2.06	0.53	97*	2.06	0.23
38*	2.06	0.32	98	2.05	0.47
39	2.06	0.52	99	2.05	0.49
40	2.06	0.58	100	2.05	0.71
41	2.06	0.56	101*	2.06	0.28
42*	2.05	0.25	102	2.06	0.50
43	2.05	0.46	103	2.06	0.56
44*	2.05	0.28	104	2.05	0.69
45	2.06	0.47	105*	2.06	0.31
46	2.06	0.44	106	2.06	0.47
47*	2.05	0.17	107	2.05	0.58
48	2.05	0.65	108	2.06	0.56
49*	2.06	0.21	109*	2.06	0.25
50	2.05	0.68	110	2.05	0.46
51	2.05	0.51	111	2.06	0.47
52	2.06	0.47	112*	2.05	0.21
53*	2.06	0.32	113	2.06	0.53
54	2.06	0.55	114	2.06	0.52
55	2.05	0.46	115	2.05	0.58
56*	2.05	0.29	116*	2.06	0.25
57	2.05	0.53	117	2.05	0.50
58	2.06	0.69	118	2.06	0.51
59	2.06	0.56	119*	2.06	0.27
60*	2.06	0.24	120	2.05	0.48

Note: Deleted item are marked with asterisks

Thus the final form of the study habit inventory consists of 80 items. The dimensions as well as the number of items in each dimension for the final tool are given below. The final form of the tool is given in Appendix II.

Table 3.10: Classification of Dimensions in The Final Tool

Sl.No.	Dimensions	No of items	Range
1	Studies at home	12	12-60
2	Reading and note taking	13	13-65
3	Planning of the subjects	10	10-50
4	Habits of concentration	10	10-50
5	Preparation for examination	15	15-75
6	General habits and attitude	10	10-50
7	Studies at school	10	10-50

Establishing Reliability

The investigator had established the test retest reliability for the study habits inventory. The Tamil version was given to the randomly selected 100 students studying in 11 standard students in Thoothukudi. After fifteen days the study habits inventory was given to the same sample of 100 students. The obtained scores were retained. Then correlation co-efficient between the two sets of scores was found. It was 0.86. Thus the reliability of the study habit inventory was found.

Tool No: 3 Self-Esteem Inventory

The researcher employed for her investigation the Self-Esteem Inventory for adolescents prepared by S. Karunanidhi (1996).

The multi-dimensional Self-esteem questionnaire consisted of 83 items in the form of statements. It has both positive and negative items. Categories are well mixed to reduce the halo effect and the logical error, and double-barreled statements are avoided. Each statement has four alternative responses such as 'Always', 'Most of the time', 'Sometimes', and 'Never'.

The inventory measures six dimensions of Self-Esteem:

Competency	(16 items)
Global Self-Esteem	(16 items)
Moral & Self-Control	(13 items)
Social-Esteem	(12 items)
Family	(11 items)
Body and Physical appearance	(9 items)

- **Competency** means ability to evaluate and understand one's personal resources. This feeling reflects esteem based on his skills, talents and unique achievements.
- **Global Self-Esteem** is the general appraisal of the self and it is based on adolescents' evolution of all parts of themselves. A positive global self-esteem would be reflected in feelings such as, 'I am a good person' or 'I respect myself'.

- **Moral and Self-Control** is the reflection of feeling good as living honest, sincere, and adhering to social values, etc. Adolescents have the feeling of goodness about themselves.
- **Social-Esteem** is the reflection of feeling good as living honest, sincere, and adhering to social values etc. Adolescents who value these are supposed to have the feeling of goodness about them.
- **Social-Esteem** encompasses the adolescents feeling about himself/herself as a friend to others. So others like him/her, value his/her ideas, and include him/her in their activities. Does he/she feel satisfied with his/her interaction and relationships with press? A child, whose social needs are living met, will feel comfortable with their aspect of himself.
- **Family Self-Esteem** reflects his/her feeling about himself/herself as a member of his/her family. A person who feels he/she is a valued member of his/her family, who makes his/her own unique contribution and who is secure in the love and respect he/she receives from parents and siblings, will have a high positive Self-Esteem in their area.
- **Body and Personal Appearance** is the body image as a contribution of physical appearance and capabilities. The adolescent's self-esteem in their area is based upon his/her satisfaction with the way his/her body looks and performs.

Scoring

The scoring key is given below:

Table 3.11: Self Esteem Scoring Pattern

Competency Scale	1, 8*, 15, 22, 29*, 36, 43, 49, 55, 61, 66*, 71, 75, 78, 80 and 82 Maximum Possible score : 64
Global Self-Esteem Scale	2, 9, 16*, 23*, 30, 37, 44*, 50, 56, 62, 67*, 72, 76*, 79*, 81* and 83 Maximum Possible Score : 64
Moral & Self-Control Scale	3, 10*, 17, 24, 31*, 38, 45, 51, 57*, 63*, 68*, 73* and 77 Maximum Possible Score : 52
Social-Esteem Scale	4, 11, 18*, 25, 32*, 39*, 46, 52*, 58, 64*, 69* and 74 Maximum Possible Score : 48
Family Scale	5, 12*, 19, 26, 33*, 40*, 47*, 53,59*, 65 and 70 Maximum Possible Score : 44
Body and Physical Appearance Scale	6, 13, 20*, 27*, 34, 41*,48, 54 and 60*. Maximum Possible Score : 36

The item numbers 7, 14,21,28,35 and 42 were considered as the lie statements. Maximum score of 24 in lie scale then it was considered as invalid for analysis

The higher the scores in each dimension the higher is the level of Self-esteem.

Response	Score
Always	4
Most of the time	3
Sometimes	2
Never	1

An Asterisk indicates reverse scoring Procedure.

Response	Score
Always	1
Most of the time	2
Sometimes	3
Never	4

Establishing Reliability

The investigator had established the reliability coefficient for the self-esteem by using test-retest method .The Tamil version was given to the randomly selected 100 students studying in XI standard students in Thoothukudi. After fifteen days the self esteem inventory was given to the same sample of 100 students. The obtained scores are retained. Then correlation co-efficient between the two sets of scores was found. The reliability of the scale has been found to be 0.91.

Achievements of Students

Teaching of science in general must fulfill the general aim of education viz., the development of all the dimensions of the child's personality, social efficacy. Apart from his general aim of education, knowledge of fundamental principles and concepts in science must be imparted. The pupils must be able to apply the acquired knowledge in their daily life.

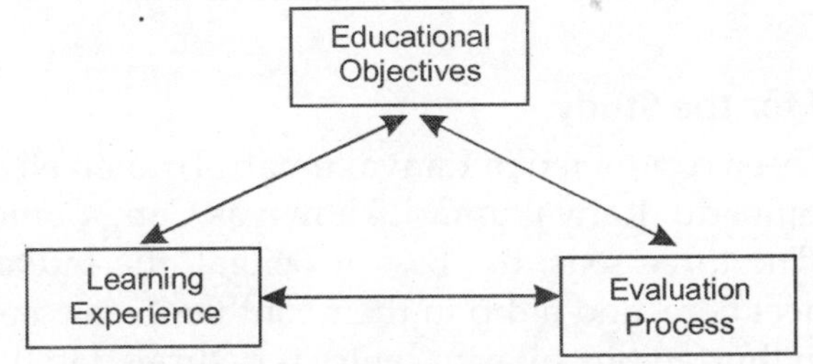

Fig. 3.1: Three Primary Aspects of The Educational Process

The above figure represents the three primary aspects of the educational process, a process for changing the behaviour and attitude of students. First, educational goals are established either explicitly or more often implicitly. Learning experiences are then designed to promote the attainments of the goals. Finally, an evaluation is conducted to determine the extent to which the objectives have been attained. The double directed victors of the above figure indicate that interacting nature of the entire process. (Stanley 1978).

Achievement Test

To test the above domains, the achievement test is constructed. According to Stanley (1978), Achievement tests are past and present oriented. They register the degree of learning or achievement after instruction. They depict present proficiency. They also represent what a person has learned. An implicit assumption in selecting an achievement test is that the examinees have been directly tested examinees have been directly exposed to the concepts needed. It does represent this level of developed ability". (P.361)

In order to assess the achievement of the students, half yearly examination marks were taken from the school register.

Procedure of Data Collection

The investigator, getting an introductory letter from the head of the institution where he is working, met the chief educational officers and the respective heads of the higher secondary schools in Kanyakumari, Tirunelveli and Thoothukudi districts. After getting their permission, the investigator contacted the higher secondary students of biology. He explained the purpose of the study to them, since the investigator personally visited the schools and administered the tools, there was the incidence of non-return of questionnaire.

Population

According to John W.Best and James V. Kahan (1992) "A population is any group of individuals that have one are more characteristics in common that are of interest to the researcher. The population may be all the individuals of a particular type, or a more restricted part of that group" (p.11)

The population of this study is the higher secondary school students studying in Kanyakumari, Tirunelveli and Thoothukudi districts in Tamilnadu.

Area Selected for the Study

This study has been conducted in Kanyakumari, Tirunelveli and Thoothukudi districts in Tamilnadu. Kanyakumari, known as Cape Comorin, is the land's end of India. The three seas, the Bay of Bengal, the Indian Ocean and the Arabian Sea-meet here, and a dip in their confluence is considered holy. The shore temple in this famous pilgrim centre is dedicated to the virgin Goddess

Devi Kanyakumari. This is the only place in India where one can enjoy the unique experience of watching the sunrise and sunset and moonrise simultaneously on full moon day Swami Vivekananda came down to Kanyakumari in 1892 and sat on the rock for meditation. The memorial was built in 1970. There is Dhyana mandapam, where one can sit in a senescent appearance and meditate. The Mahatma Gandhi memorial is located on the shore area of the Kanyakumari. This memorial to Gandhi is raised at the spot where his ashes were kept for public darshan before immersion. The architecture of the memorial is such that the sun's rays fall at the spot where the ashes were kept on 2nd October every year.

The Tirunelveli district, 4.326 square mile in extent, forms the southernmost collectorate of British India. It is bounded on the east and south by the gulf of manner. On the west is Travancore, the frontier following, with a few important exceptions the watershed of the Western Ghats. Thoothukudi is the head quarters of Thoothukudi district. Thoothukudi district is bifurcated form Tirunelveli district and came into existence form 20th October 1986. Thoothukudi town is in the gulf of manner, about 125 km north of Cape Comorin and 720 km south of Chennai.

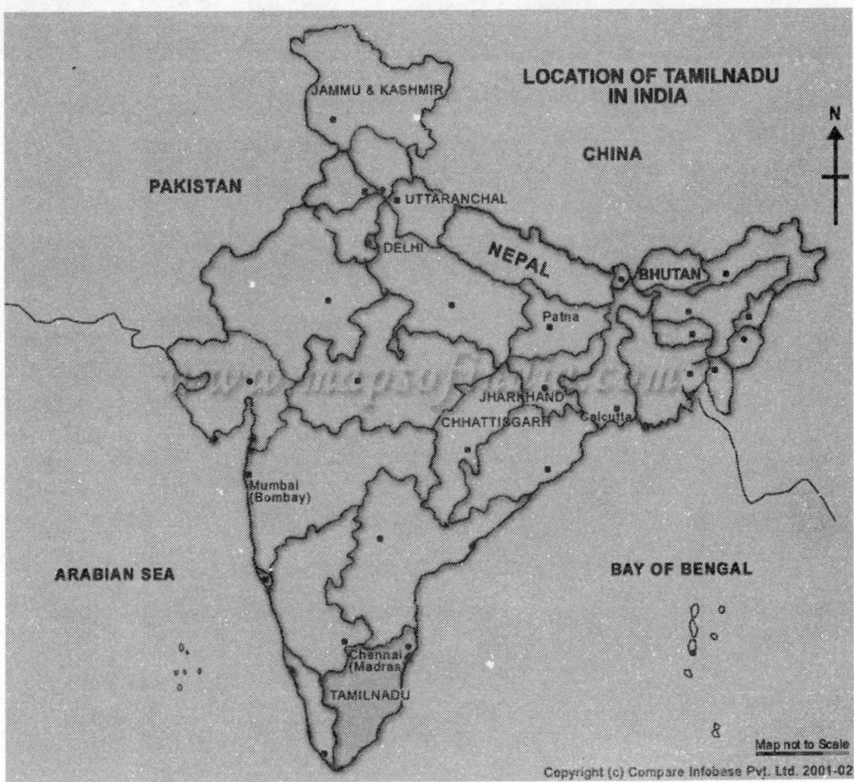

Mape 3.1: India—States

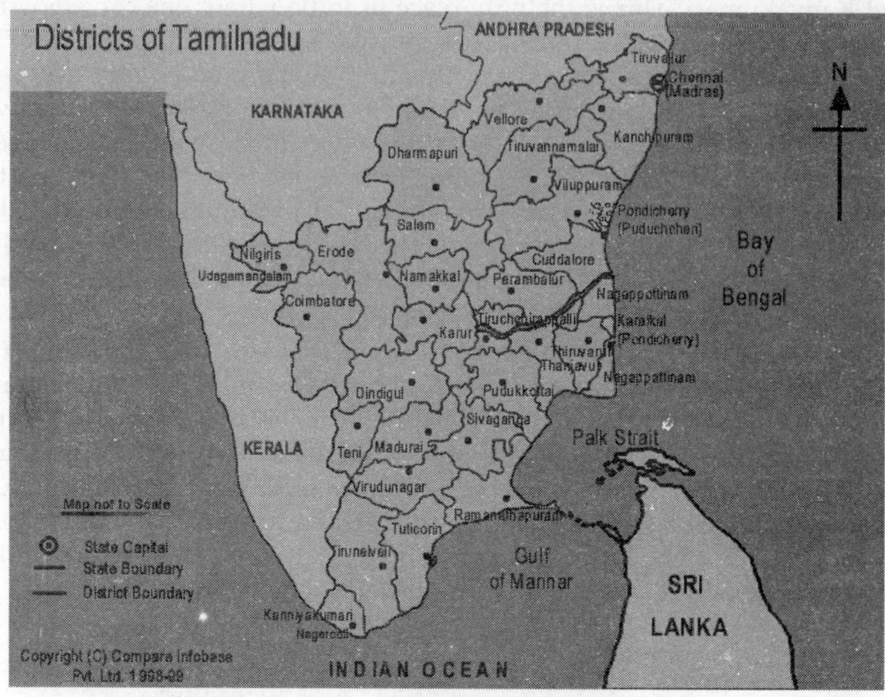

Map 3.2: Tamilnadu District

Map 3.3: Kanayakumari District

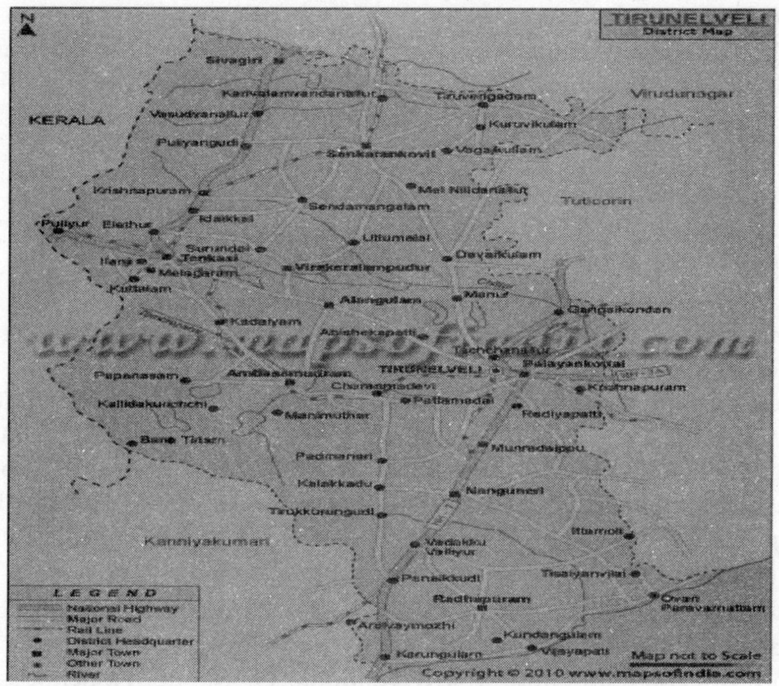

Map 3.4: Tirunelveli District

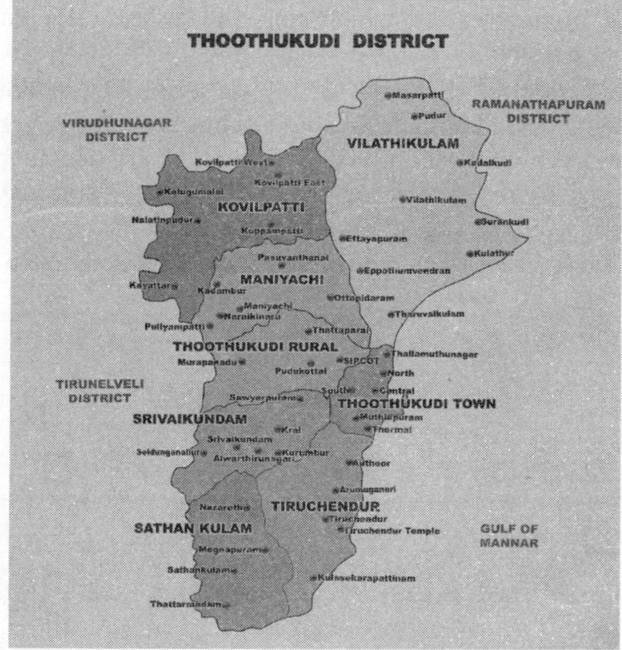

Map 3.5: Thoothukudi District

The Sample

Sampling is defined as the "process by which a relatively small number of individuals' objects or events is selected or analyzed in order to find out something about the entire population or universe from which it was selected (cornel, 1960)".

Stratified random sampling has been used to select the sample for the investigation. Stratified sampling can be adopted if the field of inquiry is not homogenous and contains variety of items.

In this method, one first divides the population known as strata, such as the items in each stratum and homogenous. From each stratum, items can then be selected by simple random sample method. Stratified random sampling technique reduces time and expense to a considerable extent. There is little possibility of any essential group of the population completely excluded. As the items in each stratum are homogenous, stratified sampling ensures greater accuracy. Stratified sampling is considered as the best technique of selecting a representative sample (Kothari, 1998). The higher secondary biology students form the population of this study.

The study was conducted in Kanyakumari, Tirunelveli and Thoothukudi districts only. In Kanyakumari district, there are 122 higher secondary schools functioning under the state board syllabus. Of the above schools 49 are government higher secondary schools 61 are management aided higher secondary schools and 12 are management unaided higher secondary schools among the 122 higher secondary schools, the investigator has selected 10 higher secondary schools.

In Tirunelveli district, there are 155 higher secondary schools functioning under the state board syllabus. The above schools 60 are government 88 are management aided higher secondary schools and 7 are management unaided higher secondary schools. Among the 155 higher secondary schools the investigator has selected 12 higher secondary schools.

Table 3.12: Distribution of Samples with Reference to Different Categories of Students

Sl.No.	Category	Variables	Total	Grand Total
1	2	3	4	5
1.	Sex	Male	438	925
		Female	487	
2.	Standard	XI	517	925
		XII	408	
3.	Locality of the school	Rural	419	925
		Urban	508	

1	2	3	4	5
4.	Nativity of the learner	Rural	405	925
		Urban	520	
5.	Nature of the school	Boys	271	925
		Girls	310	
		Co-education	344	
6.	Type of management	Government	280	925
		Govt. aided	350	
		Private	295	
7.	Medium of the school	Tamil	456	925
		English	469	
8.	Fathers' education	Illiterate	138	925
		School level	496	
		Graduate	181	
		Professional	110	
9.	Fathers' occupation	Daily wages	376	925
		Self-employed	214	
		Government Job	142	
		Private Job	193	
10.	Fathers' incomeper month	Less than Rs 5000	514	925
		Rs 5000 to Rs 10000	282	
		Above Rs 10000	129	
11.	Mothers' Education	Illiterate	215	925
		School level	470	
		Graduate	146	
		Professional	94	
12.	Mothers' Occupation	House wife	296	925
		Daily Wages	198	
		Government Job	102	
		Private Job	329	
13.	Mothers' Income per month	Less than Rs. 5000	426	925
		Rs. 5000 to Rs. 10000	202	
		Above Rs. 10000	97	
		Nil	200	
14.	Status of the family	Nuclear Family	549	925
		Joint Family	376	

In Thoothukudi district, there are 109 higher secondary schools functioning under the state board syllabus. Of the above schools 33 are government higher secondary school 71 are management aided higher secondary schools and 5 are management unaided higher secondary schools, the investigator has selected 10 higher secondary schools. The investigator has used stratified random sampling technique to select a sample of 925 students (438 males and 487 females). Adequate representations were also given.

Details of the sample are presented in the following tables

Table 3.13: Revenue District-wise Distribution of The Sample

Sl.No.	Revenue District	Number	Percentage
1.	Kanyakumari	325	35.14
2.	Tirunelveli	300	32.43
3.	Tuticorin	300	32.43
	Total	925	100

The diagrammatic representation of the revenue district-wise distribution of the sample is given in fig 3.2

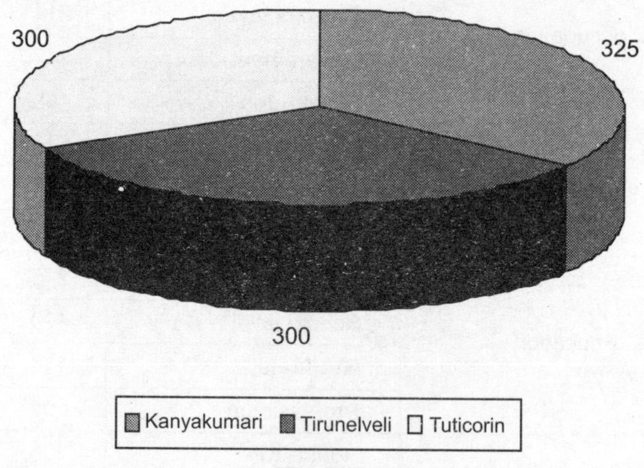

Fig. 3.2.

It may be seen from fig 3.2 that almost equal representation was given to each of the three revenue districts in the sample.

Statistical Techniques Used

For the present study, the investigator has used the following statistical techniques.

1. Percentage Analysis

$$\text{Percentage} = \frac{\text{Number of cases}}{\text{Total number of cases}} \times 100$$

2. The mean ($\bar{X}$)

Arithmetic mean is the sum of the individual scores divided by their number. The formula for mean is

$$\bar{X} = \frac{\Sigma x}{N}$$

Where
$\bar{X}$ = Mean
Σ = Sum
X = Scores of distribution
N = Total number of Scores

3. Standard Deviation

Standard Deviation (S.D) is the square-root of the mean of the squares of the deviation of the items from the arithmetic mean. It is represented by the symbol 'σ'

The formula for Standard Deviation is

$$\sigma = \frac{\sqrt{\Sigma(x-\bar{x})^2}}{N}$$

Where
σ = Standard Deviation
X = Raw scores obtained from the scale
N = Total number of Scores

4. '*t*' tests

The test of significance of the difference between two means is known as '*t*' test.

The formula to find '*t*' value is

$$t = \frac{M_1 - M_2}{\sqrt{\frac{\sigma_1^2}{N_1} + \frac{\sigma_2^2}{N_2}}}$$

Where
M_1 = Mean for the first sample
M_2 = Mean for the Second Sample
σ_1 = SD for the first sample
σ_2 = SD for the first sample
N_1 = Total number of frequency of the first sample
N_2 = Total number of frequency of the second sample

5. Chi-Square Test

Ch-square test is merely used to estimate the like hood that some factor other than chance. (Sampling error) accounts for the apparent relationship. The formula is

$$\text{Chi square } \chi^2 = \Sigma\frac{(O-E)^2}{E}$$

Where

O = Observed frequency

E = Expected frequency

6. ANOVA (Analysis of Variance)

The test of significance of the difference between more than two means, one many use what is called F test, otherwise known as Analysis of Variance. The formula to find 'F' value is

$$\sigma^2 = \frac{\Sigma x^2}{N}$$

Square of the S.D (σ^2) is called variance. Variance is also known as 'Mean Sum of Squares' (MSS). Since it stands for the average of the sum of squares of deviations of each case score from the mean it is simply termed ("SS"), and N is the total number of scores.

$$\text{F-ratio} = \frac{\text{Variance between groups (BSS)}}{\text{Variance within groups (WSS)}}$$

- Variance caused by the differences between the three group means (BSS)
- Variance due to differences within each of the groups themselves (WSS)

7. Pearson's Product Moment Correlation

$$= \frac{N\Sigma xy-(\Sigma x)(\Sigma y)}{\sqrt{N\Sigma x^2-\left(\Sigma x^2\right)}\sqrt{N\Sigma y^2-(\Sigma y)^2}}$$

Where

N = Number of the scores

ΣX = Sum of the X scores

ΣY = Sum of the Y scores

ΣX_2 = Sum of X scores squared

ΣY_2 = Sum of Y scores squared

ΣXY = Sum of the product of X, Y Scores

Delimitations

The investigation was delimited in the following aspects:

1. The study was conducted for eleventh and twelfth standard biology students in the higher secondary schools of Kanyakumari, Tirunelveli and Thoothukudi districts only.

2. The study was confined to 32 higher secondary schools in Kanyakumari, Tirnelveli and Thoothukudi districts only
3. The study has excluded special schools in three districts.
4. The study did not include any other science group than biology.
5. And study did not include central schools and public schools

Conclusion

This chapter outlines the design of the present study, the procedure followed and the nature of the sample. It describes the hypotheses to be tested, the tools used and the methods of administration and scoring. The method of investigation designed and followed is found to be quite appropriate and effective for the present study. The ensuing chapter deals with analysis of data.

4

Analysis of Data

Introduction

After the data collection, the data have to be processed and analyzed in accordance with the outline laid down for the purpose at the time of preparing the research plan. Analysis of data is the most skilled task of all the stages in the research. It is very vital for a scientific study and for ensuring that relevant data for making contemplated comparisons and analysis should be organized. The term analysis refers to the computation of certain measures along with searching for patterns of relationship that exist among data groups. This is done with the help of statistical procedures.

Good, Barr and Scates (1935) suggest four helpful modes to get started on analyzing the gathered data.

(*i*) To think in terms of significant tables that the data permit.

(*ii*) To examine carefully the statement of the problem and earlier analysis and to study the original records of the data.

(*iii*) To get away from the data and to think about the problem in layman's terms or actually discuss the problem with others.

(*iv*) To attack the data by making various statistical calculations.

In this chapter the investigator has presented the collected data and its interpretation by using statistical calculations used mean, standard deviation, t-test, ANOVA, chi-square and product moment correlation with the help of statistical package for social science (spss) .The collected data were classified, organized and analysed for testing the hypotheses formulated in the present study.

SECTION-I

Objective Testing

(a) Environmental Factors

The level of environmental factors and its dimensions of higher secondary biology Students with reference to 1. Sex 2. Standard 3. Locality of the school

4. Nativity of the student 5. Nature of the school 6. Type of management 7. Medium of the institution 8. status of the family.

Table 4.1.1 : With Reference to Sex

Dimensions	Variable	Low		Average		High	
		No	%	No	%	No	%
Home environment	Boys	77	17.6	294	67.1	67	15.1
	Girls	63	12.9	343	70.4	81	16.6
School environment	Boys	55	12.6	309	70.5	74	16.9
	Girls	82	16.8	323	66.3	82	16.8
Social environment	Boys	49	11.2	339	77.4	50	11.4
	Girls	73	15.0	348	71.5	66	13.6
Total environment	Boys	56	12.8	326	74.4	56	12.8
	Girls	69	14.2	337	69.2	81	16.6

The Level is Average

It is inferred from the above table that 17.6 percent, 67.1 percent and 15.1 percent of boys have low, average and high level of home environment respectively. Regarding girls 12.9 percent, 70.4 percent and 16.6 percent of them have low, average and high level of home environment respectively.

Among boys 12.6 percent, 70.5 percent and 16.9 percent of them have low, average and high level of school environment; and among girls 16.8 percent, 66.3 percent and 16.8 percent of them have low, average and high level of school environment respectively.

Among boys 11.2 percent, 77.4 percent and 11.4 percent of them have low, average and high level of social environment; and among girls 15.0 percent, 71.5 percent and 13.6 percent of them have low, average and high level of social environment respectively.

Table 4.1.2: With Reference to Standard

Dimensions	Variable	Low		Average		High	
		No	%	No	%	No	%
Home environment	XI standard	80	15.5	364	70.4	73	14.1
	XII standard	66	16.2	274	67.2	68	16.2
School environment	XI standard	72	13.9	373	72.1	72	13.9
	XII standard	68	16.7	272	66.7	68	16.7
Social environment	XI standard	52	10.1	386	74.1	79	15.3
	XII standard	60	14.7	290	71.1	58	14.2
Total environment	XI standard	70	13.5	374	72.3	73	14.1
	XII standard	66	16.2	287	70.3	55	13.5

The Level is Average

Among boys 12.8 percent, 74.4 percent and 12.8 percent of them have low, average and high level of total environmental factors; and among girls 14.2 percent, 69.2 percent and 16.6 percent of them have low, average and high level of total environmental factors respectively.

It is inferred from the above table that 15.5 percent, 70.4 percent and 14.1 percent of XI standard biology students have low, average and high level of home environment respectively. Regarding XII standard 16.2 percent, 67.2 percent and 16.2 percent of them have low, average and high level of home environment respectively.

Among XI standard students 13.9 percent, 72.1 percent and 13.9 percent of them have low, average and high level of school environment; and among XII standard students 16.7 percent, 66.7 percent and 16.7 percent of them have low, average and high level of school environment respectively.

Among XI standard 10.1 percent, 74.1 percent and 15.3 percent of them have low, average and high level of social environment; and among XII standard 14.7 percent, 71.1 percent and 14.2 percent of them have low, average and high level of social environment respectively.

Among XI standard13.5 percent, 72.3 percent and 14.1 percent of them have low, average and high level of total environmental factors; and among XII standard 16.2 percent, 70.3 percent and 13.5 percent of them have low, average and high level of total environmental factors respectively.

Table 4.1.3: With Reference to Locality of the School

Dimensions	Variable	Low		Average		High	
		No	%	No	%	No	%
Home environment	Rural	76	18.2	275	65.9	66	15.8
	Urban	56	11.0	365	71.9	87	17.1
School environment	Rural	48	11.5	311	74.6	58	13.9
	Urban	74	14.6	376	74.0	58	11.4
Social environment	Rural	48	11.5	311	74.6	58	13.9
	Urban	74.0	14.6	376	74.0	58	11.4
Total environment	Rural	54	12.9	292	70.0	71	17.0
	Urban	68	13.4	370	72.8	70	13.8

The Level is Average

It is inferred from the above table that 18.2 percent, 65.9 percent and 15.8 percent of rural school have low, average and high level of home environment respectively. Regarding urban school 11.0 percent, 71.9 percent and 17.1 percent of them have low, average and high level of home environment respectively.

Among rural school 11.5 percent, 74.6 percent and 13.9 percent of them have low, average and high level of school environment; and among urban school 14.6 percent, 74.0 percent and 11.4 percent of them have low, average and high level of school environment respectively.

Among rural school 11.5 percent, 74.6 percent and 13.9 percent of them have low, average and high level of social environment; and among urban school 14.6 percent, 74.0 percent and 11.4 percent of them have low, average and high level of social environment respectively.

Among rural school 12.9 percent, 70.0 percent and 17.0 percent of them have low, average and high level of total environmental factors; and among urban school 13.4 percent, 72.8 percent and 13.8 percent of them have low, average and high level of total environmental factors respectively.

Table 4.1.4: With Reference to Nativity of the Student

Dimensions	Variable	Low		Average		High	
		No	%	No	%	No	%
Home environment	Rural	70	17.3	268	66.2	67	16.5
	Urban	68	13.1	388	74.6	64	12.3
School environment	Rural	50	12.3	277	68.4	78	19.3
	Urban	84	16.2	356	68.5	80	15.4
Social environment	Rural	56	13.8	291	71.9	58	14.3
	Urban	76	14.6	386	74.2	58	11.2
Total environment	Rural	48	11.9	289	71.4	68	16.8
	Urban	70	13.5	378	72.7	72	13.8

The Level is Average

It is inferred from the above table that 17.3 percent, 66.2 percent and 16.5 percent of rural students have low, average and high level of home environment respectively. Regarding urban students 13.1 percent, 74.6 percent and 12.3 percent of them have low, average and high level of home environment respectively.

Among rural students 12.3 percent, 68.4 percent and 19.3 percent of them have low, average and high level of school environment; and among urban students 16.2 percent, 68.5 percent and 15.4 percent of them have low, average and high level of school environment respectively.

Among rural students 13.8 percent, 71.9 percent and 14.3 percent of them have low, average and high level of social environment; and among urban students 14.6 percent, 74.2 percent and 11.2 percent of them have low, average and high level of social environment respectively.

Among rural students 11.9 percent, 71.4 percent and 16.8 percent of them have low, average and high level of total environmental factors; and among urban students 13.5 percent, 72.7 percent and 13.8 percent of them have low, average and high level of total environmental factors respectively.

Table 4.1.5: With Reference to Nature of The School

Dimensions	Variable	Low		Average		High	
		No	%	No	%	No	%
Home environment	Boys	40	14.8	199	73.4	32	11.8
	Girls	42	13.5	227	73.2	41	13.2
	Co-education	66	19.2	228	66.3	50	14.5
School environment	Boys	38	14.0	182	67.2	51	18.8
	Girls	40	12.9	206	66.5	64	20.6
	Co-education	62	18.0	227	66.0	55	16.0
Social environment	Boys	30	11.1	213	78.6	28	10.3
	Girls	54	17.4	215	69.4	41	13.2
	Co-education	38	11.0	259	75.3	47	13.7
Total environment	Boys	34	12.5	205	75.6	32	11.8
	Girls	50	16.1	220	71.0	40	12.9
	Co-education	42	12.2	246	71.5	56	16.3

The Level is Average

It is inferred from the above table that 14.8 percent, 73.4 percent and 11.8 percent of boys school have low, average and high level of home environment respectively. Regarding girls school 13.5 percent, 73.2 percent and 13.2 percent of them have low, average and high level of home environment respectively. Regarding co-education school 19.2 percent, 66.3 percent and 14.5 percent of them have low, average and high level of home environment respectively.

Among boys school 14.0 percent, 67.2 percent and 18.8 percent of them have low, average and high level of school environment; and among girls school 12.9 percent, 66.5 percent and 20.6 percent of them have low, average and high level of school environment respectively. Regarding co-education school 18.0 percent, 66.0 percent and 16.0 percent of them have low, average and high level of school environment respectively.

Among boys school 11.1 percent, 78.6 percent and 10.3 percent of them have low, average and high level of social environment; and among girls school 17.4 percent, 69.4 percent and 13.2 percent of them have low, average and high level of social environment respectively. Regarding co-education school 11.0 percent, 75.3 percent and 13.7 percent of them have low, average and high level of social environment respectively.

Among boys school12.5 percent, 75.6 percent and 11.8 percent of them have low, average and high level of total environmental factors; and among girls school 16.1 percent, 71.0 percent and 12.9 percent of them have low, average and high level of total environmental factors respectively. Regarding co-education school 12.2 percent, 71.5 percent and 16.3 percent of them have low, average and high level of total environment factors respectively.

Table 4.1.6: With Reference to Type of Management

Dimensions	Variable	Low		Average		High	
		No	%	No	%	No	%
Home environment	Government	48	17.1	198	70.7	34	12.1
	Aided	48	13.7	242	69.1	60	17.1
	Private	40	13.6	217	73.6	38	12.9
School environment	Government	56	20.0	182	65.0	42	15.0
	Aided	50	14.3	252	72.0	48	13.7
	Private	34	11.5	216	73.2	45	15.3
Social environment	Government	30	10.7	222	79.3	28	10.0
	Aided	46	13.1	250	71.4	54	15.4
	Private	52	17.6	197	66.8	46	15.6
Total environment	Government	26	9.3	218	77.9	36	12.9
	Aided	52	14.9	246	70.3	52	14.9
	Private	42	14.2	209	70.8	44	14.9

The Level is Average

It is inferred from the above table that 17.1 percent, 70.7 percent and 12.1 percent of government school have low, average and high level of home environment respectively. Regarding aided school 13.7 percent, 69.1 percent and 17.1 percent of them have low, average and high level of home environment respectively. Regarding private school 13.6 percent, 73.6 percent and 12.9 percent of them have low, average and high level of home environment respectively.

Among government school 20.0 percent, 65.0 percent and 15.0 percent of them have low, average and high level of school environment; and among aided school 14.3 percent, 72.0 percent and 13.7 percent of them have low, average and high level of school environment respectively. Regarding private school 11.5 percent, 73.2 percent and 15.3 percent of them have low, average and high level of school environment respectively.

Among government school 10.7 percent, 79.3 percent and 10.0 percent of them have low, average and high level of social environment; and among aided school 13.1 percent, 71.4 percent and 15.4 percent of them have low, average and high level of social environment respectively. Regarding private school 17.6 percent, 66.8 percent and 15.6 percent of them have low, average and high level of social environment respectively.

Among Government School 9.3 percent, 77.9 percent and 12.9 percent of them have low, average and high level of total environmental factors; and among aided school 14.9 percent, 70.3 percent and 14.9 percent of them have low, average and high level of total environmental factors respectively. Regarding private school 14.2 percent, 70.8 percent and 14.9 percent of them have low, average and high level of total environment factors respectively.

Table 4.1.7: With Reference to Medium of the School

Dimensions	Variable	Low		Average		High	
		No	%	No	%	No	%
Home environment	Tamil	66	14.5	336	73.7	54	11.8
	English	66	14.1	321	68.4	82	17.5
School environment	Tamil	70	15.4	306	67.1	80	17.5
	English	68	14.5	314	67.0	87	18.6
Social environment	Tamil	52	11.4	336	73.7	68	14.9
	English	90	19.2	325	69.3	54	11.5
Total environment	Tamil	50	11.0	346	75.9	60	13.2
	English	80	17.1	310	66.1	79	16.8

The Level is Average

It is inferred from the above table that 14.5 percent, 73.7 percent and 11.8 percent of Tamil medium students have low, average and high level of home environment respectively. Regarding English medium students 14.1 percent, 68.4 percent and 17.5 percent of them have low, average and high level of home environment respectively.

Among Tamil medium students 15.4 percent, 67.1 percent and 17.5 percent of them have low, average and high level of school environment; and among English medium students 14.5 percent, 67.0 percent and 18.6 percent of them have low, average and high level of school environment respectively.

Table 4.1.8: With Reference to Status of the Family

Dimensions	Variable	Low		Average		High	
		No	%	No	%	No	%
Home environment	Nuclear	74	13.5	388	70.7	87	15.8
	Joint	52	13.8	269	71.5	55	14.6
School environment	Nuclear	72	13.1	374	68.1	103	18.8
	Joint	64	17.0	261	69.4	51	13.6
Social environment	Nuclear	80	14.6	385	70.1	84	15.3
	Joint	42	11.2	290	77.1	44	11.7
Total environment	Nuclear	80	14.6	391	71.2	78	14.2
	Joint	52	13.8	271	72.1	53	14.1

The Level is Average

Among Tamil medium students 11.4 percent, 73.7 percent and 14.9 percent of them have low, average and high level of social environment; and among English medium students 19.2 percent, 69.3 percent and 11.5 percent of them have low, average and high level of social environment respectively.

Among Tamil medium students 11.0 percent, 75.9 percent and 13.2 percent of them have low, average and high level of total environmental factors; and among English medium students 17.1 percent, 66.1 percent and 16.8 percent of them have low, average and high level of total environmental factors respectively.

It is inferred from the above table that 13.5 percent, 70.7 percent and 15.8 percent of nuclear family students have low, average and high level of home environment respectively. Regarding joint family students 13.8 percent, 71.5 percent and 14.6 percent of them have low, average and high level of home environment respectively.

Among nuclear family students 13.1 percent, 68.1 percent and 18.8 percent of them have low, average and high level of school environment; and among joint family students 17.0 percent, 69.4 percent and 13.6 percent of them have low, average and high level of school environment respectively.

Among nuclear family students 14.6 percent, 70.1 percent and 15.3 percent of them have low, average and high level of social environment; and among joint family students 11.2 percent, 77.1 percent and 11.7 percent of them have low, average and high level of social environment respectively.

Among nuclear family students 14.6 percent, 71.2 percent and 14.2 percent of them have low, average and high level of total environmental factors; and among joint family students 13.8 percent, 72.1 percent and 14.1 percent of them have low, average and high level of total environmental factors respectively.

(b) Study Habits

The level of study habits and its dimensions of higher secondary biology Students with reference to 1 Sex 2. Standard 3. Locality of the school 4. Nativity of the student 5. Nature of the school 6. Type of management 7. Medium of the institution 8. Status of the family.

Table 4.1.9: With Reference to Sex

Dimensions	Variable	Low		Average		High	
		No	%	No	%	No	%
1	2	3	4	5	6	7	8
Studies at home	Boys	74	16.9	304	69.4	60	13.7
	Girls	56	11.5	361	74.1	70	14.4
Reading and note taking	Boys	61	13.9	316	72.1	61	13.9
	Girls	62	12.7	350	71.9	75	15.4

1	2	3	4	5	6	7	8
Planning of the subject	Boys	59	13.5	339	77.4	40	9.1
	Girls	73	15.0	320	65.7	94	19.3
Habit of concentration	Boys	68	15.5	313	71.5	57	13.0
	Girls	70	14.4	358	73.5	59	12.1
Preparation for examination	Boys	58	13.2	326	74.4	54	12.3
	Girls	61	12.5	370	76.0	56	11.5
General habits and attitudes	Boys	64	14.6	330	75.3	44	10.0
	Girls	73	15.0	354	72.7	60	12.3
Studies at school	Boys	55	12.6	312	71.2	71	16.2
	Girls	77	15.8	335	68.8	75	15.4
Total study habits	Boys	70	16.0	284	64.8	84	19.2
	Girls	74	15.2	336	69.0	77	15.8

The Level is Average

It is inferred from the above table that 16.9 percent, 69.4 percent and 13.7 percent of boys have low, average and high level of studies at home respectively. Regarding girls 11.5 percent, 74.1 percent and 14.4 percent of them have low, average and high level of studies at home respectively.

Among boys 13.9 percent, 72.1 percent and 13.9 percent of them have low, average and high level of reading and note taking; and among girls 12.7 percent, 71.9 percent and 15.4 percent of them have low, average and high level of reading and note taking respectively.

Among boys 13.5 percent, 77.4 percent and 9.1 percent of them have low, average and high level of planning of the subject; and among girls 15.0 percent, 65.7 percent and 19.3 percent of them have low, average and high level of planning of the subject respectively.

Among boys 15.5 percent, 71.5 percent and 13.0 percent of them have low, average and high level of habit of concentration; and among girls 14.4 percent, 73.5 percent and 13.1 percent of them have low, average and high level of habit of concentration respectively.

Among boys 13.2 percent, 74.4 percent and 12.3 percent of them have low, average and high level of preparation for examination; and among girls 12.5 percent, 76.0 percent and 11.5 percent of them have low, average and high level of preparation for examination respectively.

Among boys 14.6 percent, 75.3 percent and 10.0 percent of them have low, average and high level of general habits and attitudes; and among girls 15.0 percent, 72.7 percent and 12.3 percent of them have low, average and high level of general habits and attitudes respectively.

Among boys 12.6 percent, 71.2 percent and 16.2 percent of them have low, average and high level of studies at school; and among girls 15.8 percent,

68.8 percent and 15.4 percent of them have low, average and high level of studies at school respectively.

Among boys 16.0 percent, 64.8 percent and 19.2 percent of them have low, average and high level of total study habits; and among girls 15.2 percent, 69.0 percent and 15.8 percent of them have low, average and high level of total study habits respectively.

Table 4.1.10: With Reference to Standard

Dimensions	Variable	Low		Average		High	
		No	%	No	%	No	%
Studies at home	XI Standard	80	15.5	370	71.6	67	13.0
	XII standard	82	20.1	263	64.5	63	15.4
Reading and note taking	XI Standard	56	10.8	384	74.3	77	14.9
	XII standard	56	13.7	287	70.3	65	15.9
Planning of the subject	XI Standard	64	12.4	375	72.5	78	15.1
	XII standard	68	16.7	280	68.6	60	14.7
Habit of concentration	XI Standard	64	12.4	382	73.9	71	13.7
	XII standard	56	13.7	290	71.1	62	15.2
Preparation for examination	XI Standard	56	10.8	391	75.6	70	13.5
	XII standard	68	16.7	289	70.8	51	12.5
General habits and attitudes	XI Standard	70	13.5	352	68.1	95	18.4
	XII standard	58	14.2	286	70.1	64	15.7
Studies at school	XI Standard	62	12.0	376	72.7	79	15.3
	XII standard	64	15.7	272	66.7	72	17.6
Total study habits	XI Standard	72	13.9	363	70.2	82	15.9
	XII standard	78	19.1	264	64.7	66	16.2

The Level is Average

It is inferred from the above table that 15.5 percent, 71.6 percent and 13.0 percent of XI standard have low, average and high level of studies at home respectively. Regarding XII standard 20.1 percent, 64.5 percent and 15.4 percent of them have low, average and high level of studies at home respectively.

Among XI standard 10.8 percent, 74.3 percent and 14.9 percent of them have low, average and high level of reading and note taking; and among XII standard 13.7 percent, 70.3 percent and 15.9 percent of them have low, average and high level of reading and note taking respectively.

Among XI standard 12.4 percent, 72.5 percent and 15.1 percent of them have low, average and high level of planning of the subject; and among XII standard 16.7 percent, 68.6 percent and 14.7 percent of them have low, average and high level of planning of the subject respectively.

Among XI standard 12.4 percent, 73.9 percent and 13.7 percent of them have low, average and high level of habit of concentration; and among XII standard 13.7 percent, 71.1 percent and 15.2 percent of them have low, average and high level of habit of concentration respectively.

Among XI standard 10.8 percent, 75.6 percent and 13.5 percent of them have low, average and high level of preparation for examination; and among XII standard 16.7 percent, 70.8 percent and 12.5 percent of them have low, average and high level of preparation for examination respectively.

Among XI standard 13.5 percent, 68.1 percent and 18.4 percent of them have low, average and high level of general habits and attitudes; and among XII standard 14.2 percent, 70.1 percent and 15.7 percent of them have low, average and high level of general habits and attitudes respectively.

Among XI standard 12.0 percent, 72.7 percent and 15.3 percent of them have low, average and high level of studies at school; and among XII standard 15.7 percent, 66.7 percent and 17.6 percent of them have low, average and high level of studies at school respectively.

Table 4.1.11: With Reference to Locality of the School

Dimensions	Variable	Low		Average		High	
		No	%	No	%	No	%
Studies at home	Rural	79	18.9	271	65.0	67	16.1
	Urban	90	17.7	317	62.4	101	19.9
Reading and note taking	Rural	52	12.5	302	72.4	63	15.1
	Urban	60	11.8	369	72.6	79	15.6
Planning of the subject	Rural	60	14.4	319	76.5	38	9.1
	Urban	84	16.5	339	66.7	85	16.7
Habit of concentration	Rural	70	16.8	304	72.9	43	10.3
	Urban	68	13.4	374	73.6	66	13.0
Preparation for examination	Rural	54	12.9	312	74.8	51	12.2
	Urban	72	14.2	357	70.3	79	15.6
General habits and attitudes	Rural	66	15.8	303	72.7	48	11.5
	Urban	80	15.7	344	67.7	84	16.5
Studies at school	Rural	76	18.2	272	65.2	69	16.5
	Urban	70	13.8	360	70.9	78	15.4
Total study habits	Rural	76	18.2	274	65.7	67	16.1
	Urban	74	14.6	346	68.1	88	17.3

The level is average

Among XI standard 13.9 percent, 70.2 percent and 15.9 percent of them have low, average and high level of total study habits; and among XII standard 19.1 percent, 64.7 percent and 16.2 percent of them have low, average and high level of total study habits respectively.

It is inferred from the above table that 18.9 percent, 65.0 percent and 16.1 percent of rural school have low, average and high level of studies at home respectively. Regarding Urban school 17.7 percent, 62.4 percent and 19.9 percent of them have low, average and high level of studies at home respectively.

Among Rural school 12.5 percent, 72.4 percent and 15.1 percent of them have low, average and high level of reading and note taking; and among urban school 11.8 percent, 72.6 percent and 15.6 percent of them have low, average and high level of reading and note taking respectively.

Among Rural school 14.4 percent, 76.5 percent and 9.1 percent of them have low, average and high level of planning of the subject; and among urban school 16.5 percent, 66.7 percent and 16.7 percent of them have low, average and high level of planning of the subject respectively.

Table 4.1.12: With Reference to Nativity of the Student

Dimensions	Variable	Low		Average		High	
		No	%	No	%	No	%
Studies at home	Rural	56	13.8	286	70.6	63	15.6
	Urban	118	22.7	335	64.4	67	12.9
Reading and note taking	Rural	54	13.3	284	70.1	67	16.5
	Urban	44	8.5	407	78.3	69	13.3
Planning of the subject	Rural	72	17.8	287	70.9	46	11.4
	Urban	88	16.9	339	65.2	93	17.9
Habit of concentration	Rural	60	14.8	285	70.4	60	14.8
	Urban	56	10.8	398	76.5	66	12.7
Preparation for examination	Rural	68	16.8	286	70.6	51	12.6
	Urban	56	10.8	385	74.0	79	15.2
General habits and attitudes	Rural	70	17.3	262	64.7	73	18.0
	Urban	80	15.4	384	73.8	56	10.8
Studies at school	Rural	60	14.8	281	69.4	64	15.8
	Urban	63	12.1	397	76.3	60	11.5
Total study habits	Rural	70	17.3	271	66.9	64	15.8
	Urban	70	13.5	358	66.8	92	17.7

The level is average

Among Rural school 16.8 percent, 72.9 percent and 10.3 percent of them have low, average and high level of habit of concentration; and among urban school 13.4 percent, 73.6 percent and 13.0 percent of them have low, average and high level of habit of concentration respectively.

Among Rural school 12.9 percent, 74.8 percent and 12.2 percent of them have low, average and high level of preparation for examination; and among urban school 14.2 percent, 70.3 percent and 15.6 percent of them have low, average and high level of preparation for examination respectively.

Among Rural school 15.8 percent, 72.7 percent and 11.5 percent of them have low, average and high level of general habits and attitudes; and among urban school 15.7 percent, 67.7 percent and 16.5 percent of them have low, average and high level of general habits and attitudes respectively.

Among Rural school 18.2 percent, 65.2 percent and 16.5 percent of them have low, average and high level of studies at school; and among urban school 13.8 percent, 70.9 percent and 15.4 percent of them have low, average and high level of studies at school respectively.

Among Rural school 18.2 percent, 65.7 percent and 16.01 percent of them have low, average and high level of total study habits; and among urban school 14.6 percent, 68.1 percent and 17.3 percent of them have low, average and high level of total study habits respectively.

It is inferred from the above table that 13.8 percent, 70.6 percent and 15.6 percent of rural students have low, average and high level of studies at home respectively. Regarding urban students 22.7 percent, 64.4 percent and 12.9 percent of them have low, average and high level of studies at home respectively.

Among Rural students 13.3 percent, 70.1 percent and 16.5 percent of them have low, average and high level of reading and note taking; and among urban students 8.5 percent, 78.3 percent and 13.3 percent of them have low, average and high level of reading and note taking respectively.

Among Rural students 17.8 percent, 70.9 percent and 11.4 percent of them have low, average and high level of planning of the subject; and among urban students 16.9 percent, 65.2 percent and 17.9 percent of them have low, average and high level of planning of the subject respectively.

Among Rural students 14.8 percent, 70.4 percent and 14.8 percent of them have low, average and high level of habit of concentration; and among urban students 10.8 percent, 76.5 percent and 12.7 percent of them have low, average and high level of habit of concentration respectively.

Among Rural students 16.8 percent, 70.6 percent and 12.6 percent of them have low, average and high level of preparation for examination; and among urban students 10.8 percent, 74.0 percent and 15.2 percent of them have low, average and high level of preparation for examination respectively.

Among Rural students 17.3 percent, 64.7 percent and 18.0 percent of them have low, average and high level of general habits and attitudes; and among urban students 15.4 percent, 73.8 percent and 10.8 percent of them have low, average and high level of general habits and attitudes respectively.

Among Rural students 14.8 percent, 69.4 percent and 15.8 percent of them have low, average and high level of studies at school; and among urban students 12.1 percent, 76.3 percent and 11.5 percent of them have low, average and high level of studies at school respectively.

Among Rural students 17.3 percent, 66.9 percent and 15.8 percent of them have low, average and high level of total study habits; and among urban students 13.5 percent, 66.8 percent and 17.7 percent of them have low, average and high level of total study habits respectively.

Table 4.1.13: With Reference to Nature of The School

Dimensions	Variable	Low		Average		High	
		No	%	No	%	No	%
Studies at home	Boys	54	19.9	165	60.9	52	19.2
	Girls	55	17.7	198	63.9	57	18.4
	Co-education	44	12.8	261	75.9	39	11.3
Reading and note taking	Boys	36	13.3	197	72.7	38	14.0
	Girls	46	14.8	226	72.9	38	12.3
	Co-education	36	10.5	263	76.5	45	13.1
Planning of the subject	Boys	44	16.2	201	74.2	26	9.6
	Girls	54	17.4	210	67.7	46	14.8
	Co-education	44	12.8	251	73.0	49	14.2
Habit of concentration	Boys	43	15.9	188	69.4	40	14.8
	Girls	42	13.5	228	73.5	40	12.9
	Co-education	53	15.4	258	75.0	33	9.6
Preparation for examination	Boys	44	16.2	195	72.0	32	11.8
	Girls	42	13.5	243	78.4	25	8.1
	Co-education	40	11.6	262	76.2	42	12.2
General habits and attitudes	Boys	48	17.7	195	72.0	28	10.3
	Girls	68	21.9	194	62.6	48	15.5
	Co-education	34	9.9	261	75.9	49	14.2
Studies at school	Boys	42	15.5	187	69.0	42	15.5
	Girls	54	17.4	208	67.1	48	15.5
	Co-education	44	12.8	256	74.4	44	12.8
Total study habits	Boys	38	14.0	191	70.5	42	15.5
	Girls	54	17.4	226	72.9	30	9.7
	Co-education	54	15.7	244	70.9	46	13.4

The level is average

It is inferred from the above table that 19.9 percent, 60.9 percent and 19.2 percent of boys' school have low, average and high level of studies at home respectively. Regarding girls school 17.7 percent, 63.9 percent and 18.4 percent of them have low, average and high level of studies at home respectively. Regarding co-education school 12.8 percent, 75.9 percent and 11.3 percent of them have low, average and high level of studies at home respectively.

Among boys school 13.3 percent, 72.7 percent and 14.0 percent of them have low, average and high level of reading and note taking; and among girls school 14.8 percent, 72.9 percent and 12.3 percent of them have low, average and high level of Reading and note taking respectively. Regarding co-education school 10.5 percent, 76.5 percent and 13.1 percent of them have low, average and high level of reading and note taking respectively.

Among boys school 16.2 percent, 74.2 percent and 9.6 percent of them have low, average and high level of planning of the subject; and among girls school 17.4 percent, 67.7 percent and 14.8 percent of them have low, average and high level of planning of the subject respectively. Regarding co-education school 12.8 percent, 73.0 percent and 14.2 percent of them have low, average and high level of planning of the subject respectively.

Among boys school 15.9 percent, 69.4 percent and 14.8 percent of them have low, average and high level of habit of concentration; and among girls school 13.5 percent, 73.5 percent and 12.9 percent of them have low, average and high level of habit of concentration respectively. Regarding co-education school 15.4 percent, 75.0 percent and 9.6 percent of them have low, average and high level of habit of concentration respectively.

Among boys school 16.2 percent, 72.0 percent and 11.8 percent of them have low, average and high level of preparation for examination; and among girls school 13.5 percent, 78.4 percent and 8.1 percent of them have low, average and high level of preparation for examination respectively. Regarding co-education school 11.6 percent, 76.2 percent and 12.2 percent of them have low, average and high level of preparation for examination respectively.

Among boys school 17.7 percent, 72.0 percent and 10.3 percent of them have low, average and high level of general habits and attitudes; and among girls school 21.9 percent, 62.6 percent and 15.5 percent of them have low, average and high level of general habits and attitudes respectively. Regarding co-education school 9.9 percent, 75.9 percent and 14.2 percent of them have low, average and high level of general habits and attitudes respectively.

Among boys school 15.5 percent, 69.0 percent and 15.5 percent of them have low, average and high level of studies at school; and among girls school 17.4 percent, 67.1 percent and 15.5 percent of them have low, average and high level of Studies at school respectively. Regarding co-education school 12.8 percent, 74.4 percent and 12.8 percent of them have low, average and high level of studies at school respectively.

Among boys school 14.0 percent, 70.5 percent and 15.5 percent of them have low, average and high level of total study habits; and among girls school 17.4 percent, 72.9 percent and 9.7 percent of them have low, average and high level of total study habit respectively. Regarding co-education school 15.7 percent, 70.9 percent and 13.4 percent of them have low, average and high level of total study habits respectively.

Table 4.1.14: With Reference to Type of Management

Dimensions	Variable	Low		Average		High	
		No	%	No	%	No	%
Studies at home	Government	38	13.6	202	72.1	40	14.3
	Aided	64	18.3	224	64.0	62	17.7
	Private	44	14.9	209	70.8	42	14.2
Reading and note taking	Government	28	10.0	210	75.0	42	15.0
	Aided	50	14.3	246	70.3	54	15.4
	Private	36	12.2	213	72.2	46	15.6
Planning of the subject	Government	32	11.4	212	75.7	36	12.9
	Aided	44	12.6	252	72.0	54	15.4
	Private	48	16.3	182	61.7	65	22.0
Habit of concentration	Government	42	15.0	196	70.0	42	15.0
	Aided	46	13.1	254	72.6	50	14.3
	Private	52	17.6	207	70.2	36	12.2
Preparation for examination	Government	34	12.1	222	79.3	24	8.6
	Aided	44	12.6	258	73.7	48	13.7
	Private	46	15.6	225	76.3	24	8.1
General habits and attitudes	Government	22	7.9	216	77.1	42	15.0
	Aided	48	13.7	240	68.6	62	17.7
	Private	46	15.6	211	71.5	38	12.9
Studies at school	Government	30	10.7	222	79.3	28	10.0
	Aided	58	16.6	210	60.0	82	23.4
	Private	50	16.9	221	74.9	24	8.1
Total study habits	Government	44	15.7	194	69.3	42	15.0
	Aided	52	14.9	238	68.0	60	17.1
	Private	52	17.6	210	71.2	33	11.2

The level is average

It is inferred from the above table that 13.6 percent, 72.1 percent and 14.3 percent of government school have low, average and high level of studies at home respectively. Regarding aided school 18.3 percent, 64.0 percent and 17.7 percent of them have low, average and high level of studies at home respectively. Regarding private school 14.9 percent, 70.8 percent and 14.2

percent of them have low, average and high level of studies at home respectively.

Among government school, 10.0 percent, 75.0 percent and 15.0 percent of them have low, average and high level of reading and note taking; and among aided school 14.3 percent, 70.3 percent and 15.4 percent of them have low, average and high level of reading and note taking respectively. Regarding private school 12.2 percent, 72.2 percent and 15.6 percent of them have low, average and high level of reading and note taking respectively.

Among government school, 11.4 percent, 75.7 percent and 12.9 percent of them have low, average and high level of planning of the subject; and among aided school, 12.6 percent, 72.0 percent and 15.4 percent of them have low, average and high level of planning of the subject respectively. Regarding private school 16.3 percent, 61.7 percent and 22.0 percent of them have low, average and high level of planning of the subject respectively.

Among government school, 15.0 percent, 70.0 percent and 15.0 percent of them have low, average and high level of habit of concentration; and among aided school 13.1 percent, 72.6 percent and 14.3 percent of them have low, average and high level of habit of concentration respectively. Regarding private school 17.6 percent, 70.2 percent and 12.2 percent of them have low, average and high level of habit of concentration respectively.

Among government school, 12.1 percent, 79.3 percent and 8.6 percent of them have low, average and high level of preparation for examination; and among aided school 12.6 percent, 73.7 percent and 13.7 percent of them have low, average and high level of preparation for examination respectively. Regarding private school 15.6 percent, 76.3 percent and 8.1 percent of them have low, average and high level of preparation for examination respectively.

Among government school, 7.9 percent, 77.1 percent and 15.0 percent of them have low, average and high level of general habits and attitudes; and among aided school 13.7 percent, 68.6 percent and 17.7 percent of them have low, average and high level of general habits and attitudes respectively. Regarding private school 15.6 percent, 71.5 percent and 12.9 percent of them have low, average and high level of general habits and attitudes respectively.

Among government school, 10.7 percent, 79.3 percent and 10.0 percent of them have low, average and high level of studies at school; and among aided school 16.6 percent, 60.0 percent and 23.4 percent of them have low, average and high level of studies at school respectively. Regarding private school 16.9 percent, 74.9 percent and 8.1 percent of them have low, average and high level of studies at school respectively.

Among government school, 15.7 percent, 69.3 percent and 15.0 percent of them have low, average and high level of total study habits; and among aided school 14.9 percent, 68.0 percent and 17.1 percent of them have low, average and high level of total study habits respectively. Regarding private school 17.6 percent, 71.2 percent and 11.2 percent of them have low, average and high level of total study habits respectively.

Table 4.1.15: With Reference To Medium Of The School

Dimensions	Variable	Low		Average		High	
		No	%	No	%	No	%
Studies at home	Tamil	70	15.4	304	66.7	82	18.0
	English	95	20.3	306	65.2	68	14.5
Reading and note taking	Tamil	52	11.4	354	77.6	50	11.0
	English	68	14.5	321	68.4	80	17.1
Planning of the subject	Tamil	62	13.6	320	70.2	74	16.2
	English	70	14.9	347	74.0	52	11.1
Habit of concentration	Tamil	76	16.7	304	66.7	76	16.7
	English	62	13.2	359	76.5	48	10.2
Preparation for examination	Tamil	56	12.3	344	75.4	56	12.3
	English	66	14.1	351	74.8	52	11.1
General habits and attitudes	Tamil	52	11.4	332	72.8	72	15.8
	English	82	17.5	323	68.9	64	13.6
Studies at school	Tamil	54	11.8	330	72.4	72	15.8
	English	78	16.6	339	72.3	52	11.1
Total study habits	Tamil	68	14.9	322	70.6	66	14.5
	English	82	17.5	326	69.5	61	13.0

The level is average

It is inferred from the above table that 15.4 percent, 66.7 percent and 18.0 percent of Tamil medium students have low, average and high level of studies at home respectively. Regarding English medium students 20.3 percent, 65.2 percent and 14.5 percent of them have low, average and high level of studies at home respectively.

Among Tamil medium students 11.4 percent, 77.6 percent and 11.0 percent of them have low, average and high level of reading and note taking; and among English medium students 14.5 percent, 68.4 percent and 17.1 percent of them have low, average and high level of reading and note taking respectively.

Among Tamil medium students 13.6 percent, 70.2 percent and 16.2 percent of them have low, average and high level of planning of the subject; and among English medium students 14.9 percent, 74.0 percent and 11.1 percent of them have low, average and high level of planning of the subject respectively.

Among Tamil medium students 16.7 percent, 66.7 percent and 16.7 percent of them have low, average and high level of habit of concentration; and among English medium students 13.2 percent, 76.5 percent and 10.2 percent of them have low, average and high level of habit of concentration respectively.

Among Tamil medium students 12.3 percent, 75.4 percent and 12.3 percent of them have low, average and high level of preparation for examination; and among English medium students 14.1 percent, 74.8 percent and 11.1 percent of them have low, average and high level of preparation for examination respectively.

Among Tamil medium students 11.4 percent, 72.8 percent and 15.8 percent of them have low, average and high level of general habits and attitudes; and among English medium students 17.5 percent, 68.9 percent and 13.6 percent of them have low, average and high level of general habits and attitudes respectively.

Among Tamil medium students 11.8 percent, 72.4 percent and 15.8 percent of them have low, average and high level of studies at school; and among English medium students 16.6 percent, 72.3 percent and 11.1 percent of them have low, average and high level of studies at school respectively.

Among Tamil medium students 14.9 percent, 70.6 percent and 14.5 percent of them have low, average and high level of total study habits; and among English medium students 17.5 percent, 69.5 percent and 13.0 percent of them have low, average and high level of total study habits respectively.

Table 4.1.16: With Reference to Status of the Family

Dimensions	Variable	Low		Average		High	
		No	%	No	%	No	%
Studies at home	Nuclear	119	21.7	338	61.6	92	16.8
	Joint	44	11.7	271	72.1	61	16.2
Reading and note taking	Nuclear	66	12.0	401	73.0	82	14.9
	Joint	32	8.5	295	78.5	49	13.0
Planning of the subject	Nuclear	94	17.1	395	71.9	60	10.9
	Joint	52	13.8	256	68.1	68	18.1
Habit of concentration	Nuclear	90	16.4	384	69.9	75	13.7
	Joint	48	12.8	278	73.9	50	13.3
Preparation for examination	Nuclear	78	14.2	404	73.6	67	12.2
	Joint	42	11.2	292	77.7	42	11.2
General habits and attitudes	Nuclear	86	15.7	362	65.9	101	18.4
	Joint	70	18.6	256	68.1	50	13.3
Studies at school	Nuclear	94	17.1	381	69.4	74	13.5
	Joint	47	12.5	269	71.5	60	16.0
Total study habits	Nuclear	94	17.1	381	69.4	74	13.5
	Joint	54	14.4	257	68.4	65	17.3

The level is average

It is inferred from the above table that 21.7 percent, 61.6 percent and 16.8 percent of nuclear family students have low, average and high level of studies at home respectively. Regarding joint family students 11.7 percent, 72.1 percent and 16.2 percent of them have low, average and high level of studies at home respectively.

Among nuclear family students, 12.0 percent, 73.0 percent and 14.9 percent of them have low, average and high level of reading and note taking; and among joint family students, 8.5 percent, 78.5 percent and 13.0 percent of them have low, average and high level of reading and note taking respectively.

Among nuclear family students, 17.1 percent, 71.9 percent and 10.9 percent of them have low, average and high level of planning of the subject; and among joint family students, 13.8 percent, 68.1 percent and 18.1 percent of them have low, average and high level of planning of the subject respectively.

Among nuclear family students, 16.4 percent, 69.9 percent and 13.7 percent of them have low, average and high level of habit of concentration; and among joint family students 12.8 percent, 73.9 percent and 13.3 percent of them have low, average and high level of habit of concentration respectively.

Among nuclear family students, 14.2 percent, 73.6 percent and 12.2 percent of them have low, average and high level of preparation for examination; and among joint family students, 11.2 percent, 77.7 percent and 11.2 percent of them have low, average and high level of preparation for examination respectively.

Among nuclear family students, 15.7 percent, 65.9 percent and 18.4 percent of them have low, average and high level of general habits and attitudes; and among joint family students, 18.6 percent, 68.1 percent and 13.3 percent of them have low, average and high level of general habits and attitudes respectively.

Among nuclear family students, 17.1 percent, 69.4 percent and 13.5 percent of them have low, average and high level of studies at school; and among joint family students, 12.5 percent, 71.5 percent and 16.0 percent of them have low, average and high level of studies at school respectively.

Among nuclear family students, 17.1 percent, 69.4 percent and 13.5 percent of them have low, average and high level of total study habits; and among joint family students, 14.4 percent, 68.4 percent and 17.3 percent of them have low, average and high level of total study habits respectively.

(c) Self -Esteem

The level of self-esteem and its dimensions of higher secondary biology Students with reference to sex 1.Sex 2.Standard 3.Locality of the school 4.Nativity of the student 5.Nature of the school 6.Type of management 7.Medium of the institution 8.Status of the family.

Table 4.1.17: With Reference to Sex

Dimensions	Variable	Low		Average		High	
		No	%	No	%	No	%
Competency	Boys	84	19.2	269	61.4	85	19.4
	Girls	66	13.6	359	73.7	62	12.7
Global self esteem	Boys	86	19.6	281	64.2	71	16.2
	Girls	68	14.0	317	65.1	102	20.9
Moral and self control	Boys	77	17.6	281	64.2	80	18.3
	Girls	65	13.3	366	75.2	56	11.5
Social esteem	Boys	59	13.5	307	70.1	72	16.4
	Girls	80	16.4	347	71.3	60	12.3
Family	Boys	73	16.7	307	70.1	58	13.2
	Girls	73	15.0	372	76.4	42	8.6
Body and physical appearance	Boys	57	13.0	326	74.4	55	12.6
	Girls	67	13.8	331	68.0	89	18.3
Total self esteem	Boys	68	15.5	291	66.4	79	18.0
	Girls	55	11.3	342	70.2	90	18.5

The level is average

It is inferred from the above table that 19.2 percent, 61.4 percent and 19.4 percent of boys have low, average and high level of competency respectively. Regarding girls, 13.6 percent, 73.7 percent and 12.7 percent of them have low, average and high level of competency respectively.

Among boys, 19.6 percent, 64.2 percent and 16.2 percent of them have low, average and high level of global self esteem; and among girls 14.0 percent, 65.1 percent and 20.9 percent of them have low, average and high level of global self esteem respectively.

Among boys, 17.6 percent, 64.2 percent and 18.3 percent of them have low, average and high level of moral and self control; and among girls 13.3 percent, 75.2 percent and 11.5 percent of them have low, average and high level of moral and self control respectively.

Among boys, 13.5 percent, 70.1 percent and 16.4 percent of them have low, average and high level of social esteem; and among girls 16.4 percent, 71.3 percent and 12.3 percent of them have low, average and high level of social esteem respectively.

Among boys, 16.7 percent, 70.1 percent and 13.2 percent of them have low, average and high level of family; and among girls 15.0 percent, 76.4 percent and 8.6 percent of them have low, average and high level of family respectively.

Among boys, 13.0 percent, 74.4 percent and 12.6 percent of them have low, average and high level of body and physical appearance; and among girls 13.8 percent, 68.0 percent and 18.3 percent of them have low, average and high level of body and physical appearance respectively.

Among boys, 15.5 percent, 66.4 percent and 18.0 percent of them have low, average and high level of total self esteem; and among girls 11.3 percent, 70.2 percent and 18.5 percent of them have low, average and high level of total self esteem respectively.

Table 4.1.18: With Reference to Standard

Dimensions	Variable	Low		Average		High	
		No	%	No	%	No	%
Competency	XI Standard	44	8.5	407	78.7	66	12.8
	XII standard	70	17.2	266	65.2	72	17.6
Global self esteem	XI Standard	67	13.0	362	70.0	88	17.0
	XII standard	45	11.0	285	69.9	78	19.1
Moral and self control	XI Standard	80	15.5	375	72.5	62	12.0
	XII standard	68	16.7	286	70.1	54	13.2
Social esteem	XI Standard	101	19.5	374	72.3	42	8.1
	XII standard	68	16.7	260	63.7	80	19.6
Family	XI Standard	88	17.0	344	66.5	85	16.4
	XII standard	68	16.7	302	74.0	38	9.3
Body and physical appearance	XI Standard	55	10.6	386	74.7	76	14.7
	XII standard	65	15.9	279	68.4	64	15.7
Total self esteem	XI Standard	59	11.4	376	72.7	82	15.9
	XII standard	52	12.7	282	69.1	74	18.1

The level is average.

It is inferred from the above table that 8.5 percent, 78.7 percent and 12.8 percent of XI standard students have low, average and high level of competency respectively. Regarding XII standard students, 17.2 percent, 65.2 percent and 17.6 percent of them have low, average and high level of competency respectively.

Among XI standard students 13.0 percent, 70.0 percent and 17.0 percent of them have low, average and high level of global self esteem; and among XII standard students 11.0 percent, 69.9 percent and 19.1 percent of them have low, average and high level of global self esteem respectively.

Among XI standard students 15.5 percent, 72.5 percent and 12.0 percent of them have low, average and high level of moral and self control; and among XII standard students 16.7 percent, 70.1 percent and 13.2 percent of them have low, average and high level of moral and self control respectively.

Among XI standard students 19.5 percent, 72.3 percent and 8.1 percent of them have low, average and high level of social esteem; and among XII standard students 16.7 percent, 63.7 percent and 19.6 percent of them have low, average and high level of social esteem respectively.

Among XI standard students 17.0 percent, 66.5 percent and 16.4 percent of them have low, average and high level of family; and among XII standard students 16.7 percent, 74.0 percent and 9.3 percent of them have low, average and high level of family respectively.

Among XI standard students 10.6 percent, 74.7 percent and 14.7 percent of them have low, average and high level of body and physical appearance; and among XII standard students 15.9 percent, 68.4 percent and 15.7 percent of them have low, average and high level of body and physical appearance respectively.

Among XI standard students 11.4 percent, 72.7 percent and 15.9 percent of them have low, average and high level of total self esteem; and among XII standard students 12.7 percent, 69.1 percent and 18.1 percent of them have low, average and high level of total self esteem respectively.

Table 4.1.19: With Reference to Locality of the School

Dimensions	Variable	Low		Average		High	
		No	%	No	%	No	%
Competency	Rural	40	9.6	307	73.6	70	16.8
	Urban	62	12.2	374	73.6	72	14.2
Global self esteem	Rural	41	9.8	306	73.4	70	16.8
	Urban	71	14.0	347	68.3	90	17.7
Moral and self control	Rural	68	16.3	307	73.6	42	10.1
	Urban	76	15.0	358	70.5	74	14.6
Social esteem	Rural	72	17.3	283	67.9	62	14.9
	Urban	88	17.3	356	70.1	64	12.6
Family	Rural	74	17.7	282	67.6	61	14.6
	Urban	76	15.0	353	69.5	79	15.6
Body and physical appearance	Rural	55	13.2	310	74.3	52	12.5
	Urban	73	14.4	345	67.9	90	17.7
Total self esteem	Rural	49	11.8	292	70.0	76	18.2
	Urban	70	13.8	356	70.1	82	16.1

The level is average

It is inferred from the above table that 9.6 percent, 73.6 percent and 16.8 percent of rural school have low, average and high level of competency respectively. Regarding urban school, 12.2 percent, 73.6 percent and 14.2 percent of them have low, average and high level of competency respectively.

Among rural school, 9.8 percent, 73.4 percent and 16.8 percent of them have low, average and high level of global self esteem; and among urban school, 14.0 percent, 68.3 percent and 17.7 percent of them have low, average and high level of global self esteem respectively.

Among rural school, 16.3 percent, 73.6 percent and 10.1 percent of them have low, average and high level of moral and self control; and among urban school, 15.0 percent, 70.5 percent and 14.6 percent of them have low, average and high level of moral and self control respectively.

Among rural school, 17.3 percent, 67.9 percent and 14.9 percent of them have low, average and high level of social esteem; and among urban school, 17.3 percent, 70.1 percent and 12.6 percent of them have low, average and high level of social esteem respectively.

Among rural school, 17.7 percent, 67.6 percent and 14.6 percent of them have low, average and high level of family; and among urban school, 15.0 percent, 69.5 percent and 15.6 percent of them have low, average and high level of family respectively.

Among rural school, 13.2 percent, 74.3 percent and 12.5 percent of them have low, average and high level of body and physical appearance; and among urban school, 14.4 percent, 67.9 percent and 17.7 percent of them have low, average and high level of body and physical appearance respectively.

Among rural school, 11.8 percent, 70.0 percent and 18.2 percent of them have low, average and high level of total self esteem; and among urban school, 13.8 percent, 70.1 percent and 16.1 percent of them have low, average and high level of total self esteem respectively.

Table 4.1.20: With Reference to Nativity of the Student

Dimensions	Variable	Low		Average		High	
		No	%	No	%	No	%
Competency	Rural	60	14.8	285	70.4	60	14.8
	Urban	66	12.7	388	74.6	66	12.7
Global self esteem	Rural	61	15.1	280	69.1	64	15.8
	Urban	71	13.7	357	68.7	92	17.7
Moral and self control	Rural	56	13.8	301	74.3	48	11.9
	Urban	68	13.1	384	73.8	68	13.1
Social esteem	Rural	68	16.8	271	66.9	66	16.3
	Urban	54	10.4	408	78.5	58	11.2
Family	Rural	78	19.3	289	71.4	38	9.4
	Urban	68	13.1	383	73.7	69	13.3
Body and physical appearance	Rural	63	15.6	288	71.1	54	13.3
	Urban	63	12.1	365	70.2	92	17.7
Total self esteem	Rural	49	12.1	280	69.1	76	18.8
	Urban	70	13.5	362	69.6	88	16.9

The level is average

It is inferred from the above table that 14.8 percent, 70.4 percent and 14.8 percent of rural students have low, average and high level of competency respectively. Regarding urban students, 12.7 percent, 74.6 percent and 12.7 percent of them have low, average and high level of competency respectively.

Among rural students, 15.1 percent, 69.1 percent and 15.8 percent of them have low, average and high level of global self esteem; and among urban students, 13.7 percent, 68.7 percent and 17.7 percent of them have low, average and high level of global self esteem respectively.

Among rural students, 13.8 percent, 74.3 percent and 11.9 percent of them have low, average and high level of moral and self control; and among urban students, 13.1 percent, 73.8 percent and 13.1 percent of them have low, average and high level of moral and self control respectively.

Table 4.1.21: With Reference to Nature of the School

Dimensions	Variable	Low		Average		High	
		No	%	No	%	No	%
Competency	Boys	48	17.7	173	63.8	50	18.5
	Girls	46	14.8	224	72.3	40	12.9
	Co-education	34	9.9	262	76.2	48	14.0
Global self esteem	Boys	29	10.7	196	72.3	46	17.0
	Girls	53	17.1	205	66.1	52	16.8
	Co-education	13	3.8	267	77.6	64	18.6
Moral and self control	Boys	48	17.7	169	62.4	54	19.9
	Girls	42	13.5	230	74.2	38	12.3
	Co-education	58	16.9	248	72.1	38	11.0
Social esteem	Boys	35	12.9	186	68.6	50	18.5
	Girls	34	11.0	236	76.1	40	12.9
	Co-education	67	19.5	245	71.2	32	9.3
Family	Boys	43	15.9	190	70.1	38	14.0
	Girls	58	18.7	201	64.8	51	16.5
	Co-education	53	15.4	263	76.5	28	8.1
Body and physical appearance	Boys	52	19.2	171	63.1	48	17.7
	Girls	37	11.9	217	70.0	56	18.1
	Co-education	50	14.5	250	72.7	44	12.8
Total self esteem	Boys	38	14.0	179	66.1	54	19.9
	Girls	41	13.2	213	68.7	56	18.1
	Co-education	40	11.6	240	69.8	64	18.6

The level is average

Among rural students, 16.8 percent, 66.9 percent and 16.3 percent of them have low, average and high level of social esteem; and among urban students, 10.4 percent, 78.5 percent and 11.2 percent of them have low, average and high level of social esteem respectively.

Among rural students, 19.3 percent, 71.4 percent and 9.4 percent of them have low, average and high level of family; and among urban students, 13.1 percent, 73.7 percent and 13.3 percent of them have low, average and high level of family respectively.

Among rural students, 15.6 percent, 71.1 percent and 13.3 percent of them have low, average and high level of body and physical appearance; and among urban students, 12.1 percent, 70.2 percent and 17.7 percent of them have low, average and high level of body and physical appearance respectively.

Among rural students, 12.1 percent, 69.1 percent and 18.8 percent of them have low, average and high level of total self esteem; and among urban students, 13.5 percent, 69.6 percent and 16.9 percent of them have low, average and high level of total self esteem respectively.

It is inferred from the above table that 17.7 percent, 63.8 percent and 18.5 percent of boys school have low, average and high level of competency respectively. Regarding girls school 14.8 percent, 72.3 percent and 12.9 percent of them have low, average and high level of competency respectively. Regarding co-education school, 9.9 percent, 76.2 percent and 14.0 percent of them have low, average and high level of competency respectively.

Among boys school, 10.7 percent, 72.3 percent and 17.0 percent of them have low, average and high level of global self esteem; and among girls school, 17.1 percent, 66.1 percent and 16.8 percent of them have low, average and high level of global self esteem respectively. Regarding co-education school, 3.8 percent, 77.6 percent and 18.6 percent of them have low, average and high level of global self esteem respectively.

Among boys school, 17.7 percent, 62.4 percent and 19.9 percent of them have low, average and high level of moral and self control; and among girls school, 13.5 percent, 74.2 percent and 12.3 percent of them have low, average and high level of moral and self control respectively. Regarding co-education school, 16.9 percent, 72.1 percent and 11.0 percent of them have low, average and high level of moral and self control respectively.

Among boys school, 12.9 percent, 68.6 percent and 18.5 percent of them have low, average and high level of social esteem; and among girls school, 11.0 percent, 76.1 percent and 12.9 percent of them have low, average and high level of social esteem respectively. Regarding co-education school, 19.5 percent, 71.2 percent and 9.3 percent of them have low, average and high level of social esteem respectively.

Among boys school, 15.9 percent, 70.1 percent and 14.0 percent of them have low, average and high level of family; and among girls school, 18.7 percent, 64.8 percent and 16.5 percent of them have low, average and high level of family respectively. Regarding co-education school, 15.4 percent, 76.5 percent and 8.1 percent of them have low, average and high level of family respectively.

Among boys school, 19.2 percent, 63.1 percent and 17.7 percent of them have low, average and high level of body and physical appearance; and among girls school, 11.9 percent, 70.0 percent and 18.1 percent of them have low, average and high level of body and physical appearance respectively. Regarding co-education school, 14.5 percent, 72.7 percent and 12.8 percent of them have low, average and high level of body and physical appearance respectively.

Among boys school, 14.0 percent, 66.1 percent and 19.9 percent of them have low, average and high level of total self esteem; and among girls school, 13.2 percent, 68.7 percent and 18.1 percent of them have low, average and high level of total self esteem respectively. Regarding co-education school, 11.6 percent, 69.8 percent and 18.6 percent of them have low, average and high level of total self esteem respectively.

Table 4.1.22: With Reference to Type of Management

Dimensions	Variable	Low		Average		High	
		No	%	No	%	No	%
Competency	Government	32	11.4	212	75.7	36	12.9
	Aided	48	13.7	240	68.6	62	17.7
	Private	49	16.6	198	67.1	48	16.3
Global self esteem	Government	12	4.3	232	82.9	36	12.9
	Aided	76	21.7	218	62.3	56	16.0
	Private	30	10.2	215	72.9	50	16.9
Moral and self control	Government	44	15.7	198	70.7	38	13.6
	Aided	64	18.3	240	68.6	46	13.1
	Private	44	14.9	225	76.3	26	8.8
Social esteem	Government	46	16.4	192	68.6	42	15.0
	Aided	60	17.1	254	72.6	36	10.3
	Private	30	10.2	203	68.8	62	21.0
Family	Government	36	12.9	212	75.7	32	11.4
	Aided	56	16.0	270	77.1	24	6.9
	Private	66	22.4	189	64.1	40	13.6
Body and physical appearance	Government	42	15.0	180	64.3	58	20.7
	Aided	52	14.9	240	68.6	58	16.6
	Private	46	15.6	197	66.8	52	17.6
Total self esteem	Government	26	9.3	210	75.0	44	15.7
	Aided	62	17.7	234	66.9	54	15.4
	Private	45	15.3	208	70.5	42	14.2

The level is average

It is inferred from the above table that 11.4 percent, 75.7 percent and 12.9 percent of government school have low, average and high level of competency respectively. Regarding aided school 13.7 percent, 68.6 percent and 17.7 percent of them have low, average and high level of competency respectively. Regarding private school 16.6 percent, 67.1 percent and 16.3 percent of them have low, average and high level of competency respectively.

Among government school, 4.3 percent, 82.9 percent and 12.9 percent of them have low, average and high level of global self esteem; and among aided school, 21.7 percent, 62.3 percent and 16.0 percent of them have low, average and high level of global self esteem respectively. Regarding private school, 10.2 percent, 72.9 percent and 16.9 percent of them have low, average and high level of global self esteem respectively.

Among government school, 15.7 percent, 70.7 percent and 13.6 percent of them have low, average and high level of moral and self control; and among aided school, 18.3 percent, 68.6 percent and 13.1 percent of them have low, average and high level of moral and self control respectively. Regarding private school, 14.9 percent, 76.3 percent and 8.8 percent of them have low, average and high level of moral and self control respectively.

Among government school, 16.4 percent, 68.6 percent and 15.0 percent of them have low, average and high level of social esteem; and among aided school, 17.1 percent, 72.6 percent and 10.3 percent of them have low, average and high level of social esteem respectively. Regarding private school, 10.2 percent, 68.8 percent and 21.0 percent of them have low, average and high level of social esteem respectively.

Among government school, 12.9 percent, 75.7 percent and 11.4 percent of them have low, average and high level of family; and among aided school, 16.0 percent, 77.1 percent and 6.9 percent of them have low, average and high level of family respectively. Regarding private school, 22.4 percent, 64.1 percent and 13.6 percent of them have low, average and high level of family respectively.

Among government school, 15.0 percent, 64.3 percent and 20.7 percent of them have low, average and high level of body and physical appearance; and among aided school, 14.9 percent, 68.6 percent and 16.6 percent of them have low, average and high level of body and physical appearance respectively. Regarding private school, 15.6 percent, 66.8 percent and 17.6 percent of them have low, average and high level of body and physical appearance respectively.

Among government school, 9.3percent, 75.0 percent and 15.7 percent of them have low, average and high level of total self esteem; and among aided school, 17.7 percent, 66.9 percent and 15.4 percent of them have low, average and high level of total self esteem respectively. Regarding private school, 15.3 percent, 70.5 percent and 14.2 percent of them have low, average and high level of total self esteem respectively.

Table 4.1.23: With Reference to Medium of the School

Dimensions	Variable	Low		Average		High	
		No	%	No	%	No	%
Competency	Tamil	50	11.0	336	73.7	70	15.4
	English	54	11.5	347	74.0	68	14.5
Global self esteem	Tamil	62	13.6	312	68.4	82	18.0
	English	50	10.7	335	71.4	84	17.9
Moral and self control	Tamil	74	16.2	296	64.9	86	18.9
	English	70	14.9	349	74.4	50	10.7
Social esteem	Tamil	66	14.5	320	70.2	70	15.4
	English	58	12.4	341	72.9	70	14.9
Family	Tamil	72	15.8	332	72.8	52	11.4
	English	78	16.6	303	64.6	88	18.8
Body and physical appearance	Tamil	64	14.0	318	69.7	74	16.2
	English	58	12.4	341	72.7	70	14.9
Total self esteem	Tamil	58	12.7	320	70.2	78	17.1
	English	61	13.0	324	69.1	84	17.9

The level is average

It is inferred from the above table that 11.0 percent, 73.7 percent and 15.4 percent of Tamil medium students have low, average and high level of competency respectively. Regarding English medium, students 11.5 percent, 74.0 percent and 14.5 percent of them have low, average and high level of competency respectively.

Among Tamil medium students, 13.6 percent, 68.4 percent and 18.0 percent of them have low, average and high level of global self esteem; and among English medium students, 10.7 percent, 71.4 percent and 17.9 percent of them have low, average and high level of global self esteem respectively.

Among Tamil medium students, 16.2 percent, 64.9 percent and 18.9 percent of them have low, average and high level of moral and self control; and English medium students, 14.9 percent, 74.4 percent and 10.7 percent of them have low, average and high level of moral and self control respectively.

Among Tamil medium students, 14.5 percent, 70.2 percent and 15.4 percent of them have low, average and high level of social esteem; and among English medium students, 12.4 percent, 72.9 percent and 14.9 percent of them have low, average and high level of social esteem respectively.

Among Tamil medium students, 15.8 percent, 72.8 percent and 11.4 percent of them have low, average and high level of family; and among English medium students, 16.6 percent, 64.6 percent and 18.8 percent of them have low, average and high level of family respectively.

Among Tamil medium students, 14.0 percent, 69.7 percent and 16.2 percent of them have low, average and high level of body and physical appearance; and among English medium students, 12.4 percent, 72.7 percent and 14.9 percent of them have low, average and high level of body and physical appearance respectively.

Among Tamil medium students, 12.7 percent, 70.2 percent and 17.1 percent of them have low, average and high level of total self esteem; and among English medium students, 13.0 percent, 69.1 percent and 17.9 percent of them have low, average and high level of total self esteem respectively.

Table 4.1.24: With Reference to Status of the Family

Dimensions	Variable	Low		Average		High	
		No	%	No	%	No	%
Competency	Nuclear	66	12.0	413	75.2	70	12.8
	Joint	48	12.8	258	68.6	70	18.6
Global self esteem	Nuclear	67	12.2	378	68.9	104	18.9
	Joint	45	12.0	269	71.5	62	16.5
Moral and self control	Nuclear	88	16.0	383	69.8	78	14.2
	Joint	54	14.4	284	75.5	38	10.1
Social esteem	Nuclear	78	14.2	402	73.2	69	12.6
	Joint	46	12.2	274	72.9	56	14.9
Family	Nuclear	96	17.5	421	76.7	32	5.8
	Joint	70	18.6	244	64.9	62	16.5
Body and physical appearance	Nuclear	94	17.1	367	66.8	88	16.0
	Joint	76	20.2	244	64.9	56	14.9
Total self esteem	Nuclear	67	12.2	388	70.7	94	17.1
	Joint	50	13.3	264	70.2	62	16.5

The level is average

It is inferred from the above table that 12.0 percent, 75.2 percent and 12.8 percent of nuclear family students have low, average and high level of competency respectively. Regarding joint family students 12.8 percent, 68.6 percent and 18.6 percent of them have low, average and high level of competency respectively.

Among nuclear family students, 12.2 percent, 68.9 percent and 18.9 percent of them have low, average and high level of global self esteem; and among joint family students, 12.0 percent, 71.5 percent and 16.5 percent of them have low, average and high level of global self esteem respectively.

Among nuclear family students, 16.0 percent, 69.8 percent and 14.2 percent of them have low, average and high level of moral and self control; and among joint family students, 14.4 percent, 75.5 percent and 10.1 percent of them have low, average and high level of moral and self control respectively.

Among nuclear family students, 14.2 percent, 73.2 percent and 12.6 percent of them have low, average and high level of social esteem; and among joint family students, 12.2 percent, 72.9 percent and 14.9 percent of them have low, average and high level of social esteem respectively.

Among nuclear family students, 17.5 percent, 76.7 percent and 5.8 percent of them have low, average and high level of family; and among joint family students, 18.6 percent, 64.9 percent and 16.5 percent of them have low, average and high level of family respectively.

Among nuclear family students, 17.1 percent, 66.8 percent and 16.0 percent of them have low, average and high level of body and physical appearance; and among joint family students, 20.2 percent, 64.9 percent and 14.9 percent of them have low, average and high level of body and physical appearance respectively.

Among nuclear family students, 12.2 percent, 70.7 percent and 17.1 percent of them have low, average and high level of total self esteem; and among joint family students, 13.3 percent, 70.2 percent and 16.5 percent of them have low, average and high level of total self esteem respectively.

(d) Academic Achievement

The level of academic achievement of higher secondary biology students with reference to background variables

It is inferred from the above table that 18.5 percent, 63.9 percent and 17.6 percent of boys have low, average and high level of academic achievement respectively. Regarding girls, 17.5 percent, 65.1 percent and 17.5 percent of them have low, average and high level of academic achievement respectively.

Among XI standard, 18.2 percent, 63.2 percent and 18.6 percent of them have low, average and high level of academic achievement; and among XII standard, 17.9 percent, 64.5 percent and 17.6 percent of them have low, average and high level of academic achievement respectively. Among rural school, 18.5 percent, 67.6 percent and 13.9 percent of them have low, average and high level of academic achievement; and among urban school, 17.3 percent, 65.0 percent and 17.7 percent of them have low, average and high level of academic achievement respectively.

Among rural students, 17.8 percent, 66.4 percent and 15.8 percent of them have low, average and high level of academic achievement: and among urban students, 17.9 percent, 65.6 percent and 16.5 percent of them have low, average and high level of academic achievement respectively. Among boys school, 14.8 percent, 69.0 percent and 16.2 percent of them have low, average and high level of academic achievement; and among girls school, 14.2 percent, 69.0 percent and 16.8 percent of them have low, average and high level of academic achievement respectively. Regarding co-education school, 17.4 percent, 64.0 percent and 18.6 percent of them have low, average and high level of academic achievement respectively.

Table 4.1.25: Level of Academic Achievement of Higher Secondary Biology Students With Reference to Background Variables

Variable	Background Variables	Low		Average		High	
		No	%	No	%	No	%
Academic Achievement	Boys	81	18.5	280	63.9	77	17.6
	Girls	85	17.5	317	65.1	85	17.5
	XI standard	94	18.2	327	63.2	96	18.6
	XII standard	73	17.9	263	64.5	72	17.6
	Rural	77	18.5	282	67.6	58	13.9
	Urban	88	17.3	330	65.0	90	17.7
	Rural	72	17.8	269	66.4	64	15.8
	Urban	93	17.9	341	65.6	86	16.5
	Boys	40	14.8	187	69.0	44	16.2
	Girls	44	14.2	214	69.0	52	16.8
	Co-education	60	17.4	220	64.0	64	18.6
	Government	50	17.9	186	66.4	44	15.7
	Aided	52	14.9	234	66.9	64	18.3
	Private	52	17.6	193	65.4	50	16.9
	Tamil	80	17.5	300	65.8	76	16.7
	English	75	16.0	322	68.7	72	15.4
	Nuclear	95	17.3	354	64.5	100	18.2
	Joint	56	14.9	263	69.9	57	15.2

The level is average

Among government school, 17.9 percent, 66.4 percent and 15.7 percent of them have low, average and high level of academic achievement; and among aided school 14.9 percent, 66.9 percent and 18.3 percent of them have low, average and high level of academic achievement respectively. Regarding private school, 17.6 percent, 65.4 percent and 16.9 percent of them have low, average and high level of academic achievement respectively.

Among Tamil medium students, 17.5 percent, 65.8 percent and 16.7 percent of them have low, average and high level of academic achievement; and among English medium students, 16.0 percent, 68.7 percent and 15.4 percent of them have low, average and high level of academic achievement respectively. Among nuclear family students, 17.3 percent, 64.5 percent and 18.2 percent of them have low, average and high level of academic achievement; and among joint family students, 14.9 percent, 69.9 percent and 15.2 percent of them have low, average and high level of academic achievement respectively.

SECTION II

Hypotheses Testing

Hypothesis-1

There is no significant difference in Environmental factors and its dimensions of higher secondary biology students with reference to sex.

Table 4.2.1: Difference in Environmental Factors and its Dimensions of Higher Secondary Biology Students with Reference to Sex

Dimensions	Boys (N= 438)		Girls (N= 487)		Calculated 't' Value	Remarks at 5% Level
	Mean	SD	Mean	SD		
Home Environment	80.90	6.90	81.48	8.49	1.13	NS
School Environment	92.38	9.23	92.57	10.61	0.28	NS
SocialEnvironment	82.57	8.19	82.26	7.97	0.59	NS
Total Environment	255.68	18.67	255.92	22.09	0.17	NS

(At 5% level of significance, the table value of 't' is 1.96)

Since the calculated value of 't' is less than the table value for 923 degrees of freedom at 5% level, the hypothesis is accepted. Therefore there is no significant difference between Boys and Girls students in their home environment, school environment, social environment and total environment.

Hypothesis-2

There is no significant difference in Environmental factors and its dimensions of higher secondary biology students with reference to standard.

Table 4.2.2: Difference in Environmental Factors and Its Dimensions of Higher Secondary Biology Students with Reference to Standard

Dimensions	XI Standard (N=517)		XII Standard (N=408)		Calculated 't' Value	Remarks at 5% Level
	Mean	SD	Mean	SD		
Home Environment	81.83	6.64	80.42	8.96	2.74	S
School Environment	91.76	8.37	93.40	11.64	2.48	S
SocialEnvironment	82.44	7.52	82.37	8.74	0.14	NS
Total Environment	255.48	17.57	256.22	23.78	0.54	NS

(At 5% level of significance, the table value of 't' is 1.96)

It is inferred from the above table that there is no significant difference between XI Standard and XII Standard students in their social environment and total environment. But there is significant difference between XI Standard and XII Standard students in their home environment and school environment.

Hypothesis-3

There is no significant difference in Environmental factors and its dimensions of higher secondary biology students with reference to locality of the school.

Table 4.2.3: Difference in Environmental Factors and Its Dimensions of Higher Secondary Biology Students With Reference to Locality of the School

Dimensions	Rural (N=417)		Urban (N=508)		Calculated 't' Value	Remarks at 5% Level
	Mean	SD	Mean	SD		
Home Environment	80.95	7.43	81.41	8.06	0.89	NS
School Environment	91.96	10.49	92.91	9.52	1.45	NS
SocialEnvironment	82.78	8.18	82.10	7.98	1.28	NS
TotalEnvironment	255.05	21.00	256.43	20.14	1.01	NS

(At 5% level of significance, the table value of 't' is 1.96)

It is inferred from the above table that there is no significant difference between rural school and urban school in their home environment, school environment, social environment and total environment.

Hypothesis-4

There is no significant difference in Environmental factors and its dimensions of higher secondary biology students with reference to nativity of the student.

Table 4.2.4: Difference in Environmental Factors and its Dimensions of Higher Secondary Biology Students with Reference to Nativity of the Student

Dimensions	Rural (N= 405)		Urban (N= 520)		Calculated 't' Value	Remarks at 5% Level
	Mean	SD	Mean	SD		
Home Environment	80.51	8.24	81.75	7.36	2.41	S
School Environment	94.46	10.01	90.94	9.68	5.40	S
Social Environment	82.00	8.93	82.72	7.33	1.34	NS
Tota lEnvironment	256.31	21.49	255.42	19.76	0.65	NS

(At 5% level of significance, the table value of't' is 1.96)

It is inferred from the above table that there is no significant difference between rural student and urban student in their social environment and total environment. But there is significant difference between rural students and urban students in their home environment and school environment.

Hypothesis-5

Table 4.2.5: Difference in Environmental Factors and its Dimensions of Higher Secondary Biology Students with Reference to Medium of The School

Dimensions	Tamil (N= 456)		English (N= 469)		Calculated 't' Value	Remarks at 5% Level
	Mean	SD	Mean	SD		
Home Environment	80.77	7.32	81.63	8.19	1.69	NS
School Environment	92.03	9.44	92.92	10.46	1.35	NS
Social Environment	81.76	8.14	83.04	7.97	2.40	S
Total Environment	253.96	19.29	257.61	21.54	2.71	S

(At 5% level of significance, the table value of 't' is 1.96)

There is no significant difference in Environmental factors and its dimensions of higher secondary biology students with reference to medium of the school.

It is inferred from the above table that there is no significant difference between Tamil medium student and English medium students in their home environment and school environment. But there is significant difference between Tamil medium student and English medium students in their social environment and total environment.

Hypothesis-6

There is no significant difference in Environmental factors and its dimensions of higher secondary biology students with reference to status of the family.

Table 4.2.6: Difference in Environmental Factors and its Dimensions of Higher Secondary Biology Students with Reference to Status of The Family

Dimensions	Nuclear (N= 549)		Joint (N= 376)		Calculated 't' Value	Remarks at 5% Level
	Mean	SD	Mean	SD		
Home Environment	81.86	8.00	80.26	7.35	3.08	S
School Environment	93.36	10.24	91.19	9.44	3.26	S
Social Environment	83.04	8.90	81.48	6.60	2.89	S
Total Environment	258.18	21.21	252.35	19.01	4.27	S

(At 5% level of significance, the table value of 't' is 1.96)

It is inferred from the above table that there is significant difference between nuclear family students and joint family students in their home environment, school environment, social environment and total environment.

Hypothesis-7

There is no significant difference in Study habits and its dimensions of higher secondary biology students with reference to sex.

Table 4.2.7: Difference in Study Habits and its Dimensions of Higher Secondary Biology Students with Reference to Sex

Dimensions	Boys (N= 438)		Girls (N= 487)		Calculated 't' Value	Remarks at 5% Level
	Mean	SD	Mean	SD		
Studies at home	41.74	4.43	42.24	4.35	1.70	NS
Reading and note taking	43.37	4.71	42.91	5.78	1.31	NS
Planning of the subject	37.89	4.23	37.77	4.05	0.44	NS
Habit of concentration	36.73	4.50	37.44	4.78	2.31	S
Preparation for examination	57.55	6.07	58.07	7.53	1.13	NS
General habits and attitudes	37.86	4.27	36.95	5.09	2.94	S
Studies at school	39.31	4.35	39.36	5.09	0.17	NS
Total study habits	294.41	22.80	294.61	24.85	0.12	NS

(At 5% level of significance, the table value of 't' is 1.96)

It is inferred from the above table that there is no significant difference between boys and girls students in their studies at home, reading and note taking, planning of the subject, preparation for examination, studies at school and total study habits. But there is significant difference between boys and girls students in their habit of concentration and general habits and attitudes.

Hypothesis-8

There is no significant difference in Study habits and its dimensions of higher secondary biology students with reference to standard.

Table 4.2.8: Difference in Study Habits and its Dimensions of Higher Secondary Biology Students with Reference to Standard

Dimensions	XI standard (N=517)		XII standard (N=408)		Calculated 't' Value	Remarks at 5% Level
	Mean	SD	Mean	SD		
Home Environment	80.77	7.32	81.63	8.19	1.69	NS
Studies at home	41.64	4.39	42.46	4.36	2.83	S
Reading and note taking	42.46	5.00	43.97	5.56	4.33	S
Planning of the subject	37.66	3.71	38.04	4.62	1.37	NS
Habit of concentration	36.98	4.03	37.27	5.35	0.96	NS
Preparation for examination	57.94	5.68	57.68	8.15	0.55	NS
General habits and attitudes	37.46	4.22	37.28	5.32	0.56	NS
Studies at school	39.45	3.90	39.20	5.65	0.79	NS
Total study habits	293.32	20.42	296.02	27.62	1.70	NS

(At 5% level of significance, the table value of 't' is 1.96)

It is inferred from the above table that there is no significant difference between XI Standard and XII Standard students in their planning of the subject, habit of concentration, preparation for examination, general habits and attitudes, studies at home, and total study habits. But there is significant difference between XI Standard and XII Standard students in their studies at home and reading and note taking.

Hypothesis-9

There is no significant difference in Study habits and its dimensions of higher secondary biology students with reference to locality of the school.

It is inferred from the above table that there is no significant difference between rural school and urban school in their planning of the subject, preparation for examination, studies at school. But there is significant difference between rural school and urban school in their studies at home, reading and note taking, habit of concentration, general habits and attitudes and total study habits.

Table 4.2.9: Difference in Study Habits and its Dimensions of Higher Secondary Biology Students with Reference to Locality of The School

Dimensions	Rural School (N=417)		Urban School (N=508)		Calculated 't' Value	Remarks at 5% Level
	Mean	SD	Mean	SD		
Studies at home	42.69	4.66	41.44	4.08	4.35	S
Reading and note taking	44.11	4.95	42.32	5.45	5.18	S
Planning of the subject	38.11	3.96	37.60	4.27	1.87	NS
Habit of concentration	36.72	4.36	37.43	4.88	2.30	S
Preparation for examination	57.68	6.96	57.94	6.81	0.56	NS
General habits and attitudes	37.89	4.53	36.96	4.86	2.98	S
Studies at school	39.55	4.32	39.16	5.08	1.24	NS
Total study habits	296.81	22.63	292.62	24.74	2.65	S

(At 5% level of significance, the table value of 't' is 1.96)

Hypothesis-10

There is no significant difference in Study habits and its dimensions of higher secondary biology students with reference to nativity of the students.

Table 4.2.10: Difference in Study Habits and Its Dimensions of Higher Secondary Biology Students with Reference to Nativity of the Students

Dimensions	Rural Student (N=405)		Urban Student (N=520)		Calculated 't' Value	Remarks at 5% Level
	Mean	SD	Mean	SD		
Studies at home	41.79	4.87	42.16	3.98	1.27	NS
Reading and note taking	43.46	5.50	42.87	5.13	1.68	NS
Planning of the subject	37.69	4.45	37.94	3.88	0.90	NS
Habit of concentration	37.14	5.17	37.08	4.23	0.18	NS
Preparation for examination	57.27	7.53	58.26	6.30	2.17	S
General habits and attitudes	36.95	4.92	37.71	4.57	2.41	S
Studies at school	39.08	5.10	39.54	4.46	1.45	NS
Total study habits	293.30	25.33	295.46	22.68	1.36	NS

(At 5% level of significance, the table value of 't' is 1.96)

It is inferred from the above table that there is no significant difference between rural students and urban students in their studies at home, reading and note taking, planning of the subject, habit of concentration, studies at school and total study habits. But there is significant difference between rural students and urban students in their preparation for examination and general habits and attitudes.

Hypothesis-11

There is no significant difference in Study habits and its dimensions of higher secondary biology students with reference to medium of the school.

Table 4.2.11: Difference in Study Habits and its Dimensions of Higher Secondary Biology Students with Reference to Medium of the School

Dimensions	Tamil (N= 456)		English (N= 469)		Calculated 't' Value	Remarks at 5% Level
	Mean	SD	Mean	SD		
Studies at home	41.16	4.43	42.82	4.20	5.82	S
Reading and note taking	42.25	4.93	43.98	5.52	4.99	S
Planning of the subject	37.64	4.12	38.01	4.15	1.36	NS
Habit of concentration	36.88	4.63	37.33	4.69	1.49	NS
Preparation for examination	57.15	6.18	58.48	7.45	2.94	S
General habits and attitudes	37.32	4.53	37.44	4.93	0.40	NS
Studies at school	39.46	4.63	39.22	4.87	0.76	NS
Total study habits	291.76	21.87	297.19	25.44	3.47	S

(At 5% level of significance, the table value of 't' is 1.96)

It is inferred from the above table that there is no significant difference between Tamil medium student and English medium student in their planning of the subject, habit of concentration, general habits and attitudes and studies at school. But there is significant difference between Tamil medium students and English medium students in their studies at home, reading and note taking, preparation for examination and total study habits.

Hypothesis-12

There is no significant difference in Study habits and its dimensions of higher secondary biology students with reference to status of the family.

Table 4.2.12: Difference in Study Habits and its Dimensions of Higher Secondary Biology Students with Reference to Status of The Family

Dimensions	Nuclear Family (N=549)		Joint Family (N=376)		Calculated 't' Value	Remarks at 5% Level
	Mean	SD	Mean	SD		
Studies at home	42.50	4.38	41.28	4.32	4.16	S
Reading and note taking	43.51	5.64	42.56	4.72	2.67	S
Planning of the subject	37.70	4.40	38.01	3.72	1.10	NS
Habit of concentration	36.88	4.58	37.45	4.76	1.82	NS
Preparation for examination	58.10	7.54	57.42	5.77	1.48	NS
General habits and attitudes	37.15	4.78	37.71	4.66	1.77	NS
Studies at school	39.21	4.98	39.53	4.40	1.00	NS
Total study habits	294.94	25.54	293.89	21.26	0.65	NS

(At 5% level of significance, the table value of 't' is 1.96)

It is inferred from the above table that there is no significant difference between nuclear family and joint family students in their planning of the subject, habit of concentration, preparation for examination, general habits and attitudes, studies at school and total study habits. But there is significant difference between nuclear family and joint family students in their studies at home and reading and note taking.

Hypothesis-13

There is no significant difference in Self esteem and its dimensions of higher secondary biology students with reference to sex

Table 4.2.13: Difference in Self Esteem and its Dimensions of Higher Secondary Biology Students with Reference to Sex

Dimensions	Boys (N= 438)		Girls (N= 487)		Calculated 't' Value	Remarks at 5% Level
	Mean	SD	Mean	SD		
Competency	45.15	4.76	44.79	6.32	0.96	NS
Global self esteem	45.26	5.10	46.23	7.35	2.31	S
Moral and self control	37.96	3.78	38.65	4.80	2.40	S
Social esteem	35.39	3.96	36.36	4.26	3.59	S
Family	32.51	3.70	34.25	4.43	6.41	S
Body and physical appearance	24.97	3.26	26.02	3.49	4.71	S
Total Self esteem	224.17	17.59	229.45	21.97	4.00	S

(At 5% level of significance, the table value of 't' is 1.96)

It is inferred from the above table that there is no significant difference between boys and girls students in their competency. But there is significant difference between boys and girls students in their global self esteem, moral and self control, social esteem, family, body and physical appearance and total self esteem.

Hypothesis-14

There is no significant difference in Self esteem and its dimensions of higher secondary biology students with reference to standard.

Table 4.2.14: Difference in Self Esteem and its Dimensions of Higher Secondary Biology Students with Reference to Standard

Dimensions	XI standard (N=517)		XII standard (N=408)		Calculated 't' Value	Remarks at 5% Level
	Mean	SD	Mean	SD		
Competency	45.12	5.57	44.76	5.72	0.96	NS
Global self esteem	45.29	5.91	46.38	6.94	2.58	S
Moral and self control	38.56	4.13	38.03	4.62	1.80	NS
Social esteem	36.10	4.00	35.65	4.33	1.66	NS
Family	32.89	3.95	34.10	4.38	4.41	S
Body and physical appearance	25.29	3.36	25.82	3.48	2.36	S
Total Self esteem	226.55	18.73	227.46	21.90	0.68	NS

(At 5% level of significance, the table value of 't' is 1.96)

It is inferred from the above table that there is no significant difference between XI and XII standard students in their competency, moral and self control, social esteem and total self esteem. But there is significant difference between XI and XII standard students in their global self esteem, family and body and physical appearance.

Hypothesis-15

There is no significant difference in Self esteem and its dimensions of higher secondary biology students with reference to locality of the school.

Table 4.2.15: Difference in Self Esteem and its Dimensions of Higher Secondary Biology Students with Reference to Locality of the School

Dimensions	Rural School (N=417)		Urban School (N=508)		Calculated 't' Value	Remarks at 5% Level
	Mean	SD	Mean	SD		
Competency	44.97	4.99	44.96	6.12	0.035	NS
Global self esteem	45.29	5.73	46.16	6.89	2.04	S
Moral and self control	38.46	4.00	38.22	4.63	0.81	NS
Social esteem	35.14	3.84	36.53	4.29	5.11	S
Family	32.97	4.53	33.79	3.85	2.97	S
Body and physical appearance	24.93	3.39	26.01	3.38	4.82	S
Total Self esteem	225.85	18.69	227.85	21.30	1.50	NS

(At 5% level of significance, the table value of 't' is 1.96)

It is inferred from the above table that there is no significant difference between rural school and urban school students in their competency, moral and self control and total self esteem. But there is significant difference between rural school and urban school students in their global self esteem, social esteem, family and body and physical appearance.

Hypothesis-16

Table 4.2.16: Difference in Self Esteem and its Dimensions of Higher Secondary Biology Students with Reference to Nativity of the Students

Dimensions	Rural Students (N=405)		Urban Students (N=520)		Calculated 't' Value	Remarks at 5% Level
	Mean	SD	Mean	SD		
Competency	45.90	5.29	44.23	5.79	4.51	S
Global self esteem	46.32	5.95	45.34	6.71	2.31	S
Moral and self control	37.67	4.72	38.83	3.98	4.04	S
Social esteem	34.94	4.28	36.65	3.89	6.32	S
Family	33.25	4.87	33.56	3.57	1.12	NS
Body and Physical appearance	24.72	3.53	26.15	3.20	6.46	S
Total Self esteem	228.29	2054	225.91	19.86	1.77	NS

(At 5% level of significance, the table value of 't' is 1.96)

There is no significant difference in Self esteem and its dimensions of higher secondary biology students with reference to nativity of the students.

It is inferred from the above table that there is no significant difference between rural and urban students in their family and total self esteem. But there is significant difference between rural school and urban school students in their competency, global self esteem, moral and self control, social esteem and body and physical appearance.

Hypothesis-17

There is no significant difference in Self esteem and its dimensions of higher secondary biology students with reference to medium of the school.

Table 4.2.17: Difference in Self Esteem and its Dimensions of Higher Secondary Biology Students With Reference to Medium of the School

Dimensions	Tamil Medium (N= 456)		English Medium (N= 469)		Calculated 't' Value	Remarks at 5% Level
	Mean	SD	Mean	SD		
Competency	45.09	5.12	44.84	6.10	0.66	NS
Global self esteem	45.17	5.84	46.35	6.87	2.79	S
Moral and self control	37.72	4.21	38.92	4.42	4.21	S
Social esteem	35.46	3.78	36.34	4.44	3.23	S
Family	33.03	4.25	33.81	4.09	2.83	S
Body and physical appearance	24.94	3.62	26.09	3.12	5.15	S
Total Self esteem	226.36	18.78	227.53	21.47	0.87	NS

(At 5% level of significance, the table value of 't' is 1.96)

It is inferred from the above table that there is no significant difference between English and Tamil medium students in their competency and total self esteem. But there is significant difference between English and Tamil medium students in their global self esteem, moral and self control, social esteem, family and body and physical appearance.

Hypothesis-18

There is no significant difference in self esteem and its dimensions of higher secondary biology students with reference to status of the family.

Table 4.2.18: Difference in Self Esteem and its Dimensions of Higher Secondary Biology Students with Reference to Status of the Family

Dimensions	Nuclear Family (N=549)		Joint Family (N=376)		Calculated 't' Value	Remarks at 5% Level
	Mean	SD	Mean	SD		
Competency	45.07	6.04	44.80	4.99	0.72	NS
Global self esteem	46.13	6.68	45.25	5.93	2.06	S
Moral and self control	38.28	4.53	38.39	4.11	0.39	NS
Social esteem	36.05	4.43	35.69	3.70	1.36	NS
Family	33.71	4.35	33.00	3.91	2.55	S
Body and physical appearance	25.58	3.45	25.45	3.38	0.56	NS
Total Self esteem	227.76	21.04	225.77	18.83	1.47	NS

(At 5% level of significance, the table value of 't' is 1.96)

It is inferred from the above table that there is no significant difference between joint and nuclear family students in their competency, moral and self control, social esteem, body and physical appearance and total self esteem. But there is significant difference between joint and nuclear family students in their global self esteem and family.

Hypothesis-19

There is no significant difference in Academic achievement of higher secondary students in biology with reference to 1.Sex 2.Standard 3.Locality of the school 4.Nativity of the student 5.Medium of the institution and 6.Status of the family

Table 4.2.19: Difference between Academic Achievements of Higher Secondary Students in Biology with Reference to Background Variables

Variables	Background Variables	Mean	SD	Count N	Calculated value 't'	Remarks
Academic Achievement	Boys	126.18	27.05	438	3.30	S
	Girls	132.05	26.82	487		
	XI	127.64	26.79	517	2.05	S
	XII	131.33	27.32	408		
	Rural	126.49	25.62	417	2.84	S
	Urban	131.55	28.03	508		
	Rural	126.86	26.32	405	2.39	S
	Urban	131.15	27.53	520		
	Tamil	123.96	25.52	456	5.98	S
	English	134.43	27.57	469		
	Nuclear	132.37	27.57	549	4.24	S
	Joint	124.74	25.71	376		

(At 5% level of significance, the table value't' is 1.96)

Since the calculated value of't' is greater than the table value for 923 degrees of freedom of 5% level, the hypothesis is rejected. Therefore there is significant difference in academic achievement of higher secondary students in biology with reference to background variables.

SECTION-III

Hypothesis-1

There is no significant difference among boys, girls and coeducation school students in their Environmental factors and its dimensions.

It is inferred from the above table that there is no significant difference among boys, girls and coeducation school students in their social environment and total environment. But there is significant difference among boys, girls and coeducation school students in their home environment and school environment.

Table 4.3.1: Difference among Boys, Girls and Coeducation School Students in their Environmental Factors

Dimensions	Source of variation	Sum of squares	Degrees of freedom	Mean square value	Calculated 'F' value	Remarks at 5% level
Home environment	Between	673.39	2	336.69	5.61	S
	Within	55330.49	922	60.01		
School environment	Between	1172.05	2	586.02	5.94	S
	Within	90823.02	922	98.50		
Social environment	Between	0.345	2	0.173	0.03	NS
	Within	60313.89	922	65.41		
Total environment	Between	2352.75	2	1176.37	2.80	NS
	Within	387367.90	922	420.13		

(At 5% level of significance for 2,922 df,, the table value of 'F' is 3.00)

While comparing the mean score of higher secondary biology students in boys, girls and coeducation schools, the girls school higher secondary biology students are better in home environment (mean 82.00) than the boys school (mean 79.92)and coeducation school (mean 81.50) higher secondary biology students.

While comparing the mean score of higher secondary biology students in boys, girls and coeducation schools, the girls school higher secondary biology students are better in school environment (mean 93.62) than the boys school (mean 92.98) and coeducation school (mean 91.06) higher secondary biology students

Hypothesis-2

There is no significant difference among boys, girls and coeducation school students in their Study habits and its dimensions.

It is inferred from the above table that there is no significant difference among boys, girls and coeducation school students in their general habits and attitudes. But there is significant difference among boys, girls and coeducation school students in their studies at home, Reading and note taking, planning of the subject, Habit of concentration, preparation for examination, studies at school and total study habits.

While comparing the mean score of higher secondary biology students in boys, girls and coeducation schools, the girls school higher secondary biology students are better in studies at home (mean 43.48) than the boys school (mean 41.03)and coeducation school (mean 41.44) higher secondary biology students.

Table 4.3.2: Difference Among Boys, Girls and Coeducation School Students in Their Study Habits

Dimensions	Source of variation	Sum of squares	Degrees of freedom	Mean square value	Calcu-lated 'F' value	Remarks at 5% level
Studies at home	Between	1043.00	2	521.50	28.57	S
	Within	16824.95	922	18.24		
Reading and note taking	Between	807.68	2	403.84	14.75	S
	Within	25238.22	922	27.37		
Planning of the subject	Between	201.63	2	100.81	5.93	S
	Within	15664.72	922	16.99		
Habit of concentration	Between	332.71	2	166.35	7.753	S
	Within	19784.37	922	21.45		
Preparation for examination	Between	721.02	2	360.51	7.71	S
	Within	43059.32	922	46.70		
General habits and attitudes	Between	60.75	2	30.38	1.35	NS
	Within	20701.99	922	22.45		
Studies at school	Between	235.08	2	117.54	5.24	S
	Within	20677.58	922	22.42		
Total study habits	Between	16235.92	2	8117.96	14.63	S
	Within	511323.00	922	554.58		

(At 5% level of significance for 2,922 df, the table value of 'F' is 3.00)

While comparing the mean score of higher secondary biology students in boys, girls and coeducation schools, the girls school higher secondary biology students are better in reading and note taking (mean 44.11) than the boys school (mean 43.49)and coeducation school (mean 41.95) higher secondary biology students.

While comparing the mean score of higher secondary biology students in boys, girls and coeducation schools, the boys, girls school higher secondary biology students are better in planning of the subject (mean 38.19) than the coeducation school (mean 37.22) higher secondary biology students.

While comparing the mean score of higher secondary biology students in boys, girls and coeducation schools, the girls school higher secondary biology students are better in habit of concentration (mean 37.70) than the boys school (mean 37.40)and coeducation school (mean 36.34) higher secondary biology students.

While comparing the mean score of higher secondary biology students in boys, girls and coeducation schools, the girls school higher secondary biology students are better in preparation for examination (mean 58.75) than the boys school (mean 58.11)and coeducation school (mean 56.73) higher secondary biology students.

While comparing the mean score of higher secondary biology students in boys, girls and coeducation schools, the girls school higher secondary biology students are better in studies at school (mean 39.90) than the boys school (mean 39.49)and coeducation school (mean 38.72) higher secondary biology students.

While comparing the mean score of higher secondary biology students in boys, girls and coeducation schools, the girls school higher secondary biology students are better in total study habits (mean 299.39) than the boys school (mean 295.32)and coeducation school (mean 289.49) higher secondary biology students.

Hypothesis-3

There is no significant difference among boys, girls and coeducation school students in their Self esteem and its dimensions.

Table 4.3.3: Difference among Boys, Girls and Coeducation School Students in their Self Esteem

Dimensions	Source of variation	Sum of squares	Degrees of freedom	Mean square value	Calcu-lated 'F' value	Remarks at 5% level
Competency	Between	279.62	2	139.81	4.42	S
	Within	29114.33	922	31.57		
Global self esteem	Between	2755.71	2	1377.85	36.11	S
	Within	35175.51	922	38.15		
Moral and self control	Between	100.75	2	50.37	2.65	NS
	Within	17486.01	922	18.96		
Social esteem	Between	117.33	2	58.66	3.41	S
	Within	15840.67	922	17.18		
Family	Between	260.77	2	130.38	7.52	S
	Within	15973.84	922	17.32		
Body and physical appearance	Between	247.84	2	123.92	10.76	S
	Within	10610.64	922	11.50		
Total Self esteem	Between	4239.66	2	2119.83	5.249	S
	Within	372329.50	922	403.82		

(At 5% level of significance for 2,922 df,, the table value of 'F' is 3.00)

It is inferred from the above table that there is no significant difference among boys, girls and coeducation school students in their moral and self control. But there is significant difference among boys, girls and coeducation school students in their competency, global self esteem, social esteem, family, body and physical appearance and total self esteem.

While comparing the mean score of higher secondary biology students in boys, girls and coeducation schools, the boys school higher secondary biology students are better in competency (mean 45.50) than the girls school (mean 45.27)and coeducation school (mean 44.26) higher secondary biology students.

While comparing the mean score of higher secondary biology students in boys, girls and coeducation schools, the girls school higher secondary biology students are better in global self esteem (mean 48.01) than the boys school (mean 45.56)and coeducation school (mean 43.92) higher secondary biology students.

While comparing the mean score of higher secondary biology students in boys, girls and coeducation schools, the girls school higher secondary biology students are better in social esteem (mean 36.15) than the boys school (mean 35.35)and coeducation school (mean 36.11) higher secondary biology students.

While comparing the mean score of higher secondary biology students in boys, girls and coeducation schools, the girls school higher secondary biology students are better in family (mean 33.80) than the boys school (mean 32.60)and coeducation school (mean 33.74) higher secondary biology students.

While comparing the mean score of higher secondary biology students in boys, girls and coeducation schools, the girls school higher secondary biology students are better in body and physical appearance (mean 26.15) than the boys school (mean 25.57)and coeducation school (mean 24.92) higher secondary biology students.

While comparing the mean score of higher secondary biology students in boys, girls and coeducation schools, the girls school higher secondary biology students are better in total self esteem (mean 229.84) than the boys school (mean 224.65)and coeducation school (mean 226.16) higher secondary biology students.

Hypothesis-4

There is no significant difference among boys, girls and coeducation school students in their Academic achievement.

Table 4.3.4: Difference among Boys, Girls and Coeducation School Students in their Academic Achievement

Dimensions	Source of variation	Sum of squares	Degrees of freedom	Mean square value	Calcu-lated 'F' value	Remarks at 5% level
Academic achievement	Between	31282.81	2	15641.40	22.31	S
	Within	646253.00	922	700.92		

(At 5% level of significance for 2,922 df,, the table value of 'F' is 3.00)

It is inferred from the above table that there is significant difference among boys school, girls school and coeducation school biology students in their academic achievement.

While comparing the mean score of higher secondary biology students in boys, girls and coeducation schools, the girls school higher secondary biology students are better in academic achievement (mean 136.10) than the boys school (mean 121.39)and coeducation school (mean 129.32) higher secondary biology students.

Hypothesis-5

There is no significant difference among government, aided and self financing school students in their Environmental factors and its dimensions.

Table 4.3.5: Difference among Government, Aided and Self Financing School Students in their Environmental Factors

Dimensions	Source of variation	Sum of squares	Degrees of freedom	Mean square value	Calcu-lated 'F' value	Remarks at 5% level
Home Environment	Between	10.99	2	5.49	0.91	NS
	Within	55992.89	922	60.73		
School Environment	Between	8611.22	2	4305.61	47.6	S
	Within	83383.86	922	90.43		
Social Environment	Between	473.55	2	236.77	3.64	S
	Within	59840.68	922	64.90		
Total Environment	Between	16837.75	2	8418.87	20.81	S
	Within	372882.9	922	404.42		

(At 5% level of significance for 2,922 df,, the table value of 'F' is 3.00)

It is inferred from the above table that there is no significant difference among government, aided and self financing school students in their home environment. But there is significant difference among government, aided and self financing school students in their school environment, social environment and total environment.

While comparing the mean score of higher secondary biology students in government aided and self financing schools, the aided school higher secondary biology students are better in school environment (mean 95.81) than the government school (mean 88.37) and self financing school (mean 92.44) higher secondary biology students.

While comparing the mean score of higher secondary biology students in government aided and self financing schools, the aided school higher secondary biology students are better in social environment (mean 83.01) than the government school (mean 81.34) and self financing school (mean 82.71) higher secondary biology students.

While comparing the mean score of higher secondary biology students in government aided and self financing schools, the aided school higher secondary biology students are better in total environmental factor (mean

260.15) than the government school (mean 249.79) and self financing school (mean 256.37) higher secondary biology students.

Hypothesis-6

There is no significant difference among government, aided and self financing school students in their Study habits and its dimensions.

Table 4.3.6: Difference among Government, Aided and Self Financing School Students in Their Study Habits

Dimensions	Source of variation	Sum of squares	Degrees of freedom	Mean square value	Calculated 'F' value	Remarks at 5% level
Studies at home	Between	348.87	2	174.43	9.180	S
	Within	17519.08	922	19.001		
Reading and note taking	Between	487.25	2	243.62	8.78	S
	Within	25558.65	922	27.72		
Planning of the subject	Between	90.22	2	45.11	2.63	NS
	Within	15776.13	922	17.11		
Habit of concentration	Between	617.04	2	308.52	14.58	S
	Within	19500.03	922	21.15		
Preparation for examination	Between	1014.40	2	507.20	10.93	S
	Within	42765.94	922	46.38		
General habits and attitudes	Between	418.43	2	209.21	9.48	S
	Within	20344.32	922	22.06		
Studies at school	Between	96.90	2	48.45	2.14	NS
	Within	20815.76	922	22.57		
Total study habits	Between	10303.97	2	5151.98	9.18	S
	Within	517255.0	922	561.01		

(At 5% level of significance for 2,922 df, the table value of 'F' is 3.00)

It is inferred from the above table that there is no significant difference among government, aided and self financing school students in their planning of the subject and studies at school. But there is significant difference among government, aided and self financing school students in their studies at home, reading and note taking, habit of concentration, preparation for examination, general habit and attitudes and total study habits.

While comparing the mean score of higher secondary biology students in government, aided and self financing schools, the self financing school higher secondary biology students are better in studies at home (mean 42.48) than the boys school (mean 41.03)and coeducation school (mean 40.44) higher secondary biology students. While comparing the mean score of higher secondary biology students in government aided and self financing schools, the self financing school higher secondary biology students are better in reading and note taking (mean 43.77) than the government school (mean 42.05) and aided school (mean 43.15) higher secondary biology students.

While comparing the mean score of higher secondary biology students in government aided and self financing schools, the self financing school higher secondary biology students are better in habit of concentration (mean 38.11) than the government school (mean 36.04) and aided school (mean 37.12) higher secondary biology students. While comparing the mean score of higher secondary biology students in government aided and self financing schools, the self financing school higher secondary biology students are better in preparation for examination (mean 58.80 than the government school (mean 56.30) and aided school (mean 58.12) higher secondary biology students.

While comparing the mean score of higher secondary biology students in government aided and self financing schools, the self financing school higher secondary biology students are better in general habit and attitude (mean 38.23) than the government school (mean 37.45) and aided school (mean 36.61) higher secondary biology students. While comparing the mean score of higher secondary biology students in government aided and self financing schools, the self financing school higher secondary biology students are better in total study habit (mean 297.46) than the government school (mean 289.53) and aided school (mean 296.01) higher secondary biology students.

Hypothesis-7

There is no significant difference among government, aided and self financing school students in their Self esteem and its dimensions.

It is inferred from the above table that there is no significant difference among government, aided and self financing school students in their moral and self control and social esteem. But there is significant difference among government, aided and self financing school students in their competency, global self esteem, family, body and physical appearance and total self esteem.

While comparing the mean score of higher secondary biology students in government aided and self financing schools, the aided school higher secondary biology students are better in competency (mean 46.32) than the government school (mean 43.37) and self financing schools (mean 44.86) higher secondary biology students.

While comparing the mean score of higher secondary biology students in government aided and self financing schools, the aided school higher secondary biology students are better in global self esteem (mean 49.32) than the government school (mean 42.67) and self financing schools (mean 44.50) higher secondary biology students.

While comparing the mean score of higher secondary biology students in government aided and self financing schools, the aided school higher secondary biology students are better in family (mean 34.78) than the government school (mean 32.92) and self financing schools (mean 32.30) higher secondary biology students.

Table 4.3.7: Difference among Government, Aided and Self Financing School Students in their Self Esteem

Dimensions	Source of variation	Sum of squares	Degrees of freedom	Mean square value	Calcu-lated 'F' value	Remarks at 5% level
Competency	Between	1355.91	2	677.96	22.29	S
	Within	28038.04	922	30.41		
Global self esteem	Between	7556.26	2	3778.13	114.68	S
	Within	30374.96	922	32.94		
Moral and self control	Between	32.63	2	16.31	0.85	NS
	Within	17554.14	922	19.03		
Social esteem	Between	52.43	2	26.21	1.52	NS
	Within	15905.57	922	17.25		
Family	Between	1086.30	2	543.15	33.05	S
	Within	15148.31	922	16.43		
Body and physical appearance	Between	744.35	2	372.17	33.92	S
	Within	10114.13	922	10.97		
Total Self esteem	Between	24203.45	2	12101.72	31.66	S
	Within	352365.7	922	382.17		

(At 5% level of significance for 2,922 df, the table value of 'F' is 3.00)

While comparing the mean score of higher secondary biology students in government aided and self financing schools, the aided school higher secondary biology students are better in body and physical appearance (mean 26.60) than the government school (mean 24.46) and self financing schools (mean 25.26) higher secondary biology students.

While comparing the mean score of higher secondary biology students in government aided and self financing schools, the aided school higher secondary biology students are better in total self esteem (mean 233.50) than the government school (mean 223.18) and self financing schools (mean 222.75) higher secondary biology students.

Hypothesis-8

There is no significant difference among government, aided and self financing school students in their Academic achievement.

It is inferred from the above table that there is significant difference among government, aided and self financing school students in their academic achievement

While comparing the mean score of higher secondary biology students in government aided and self financing schools, the self financing school higher secondary biology students are better in academic achievement (mean 134.48) than the government school (mean 122.70) and self financing schools (mean 130.13) higher secondary biology students.

Table 4.3.8: Difference among Government, Aided and Self Financing School Students in their Academic Achievement

Dimensions	Source of variation	Sum of squares	Degrees of freedom	Mean square value	Calcu-lated 'F' value	Remarks at 5% level
Academic achievement	Between	20352.15	2	10176.07	14.27	S
	Within	657183.6	922	712.78		

(At 5% level of significance for 2,922 df, the table value of 'F' is 3.00)

SECTION-IV

Hypothesis-1

There is no significant association between fathers' education and their children's Environmental factors and its dimensions.

Table 4.4.1: Association between Fathers' Education and their Children's Environmental Factors

Sl.No.	Dimensions	df	Calculated χ^2value	Remarks at 5% level
1.	Home environment	6	6.14	NS
2.	School environment		1.90	NS
3.	Social environment		5.04	NS
4.	Total environment		11.34	NS

(At 5% level of significance for 6 df the table value of c^2 is 12.6)

It is inferred from the above table that there is no significant association between father's education and their children's home environment, school environment, social environment and total environment.

Hypothesis-2

There is no significant association between fathers' education and their children's Study habits and its dimensions.

Table 4.4.2: Association between Fathers' Education and their Children's Study Habits

Sl.No.	Dimensions	df	Calculated χ^2value	Remarks at 5% level
1.	Studies at home	6	10.89	NS
2.	Reading and note taking		3.04	NS
3.	Planning of the subject		8.82	NS
4.	Habit of concentration		2.18	NS
5.	Preparation for examination		5.40	NS
6.	General habits and attitudes		6.52	NS
7.	Studies at school		4.36	NS
8.	Total study habits		19.21	S

(At 5% level of significance for 6 df the table value of χ^2 is 12.6)

It is inferred from the above table that there is no significant association between fathers' education and their children's studies at home, Reading and note taking, planning of the subject, Habit of concentration, preparation for examination, general habit and attitudes and studies at school. But there is significant association between father's education and their children's total study habits.

Hypothesis-3

There is no significant association between fathers' education and their children's Self esteem and its dimensions.

Table 4.4.3: Association between Fathers' Education and their Children's Self Esteem

Sl.No.	Dimensions	df	Calculated χ^2value	Remarks at 5% level
1.	Competency	6	2.03	NS
2.	Global self esteem		27.98	S
3.	Moral and self control		7.00	NS
4.	Social esteem		15.32	S
5.	Family		5.26	NS
6.	Body and physical appearance		5.00	NS
7.	Total Self esteem		2.63	NS

(At 5% level of significance for 6 df the table value of c^2 is 12.6)

It is inferred from the above table that there is no significant association between father's education and their children's competency, moral and self control, family, body and physical appearance and total self esteem. But there is significant association between father education and their children's global self esteem and social esteem.

Hypothesis-4

There is no significant association between fathers' education and their children's academic achievement.

Table 4.4.4: Association between Fathers' Education and their Children's Academic Achievement

Academic achievement		Low	Average	High	Calculated value	Remarks at 5% level
Father Education	Illiterate	30 (24)	86 (92)	22 (22)	7.59	NS
	School	80 (87)	334 (331)	82 (78)		
	Graduate	39 (32)	116 (121)	26 (29)		
	Professional	13 (19)	81 (73)	16 (17)		

(At 5% level of significance for 6 df the table value of χ^2 is 12.6)

It is inferred from the above table that there is no significant difference association between father's educations and their children's academic achievement.

Hypothesis-5

There is no significant association between fathers' occupation and their children's Environmental factors and its dimensions.

Table 4.4.5: Association between Fathers' Occupation and their Children's Environmental Factors

Sl.No.	Dimensions	df	Calculated χ^2value	Remarks at 5% level
1.	Home environment	6	8.69	NS
2.	School environment		5.63	NS
3.	Social environment		8.32	NS
4.	Total environment		2.94	NS

(At 5% level of significance for 6 df the table value of χ^2 is 12.6

It is inferred from the above table that there is no significant difference association between father's occupation and their children's home environment, school environment, social environment and total environment.

Hypothesis-6

There is no significant association between fathers' occupation and their children's Study habits and its dimensions.

Table 4.4.6: Association between Fathers' Occupation and their Children's Study Habits

Sl.No.	Dimensions	df	Calculated χ^2value	Remarks at 5% level
1.	Studies at home	6	11.30	NS
2.	Reading and note taking		14.29	S
3.	Planning of the subject		14.99	S
4.	Habit of concentration		7.74	NS
5.	Preparation for examination		17.65	S
6.	General habits and attitudes		23.83	S
7.	Studies at school		9.58	NS
8.	Total study habits		4.03	NS

(At 5% level of significance for 6 df the table value of c^2 is 12.6)

It is inferred from the above table that there is no significant association between father's occupation and their children's studies at home, Habit of concentration, studies at school and total study habits. But there is significant association between father's occupation in their children's reading and note taking, planning of the subject, preparation for examination and general habit and attitudes.

Hypothesis-7

There is no significant association between fathers' occupation and their children's Self esteem and its dimensions.

Table 4.4.7: Association between Fathers' Occupation and their Children's Self Esteem

Sl.No.	Dimensions	df	Calculated χ^2value	Remarks at 5% level
1.	Competency	6	11.49	NS
2.	Global self esteem		5.36	NS
3.	Moral and self control		14.01	S
4.	Social esteem		23.92	S
5.	Family		17.79	S
6.	Body and physical appearance		4.23	NS
7.	Total Self esteem		7.32	NS

(At 5% level of significance for 6 df the table value of χ^2 is 12.6)

It is inferred from the above table that there is no significant association between fathers' occupations and their children's competency, global self esteem, body and physical appearance and total self esteem. But there is significant association between father's occupation in their children's moral and self control, social esteem and family.

Hypothesis-8

There is no significant association between fathers' occupation and their children's Academic achievement.

Table 4.4.8: Association between Fathers' Occupation and their Children's Academic Achievement

Academic achievement		Low	Average	High	Calculated value	Remarks at 5% level
Fathers' Occupation	Daily wages	65 (67)	253 (247)	58 (62)	2.24	NS
	Self employed	38 (38)	136 (141)	40 (35)		
	Government Job	29 (25)	89 (94)	24 (23)		
	Private Job	33 (34)	130 (127)	30 (32)		

(At 5% level of significance for 6 df the table value of c^2 is 12.6)

It is inferred from the above table that there is no significant difference association between fathers' occupation and their children's academic achievement.

Hypothesis-9

There is no significant association between fathers' income and their children's Environmental factors and its dimensions.

It is inferred from the above table that there is no significant difference association between father's income and their children's home environment, social environment and total environment. But there is significant difference association between father's incomes and their children's school environment.

Table 4.4.9: Association Between Fathers' Income and their Children's Environmental Factors

Sl.No.	Dimensions	df	Calculated χ^2value	Remarks at 5% level
1.	Home environment		3.06	NS
2.	School environment	4	9.72	S
3.	Social environment		7.04	NS
4.	Total environment		4.79	NS

(At 5% level of significance for 4 df the table value of χ^2 is 9.49)

Hypothesis-10

There is no significant association between fathers' income and their children's Study habits and its dimensions.

Table 4.4.10: Association between Fathers' Income and their Children's Study Habits

Sl.No.	Dimensions	df	Calculated χ^2value	Remarks at 5% level
1.	Studies at home		2.09	NS
2.	Reading and note taking		5.29	NS
3.	Planning of the subject		14.87	S
4.	Habit of concentration	4	5.20	NS
5.	Preparation for examination		5.24	NS
6.	General habits and attitudes		4.92	NS
7.	Studies at school		2.88	NS
8.	Total study habits		3.14	NS

(At 5% level of significance for 4 df the table value of χ^2 is 9.49)

It is inferred from the above table that there is no significant association between father's income and their children's studies at home, Reading and note taking, Habit of concentration, preparation for examination, general habits and attitudes, studies at school and total study habits. But there is significant association between fathers' occupations in their children's planning of the subject.

Hypothesis-11

There is no significant association between fathers' income and their children's Self esteem and its dimensions.

It is inferred from the above table that there is no significant association between fathers' income and their children's moral and self control, body and physical appearance and total self esteem. But there is significant association between fathers' income and their children's competency, global self esteem, social esteem and family.

Table 4.4.11: Association between Father's Income and their Children's Self Esteem

Sl.No.	Dimensions	df	Calculated χ^2value	Remarks at 5% level
1.	Competency	4	15.18	S
2.	Global self esteem		14.80	S
3.	Moral and self control		8.40	NS
4.	Social esteem		14.19	S
5.	Family		14.0	S
6.	Body and physical appearance		8.06	NS
7.	Total self esteem		5.24	NS

(At 5% level of significance for 4 df the table value of c^2 is 9.49)

Hypothesis-12

There is no significant association between fathers' income and their children's Academic achievement.

Table 4.4.12: Association Between Father's Income and their Children's Academic Achievement

Academic achievement		Low	Average	High	Calculated value	Remarks at 5% level
Father s' income	Less than Rs.5000	90 (94)	348 (335)	76 (86)	5.92	NS
	Rs.5000-Rs.10000	59 (52)	169 (184)	54 (47)		
	Above Rs.10000	20 (24)	85 (84)	24 (21)		

(At 5% level of significance for 4 df the table value of χ^2 is 9.49)

It is inferred from the above table that there is no significant association between father's income and their children's academic achievement.

Hypothesis-13

There is no significant association between mothers' education and their children's Environmental factors and its dimensions

Table 4.4.13: Association between Mothers' Education and their Children's Environmental Factors

Sl.No.	Dimensions	df	Calculated χ^2value	Remarks at 5% level
1.	Home environment	6	6.77	NS
2.	School environment		13.55	S
3.	Social environment		13.66	S
4.	Total environment		2.61	NS

(At 5% level of significance for 6 df the table value of χ^2 is 12.6)

It is inferred from the above table that there is no significant association between mothers' education and their children's home environment and total environment. But there is significant association between mothers' education and their children school environment and social environment.

Hypothesis-14

There is no significant association between mothers' education and their children's Study habits and its dimensions.

Table 4.4.14: Association between Mothers' Education and their Children's Study Habits

Sl.No.	Dimensions	df	Calculated χ^2value	Remarks at 5% level
1.	Studies at home	6	11.96	NS
2.	Reading and note taking		10.66	NS
3.	Planning of the subject		6.29	NS
4.	Habit of concentration		5.08	NS
5.	Preparation for examination		21.50	S
6.	General habits and attitudes		5.91	NS
7.	Studies at school		11.95	NS
8.	Total study habits		7.69	NS

(At 5% level of significance for 6 df the table value of χ^2 is 12.6)

It is inferred from the above table that there is no significant association between mothers' education and their children's studies at home, reading and note taking, planning of the subject, habit of concentration, general habit and attitudes, studies at school and total study habits. But there is significant association between mothers' education and their children's preparation for examination.

Hypothesis-15

There is no significant association between mothers' education and their children's Self esteem and its dimensions.

Table 4.4.15: Association Between Mothers' Education and their Children's Self Esteem

Sl.No.	Dimensions	df	Calculated χ^2value	Remarks at 5% level
1.	Competency	6	5.63	NS
2.	Global self esteem		13.55	S
3.	Moral and self control		14.96	S
4.	Social esteem		20.81	S
5.	Family		36.39	S
6.	Body and physical appearance		19.88	S
7.	Total Self esteem		12.25	NS

(At 5% level of significance for 6 df the table value of χ^2 is 12.6)

It is inferred from the above table that there is no significant association between mothers' education and their children's competency and total self esteem. But there is significant association between mothers' education and their children's global self esteem, moral and self control, social esteem, family and body and physical appearance.

Hypothesis-16

There is no significant association between mothers' education and their children's academic achievement.

Table 4.4.16: Association between Mothers' Education and their Children's Academic Achievement

Academic achievement		Low	Average	High	Calculated value	Remarks at 5% level
Mothers' Education	Illiterate	51 (40)	136 (141)	28 (33)	7.93	NS
	School	81 (88)	309 (309)	80 (73)		
	College	27 (27)	101 (96)	18 (23)		
	Professional	14 (18)	62 (62)	18 (15)		

(At 5% level of significance for 6 df the table value of χ^2 is 12.6)

It is inferred from the above table that there is no significant difference association between mothers' educations and their children's academic achievement.

Hypothesis-17

There is no significant association between mothers' occupation and their children's Environmental factors and its dimensions.

Table 4.4.17: Association between Mothers' Occupation and their Children's Environmental Factors

Sl.No.	Dimensions	df	Calculated χ^2value	Remarks at 5% level
1.	Home environment	6	12.61	S
2.	School environment		8.97	NS
3.	Social environment		10.82	NS
4.	Total environment		2.20	NS

(At 5% level of significance for 6 df the table value of χ^2 is 12.6)

It is inferred from the above table that there is no significant difference association between mothers' occupation and their children's school environment, social environment and total environment. But there is significant difference association between mothers' occupation and their children's home environment.

Hypothesis-18

There is no significant association between mothers' occupation and their children's Study habits and its dimensions.

Table 4.4.18: Association between Mothers' Occupation and their Children's Study Habits

Sl.No.	Dimensions	df	Calculated χ^2value	Remarks at 5% level
1.	Studies at home		22.10	S
2.	Reading and note taking		7.35	NS
3.	Planning of the subject		6.14	NS
4.	Habit of concentration		7.78	NS
5.	Preparation for examination	6	22.29	S
6.	General habits and attitudes		5.73	NS
7.	Studies at school		9.68	NS
8.	Total study habits		4.18	NS

(At 5% level of significance for 6 df the table value of χ^2 is 12.6)

It is inferred from the above table that there is no significant association between mothers' occupation and their children's reading and note taking, planning of the subject, habit of concentration, general habit and attitudes, studies at school and total study habits. But there is significant association between mothers' occupation and their children's studies at home and preparation for examination.

Hypothesis-19

There is no significant association between mothers' occupation and their children's Self esteem and its dimensions.

Table 4.4.19: Association between Mothers' Occupation and their Children's Self Esteem

Sl.No.	Dimensions	df	Calculated χ^2value	Remarks at 5% level
1.	Competency		5.87	NS
2.	Global self esteem		12.71	S
3.	Moral and self control		12.20	NS
4.	Social esteem	6	13.14	S
5.	Family		19.55	S
6.	Body and physical appearance		6.20	NS
7.	Total Self esteem		5.81	NS

(At 5% level of significance for 6 df the table value of c^2 is 12.6)

It is inferred from the above table that there is no significant association between mothers' occupation and their children's competency, moral and self control, body and physical appearance and total self esteem. But there is significant association between mothers' occupation and their children's global self esteem, social esteem and family.

Hypothesis-20

There is no significant association between mothers' occupation and their children's Academic achievement.

Table 4.4.20: Association Between Mothers' Occupation and their Children's Academic Achievement

Academic achievement		Low	Average	High	Calculated value	Remarks at 5% level
Mothers' Occupation	House Wife	51 (49)	203 (200)	42 (48)	4.15	NS
	Daily wages	33 (33)	133 (134)	32 (32)		
	Government job	16 (17)	63 (69)	23 (16)		
	Private job	52 (54)	225 (222)	52 (53)		

(At 5% level of significance for 6 df the table value of χ^2 is 12.6)

It is inferred from the above table that there is no significant difference association between mothers' occupations and their children's academic achievement

Hypothesis-21

There is no significant association between mothers' income and their children's Environmental factors and its dimensions.

Table 4.4.21: Association between Mothers' Income and their Children's Environmental Factors

Sl.No.	Dimensions	df	Calculated χ^2value	Remarks at 5% level
1.	Home environment	6	12.46	NS
2.	School environment		3.40	NS
3.	Social environment		9.69	NS
4.	Total environment		6.07	NS

(At 5% level of significance for 6 df the table value of χ^2 is 12.6)

It is inferred from the above table that there is no significant association between mothers' income and their children's home environment, school environment, social environment and total environment.

Hypothesis-22

There is no significant association between mothers' income and their children's Study habits and its dimensions.

It is inferred from the above table that there is no significant association between mothers' income and their children's studies at home, reading and note taking, planning of the subject, habit of concentration, general habit and attitudes and total study habits. But there is significant association between mothers' income and their children's preparation for examination and studies at school.

Table 4.4.22: Association between Mothers' Income and their Children's Study Habits

Sl.No.	Dimensions	df	Calculated χ^2value	Remarks at 5% level
1.	Studies at home		12.37	NS
2.	Reading and note taking		8.39	NS
3.	Planning of the subject		11.26	NS
4.	Habit of concentration	6	3.54	NS
5.	Preparation for examination		26.98	S
6.	General habits and attitudes		11.23	NS
7.	Studies at school		14.55	S
8.	Total study habits		7.38	NS

(At 5% level of significance for 6 df the table value of c^2 is 12.6)

Hypothesis-23

There is no significant association between mothers' income and their children's Self esteem and its dimensions.

Table 4.4.23: Association between Mothers' Income and their Children's Self Esteem

Sl.No.	Dimensions	df	Calculated χ^2value	Remarks at 5% level
1.	Competency		10.94	NS
2.	Global self esteem		9.31	NS
3.	Moral and self control		13.03	S
4.	Social esteem	6	25.35	S
5.	Family		17.19	S
6.	Body and physical appearance		10.75	NS
7.	Total Self esteem		10.85	NS

(At 5% level of significance for 6 df the table value of c^2 is 12.6)

It is inferred from the above table that there is no significant association between mothers' income and their children's competency, global self esteem, body and physical appearance and total self esteem. But there is significant association between mothers' income and their children's moral and self control, social esteem and family.

Hypothesis-24

There is no significant association between mothers' income and their children's Academic achievement.

Table 4.4.24: Association between Mothers' Income and their Children's Academic Achievement

Academic achievement		Low	Average	High	Calculated value	Remarks at 5% level
Mothers' Income	Less than Rs.5000	70 (71)	284 (280)	72 (74)	1.28	NS
	Rs.5000-Rs.10000	37 (34)	131 (133)	34 (35)		
	Above Rs.10000	14 (16)	66 (64)	17 (17)		
	Nil	34 (34)	128 (132)	38 (35)		

(At 5% level of significance for 6 df the table value of χ^2 is 12.6)

It is inferred from the above table that there is no significant association between mothers' income and their children's academic achievement.

SECTION-V

Hypothesis-1

There is no significant relationship between Environmental factors and Academic achievement with reference to background variables.

Table 4.5.1: Relationship between Environmental Factor S and Achievement with Reference to Background Variables

Sl.No.	Variable	Categories	"r" value	Table value	Result
1.	Sex	Male	0.238	0.088	S
		Female	0.115	0.088	S
2.	Standard	XI standard	0.106	0.088	S
		XII standard	0.225	0.088	S
3.	Locality of the school	Rural	0.196	0.088	S
		Urban	0.141	0.088	S
4.	Nativity of the learner	Rural	0.213	0.088	S
		Urban	0.135	0.088	S
5.	Nature of the school	Boys	0.294	0.169	S
		Girls	0.055	0.139	NS
		Co-education	0.181	0.139	S
6.	Type of the management	Government	0.144	0.160	NS
		Aided	0.118	0.139	NS
		Self financing	0.180	0.160	S
7.	Medium of the institution	Tamil	0.196	0.088	S
		English	0.119	0.088	S
8.	Family status	Nuclear	0.313	0.088	S
		joint	0.136	0.088	S

Since the calculated value of 'r' is greater than the table value at 5 % level of significance, the hypothesis is rejected except girls school, government and aided school. Therefore there is significant relationship between environmental factors and academic achievement with reference to background variables.

Hypothesis-2

There is no significant relationship between Home environment and Academic achievement with reference to background variables.

Table 4.5.2: Relationship between Home Environment and Academic Achievement with Reference to Background Variables

Sl.No.	Variable	Categories	"r" value	Table value	Result
1.	Sex	Male	0.180	0.088	S
		Female	0.131	0.088	S
2.	Standard	XI standard	0.114	0.088	S
		XII standard	0.207	0.088	S
3.	Locality of the school	Rural	0.095	0.088	S
		Urban	0.191	0.088	S
4.	Nativity of the learner	Rural	0.069	0.088	NS
		Urban	0.215	0.088	S
5.	Nature of the school	Boys	0.195	0.169	S
		Girls	0.137	0.139	NS
		Co-education	0.087	0.139	NS
6.	Type of the management	Government	0.061	0.160	NS
		Aided	0.106	0.139	NS
		Self financing	0.283	0.160	S
7.	Medium of the institution	Tamil	0.095	0.088	S
		English	0.186	0.088	S
8.	Family status	Nuclear	0.290	0.088	S
		joint	0.115	0.088	S

Since the calculated value of 'r' is greater than the table value at 5 % level of significance, the hypothesis is rejected except rural students, girls school, co-education school, government school and aided school. Therefore there is significant relationship between home environment and academic achievement with reference to background variables.

Hypothesis-3

There is no significant relationship between School environment and Academic achievement with reference to background variables.

Table 4.5.3: Relationship between School Environment and Academic Achievement with Reference to Background Variables

Sl.No.	Variable	Categories	"r" value	Table value	Result
1.	Sex	Male	0.226	0.088	S
		Female	0.113	0.088	S
2.	Standard	XI standard	0.077	0.088	NS
		XII standard	0.234	0.088	S
3.	Locality of the school	Rural	0.233	0.088	S
		Urban	0.098	0.088	S
4.	Nativity of the learner	Rural	0.246	0.088	S
		Urban	0.129	0.088	S
5.	Nature of the school	Boys	0.258	0.169	S
		Girls	0.046	0.139	NS
		Coeducation	0.220	0.139	S
6.	Type of the management	Government	0.206	0.160	S
		Aided	0.072	0.139	NS
		Self financing	0.163	0.160	S
7.	Medium of the institution	Tamil	0.201	0.088	S
		English	0.121	0.088	S
8.	Family status	Nuclear	0.128	0.088	S
		joint	0.232	0.088	S

Since the calculated value of 'r' is greater than the table value at 5 % level of significance, the hypothesis is rejected except XI standard students, girls school and aided school. Therefore there is significant relationship between school environment and academic achievement with reference to background variables.

Hypothesis-4

There is no significant relationship between Social environment and Academic achievement with reference to background variables.

Since the calculated value of 'r' is greater than the table value at 5 % level of significance, the hypothesis is rejected. Except rural, urban, girls school, government and aided schools. Therefore there is significant relationship between social environment and academic achievement with reference to background variables.

Table 4.5.4: Relationship between Social Environment and Academic Achievement with Reference to Background Variables

Sl.No.	Variable	Categories	"r" value	Table value	Result
1.	Sex	Male	0.173	0.088	S
		Female	0.125	0.088	S
2.	Standard	XI standard	0.095	0.088	S
		XII standard	0.093	0.088	S
3.	Locality of the school	Rural	0.073	0.088	NS
		Urban	0.072	0.088	NS
4.	Nativity of the learner	Rural	0.143	0.088	S
		Urban	0.126	0.088	S
5.	Nature of the school	Boys	0.214	0.169	S
		Girls	0.030	0.139	NS
		Coeducation	0.150	0.139	S
6.	Type of the management	Government	0.039	0.160	NS
		Aided	0.076	0.139	NS
		Self financing	0.166	0.160	S
7.	Medium of the institution	Tamil	0.134	0.088	S
		English	0.124	0.088	S
8.	Family status	Nuclear	0.162	0.088	S
		joint	0.140	0.088	S

Hypothesis-5

There is no significant relationship between Study habits and Academic achievement with reference to background variables.

Table 4.5.5: Relationship Between Study Habits and Academic Achievement with Reference to Background Variables

Sl.No.	Variable	Categories	"r" value	Table value	Result
1.	Sex	Male	0.290	0.088	S
		Female	0.245	0.088	S
2.	Standard	XI standard	0.294	0.088	S
		XII standard	0.236	0.088	S
3.	Locality of the school	Rural	0.285	0.088	S
		Urban	0.267	0.088	S
4.	Nativity of the learner	Rural	0.237	0.088	S
		Urban	0.284	0.088	S
5.	Nature of the school	Boys	0.351	0.169	S
		Girls	0.140	0.139	S
		Coeducation	0.333	0.139	S
6.	Type of the management	Government	0.266	0.160	S
		Aided	0.262	0.139	S
		Self financing	0.222	0.160	S
7.	Medium of the institution	Tamil	0.328	0.088	S
		English	0.187	0.088	S
8.	Family status	Nuclear	0.162	0.088	S
		joint	0.140	0.088	S

Since the calculated value of 'r' is greater than the table value at 5 % level of significance, the hypothesis is rejected. Therefore there is significant relationship between study habits and academic achievement with reference to background variables.

Hypothesis-6

There is no significant relationship between Self esteem and Academic achievement with reference to background variables.

Table 4.5.6: Relationship between Self Esteem and Academic Achievement With Reference To Background Variables

Sl.No.	Variable	Categories	"r" value	Table value	Result
1.	Sex	Male	0.376	0.088	S
		Female	0.234	0.088	S
2	Standard	XI standard	0.311	0.088	S
		XII standard	0.292	0.088	S
3	Locality of the school	Rural	0.455	0.088	S
		Urban	0.196	0.088	S
4	Nativity of the learner	Rural	0.392	0.088	S
		Urban	0.244	0.088	S
5	Nature of the school	Boys	0.492	0.169	S
		Girls	0.159	0.139	S
		Coeducation	0.287	0.139	S
6	Type of the management	Government	0.265	0.160	S
		Aided	0.240	0.139	S
		Self financing	0.485	0.160	S
7	Medium of the institution	Tamil	0.304	0.088	S
		English	0.300	0.088	S
8	Family status	Nuclear	0.262	0.088	S
		joint	0.116	0.088	S

Since the calculated value of 'r' is greater than the table value at 5 % level of significance, the hypothesis is rejected. Therefore there is significant relationship between self esteem and academic achievement with reference to background variables.

Conclusion

A detailed analysis of the hypotheses has been done in this chapter. Different statistical techniques like "percentage analyzes", "t" test, "F" test, chi-square analysis c^2 and Product Moment Correlation (r) have been used in verifying the various hypotheses. The statistical analyzes of the data revealed the significant relationship among the environmental factors, study habits and self esteem on academic achievement with reference to some selected variables. The ensuing chapter deals with findings, interpretation, recommendation and suggestions.

5

Findings, Interpretations, Recommendations and Suggestions

Introduction

This chapter is concluding chapter of these findings, interpretations, recommendation and educational implications and scope of the further research are described.

Once the research data have been collected and the analysis has been made, the researcher can proceed to the stage of interpreting the data. Interpretation refers to task of drawing inferences from the collected facts after the analytical study. In fact, it is search for broader meaning of research findings.

According to Carter V. Good (1994) "The process of interpretation is essentially one of starting what the findings convey, what is their significance and what is the answer to the original problem".

According to Lokesh Koul (1997) "Interpretation calls for a careful, logical and critical examination of the sample chosen, the tools selected and used in the study".

In one sense, interpretation is concerned with relationship with in the collected data. Interpretation also extends beyond the data of the study to include the results of other researches, theories and hypotheses. Thus, interpretation is the device through which the factors the seem to explain what has been observed by the researcher in the course of the study can be better understood and it also provides a theoretical conception, which can serve as a guide for further researches.

There is always an element of subjectivity and researches generally commit certain errors while interpreting the results of his study. Educational researchers have to exercise all care and caution in formulating his conclusions and arriving at generalization on the basis of his data. Like interpretation of results, the formulation of conclusions and generalizations also demand keen observation, broad outlook and power of logical thinking.

Findings

Section-I

1. The level of environmental factors and its dimensions of higher secondary biology students with reference to sex is average. Among the average value, boys higher secondary biology students have high score (74.4 percent). The level of boys higher secondary biology students in the dimension social environment is high (77.4 percent). The level of girls higher secondary biology students in school environment is low (66.3 percent).
2. The level of environmental factors and its dimensions of higher secondary biology students with reference to standard is average. Among the average value, XI standard higher secondary biology students have high score (72.3 percent). The level of XI standard higher secondary biology students in the dimension social environment is high (74.1 percent). The level of XII standard higher secondary biology students in school environment is low (66.7 percent).
3. The level of environmental factors and its dimensions of higher secondary biology students with reference to locality of the school is average. Among the average value, urban school higher secondary biology students have high score (72.8 percent). The level of rural school higher secondary biology students in the dimensions school environment and social environment is high (74.6 and 74.6 percent). The level of rural school higher secondary biology students in home environment is low (65.9 percent).
4. The level of environmental factors and its dimensions of higher secondary biology students with reference to nativity of the students is average. Among the average value, urban higher secondary biology students have high score (72.7 percent). The level of urban higher secondary biology students in the dimensions home environment is high (74.6 percent). The level of rural higher secondary biology students in home environment is low (66.2 percent).
5. The level of environmental factors and its dimensions of higher secondary biology students with reference to nature of the school is average. Among the average value, boys school higher secondary biology students have high score (75.6 percent). The level of boys school higher secondary biology students in the dimensions social environment is high (78.6 percent). The level of co-education school higher secondary biology students in school environment is low (66.0 percent).
6. The level of environmental factors and its dimensions of higher secondary biology students with reference to type of management is

average. Among the average value, government higher secondary biology students have high score (77.9 percent). The level of government higher secondary biology students in the dimensions social environment is high (79.3 percent). The level of government higher secondary biology students in school environment is low (65.0 percent).

7. The level of environmental factors and its dimensions of higher secondary biology students with reference to medium of institution is average. Among the average value, Tamil medium higher secondary biology students have high score (75.9 percent). The level of Tamil medium higher secondary biology students in the dimensions home environment and social environment is high (73.7 and 73.7 percent). The level of English medium higher secondary biology students in school environment is low (67.0 percent).
8. The level of environmental factors and its dimensions of higher secondary biology students with reference to status of the family is average. Among the average value, Joint family higher secondary biology students have high score (72.1 percent). The level of joint family higher secondary biology students in the dimensions social environment is high (77.1 percent). The level of nuclear family higher secondary biology students in school environment is low (68.1 percent).
9. The level of study habits and its dimensions of higher secondary biology students with reference to sex is average. Among the average value, girls higher secondary biology students have high score (69.0 percent). The level of boys higher secondary biology students in the dimension planning of the subject is high (77.4 percent). The level of girls higher secondary biology students in planning of the subject is low (65.7 percent).
10. The level of study habits and its dimensions of higher secondary biology students with reference to standard is average. Among the average value, XI standard higher secondary biology students have high score (70.2 percent). The level of XI standard higher secondary biology students in the dimensions preparation for examination is high (75.6 percent). The level of XII standard higher secondary biology students in studies at home is low (64.5 percent).
11. The level of study habits and its dimensions of higher secondary biology students with reference to locality of the school is average. Among the average value, urban school higher secondary biology students have high score (68.1 percent). The level of rural school higher secondary biology students in the dimension planning of the subject is high (76.5 percent). The level of urban school higher secondary biology students in studies at home is low (62.4 percent).

12. The level of study habits and its dimensions of higher secondary biology students with reference to nativity of the student is average. Among the average value, rural higher secondary biology students have high score (66.9 percent). The level of urban higher secondary biology students in the dimension reading and note taking is high (78.3 percent). The level of urban school higher secondary biology students in studies at home is low (64.4 percent).
13. The level of study habits and its dimensions of higher secondary biology students with reference to nature of the school is average. Among the average value, girls school higher secondary biology students have high score (72.9 percent). The level of girls school higher secondary biology students in the dimension preparation for examination is high (78.4 percent). The level of boys school higher secondary biology students in studies at home is low (60.9 percent).
14. The level of study habits and its dimensions of higher secondary biology students with reference to type of management is average. Among the average value, private higher secondary biology students have high score (71.2 percent). The level of government higher secondary biology students in the dimension preparation for examination and studies at school is high (79.3 percent). The level of aided school higher secondary biology students in studies at school is low (60.0 percent).
15. The level of study habits and its dimensions of higher secondary biology students with reference to medium of institution is average. Among the average value, Tamil medium higher secondary biology students have high score (70.6 percent). The level of Tamil medium higher secondary biology students in the dimension reading and note taking is high (77.6 percent). The level of English medium higher secondary biology students in studies at home is low (65.2 percent).
16. The level of study habits and its dimensions of higher secondary biology students with reference to status of the family is average. Among the average value, nuclear family higher secondary biology students have high score (69.4 percent). The level of joint family higher secondary biology students in the dimension reading and note taking is high (78.5 percent). The level of nuclear family higher secondary biology students in studies at home is low (61.6 percent).
17. The level of self esteem and its dimensions of higher secondary biology students with reference to sex is average. Among the average value, girls higher secondary biology students have high score (70.2 percent). The level of girls higher secondary biology students in the dimension family is high (76.4 percent). The level of boys higher secondary biology students in competency is low (61.4 percent).

18. The level of self esteem and its dimensions of higher secondary biology students with reference to standard is average. Among the average value, XI standard higher secondary biology students have high score (72.7 percent). The level of XI standard higher secondary biology students in the dimension competency is high (78.7 percent). The level of XII standard higher secondary biology students in social esteem is low (63.7 percent).
19. The level of self esteem and its dimensions of higher secondary biology students with reference to locality of the school is average. Among the average value, urban higher secondary biology students have high score (70.1 percent). The level of rural school higher secondary biology students in the dimension body and physical appearance is high (74.3 percent). The level of rural school higher secondary biology students in family is low (67.6 percent).
20. The level of self esteem and its dimensions of higher secondary biology students with reference to nativity of the student is average. Among the average value, urban higher secondary biology students have high score (69.6 percent). The level of urban higher secondary biology students in the dimension social esteem is high (78.5 percent). The level of rural school higher secondary biology students in social esteem is low (66.9 percent).
21. The level of self esteem and its dimensions of higher secondary biology students with reference to nature of the school is average. Among the average value, co-education school higher secondary biology students have high score (69.8 percent). The level of co-education higher secondary biology students in the dimension global self esteem is high (77.6 percent). The level of boys school higher secondary biology students in moral and self control is low (62.4 percent).
22. The level of self esteem and its dimensions of higher secondary biology students with reference to type of management is average. Among the average value, government higher secondary biology students have high score (75.0 percent). The level of government higher secondary biology students in the dimension global self esteem is high (82.9 percent). The level of aided higher secondary biology students in global self esteem is low (62.3 percent).
23. The level of self esteem and its dimensions of higher secondary biology students with reference to medium of the school is average. Among the average value, Tamil medium higher secondary biology students have high score (70.2 percent). The level of English medium higher secondary biology students in the dimension moral and self control is high (74.4 percent). The level of English medium higher secondary biology students in family is low (64.6 percent).

24. The level of self esteem and its dimensions of higher secondary biology students with reference to Status of the family is average. Among the average value, nuclear family higher secondary biology students have high score (70.7 percent). The level of nuclear family higher secondary biology students in the dimension family is high (76.7 percent). The level of joint family higher secondary biology students in family, body and physical appearance is low (64.9 and 64.9 percent).
25. (*a*) The level of academic achievement of higher secondary biology students with reference to sex is average. Among the average value girls higher secondary biology students have high score (65.1 percent). The level of boys higher secondary biology students is low (63.9 percent).
    (*b*) The level of academic achievement of higher secondary biology students with reference to standard is average. Among the average value XII standard higher secondary biology students have high score (64.5 percent). The level of XI standard higher secondary biology students is low (63.2 percent).
    (*c*) The level of academic achievement of higher secondary biology students with reference to locality of the school is average. Among the average value rural school higher secondary biology students have high score (67.6 percent). The level of urban school higher secondary biology students is low (65.0 percent).
    (*d*) The level of academic achievement of higher secondary biology students with reference to nativity of the student is average. Among the average value rural higher secondary biology students have high score (66.4 percent). The level of urban school higher secondary biology students is low (65.6 percent).
    (*e*) The level of academic achievement of higher secondary biology students with reference to nature of the school is average. Among the average value boys, girls school higher secondary biology students have high score (69.0 and 69.0 percent). The level of coeducation school higher secondary biology students is low (64.0 percent).
    (*f*) The level of academic achievement of higher secondary biology students with reference to type of management is average. Among the average value aided higher secondary biology students have high score (66.9 percent). The level of private school higher secondary biology students is low (65.4 percent).
    (*g*) The level of academic achievement of higher secondary biology students with reference to medium of the school is average. Among the average value English medium higher secondary biology students have high score (68.7 percent). The level of Tamil medium higher secondary biology students is low (65.8 percent).

(*h*) The level of academic achievement of higher secondary biology students with reference to status of the family is average. Among the average joint family higher secondary biology students have high score (69.9 percent). The level of nuclear family higher secondary biology students is low (64.5 percent).

Section-II

1. There is no significant difference in environmental factors and its dimensions of higher secondary biology students with reference to sex.
2. There is no significant difference between XI standard and XII standard students in their social environment and total environment. But there is significant difference between XI standard and XII standard students in their home environment and school environment.
3. There is no significant difference in environmental factor and its dimensions of higher secondary biology students with reference to locality of the school.
4. There is no significant difference between rural students and urban students in their social environment and total environment. But there is significant difference between rural students and urban students in their home environment and school environment.
5. There is no significant difference between Tamil medium and English medium students in their home environment and school environment. But there is significant difference between Tamil medium and English medium students in their social environment and total environment.
6. There is significant difference between nuclear family student and joint family students in their home environment, school environment, social environment and total environment
7. There is no significant difference between boys and girls students in their studies at home, reading and note taking, planning of the subject, preparation for examination, studies at school and total study habits. But there is significant difference between boys and girls students in their habit of concentration and general habits and attitudes.
8. There is no significant difference between XI standard and XII standard students in their planning of the subject, habit of concentration, preparation for examination, general habits and attitudes, studies at school and total study habits. But there is significant difference between XI standard and XII standard students in their studies at home and reading and note taking.
9. There is no significant difference between rural school and urban school in their planning of the subject, preparation for examination

and studies at school. But there is significant difference between rural school and urban school in their studies at home, reading and note taking, habit of concentration, general habits and attitudes and total study habits.

10. There is no significant difference between rural students and urban students in their studies at home, reading and note taking, planning of the subject, habit of concentration, studies at school and total study habits. But there is significant difference between rural students and urban students in their preparation for examination and general habits and attitudes.
11. There is no significant difference between Tamil medium and English medium students in their planning of the subject, habit of concentration, general habits and attitudes and studies at school. But there is significant difference between Tamil medium and English medium students in their studies at home, reading and note taking, preparation for examination and total study habits.
12. There is no significant difference between nuclear family and joint family students in their planning of the subject, habit of concentration, preparation for examination, general habits and attitudes, studies at school and total study habits. But there is significant difference between nuclear family and joint family students in their studies at home and reading and note taking.
13. There is no significant difference between boys and girls students in their competency. But there is significant difference between boys and girls students in their global self esteem, moral and self control, social esteem, family, body and physical appearance and total self esteem.
14. There is no significant difference between XI and XII standard students in their competency, moral and self control, social esteem and total self esteem. But there is significant difference between XI and XII standard students in their global self esteem, family and body and physical appearance.
15. There is no significant difference between rural school and urban school students in their competency, moral and self control and total self esteem. But there is significant difference between rural school and urban school students in their global self esteem, social esteem, family and body and physical appearance.
16. There is no significant difference between rural and urban school students in their family and total self esteem. But there is significant difference between rural and urban school students in their competency, global self esteem, moral and self control, social esteem and body and physical appearance.

17. There is no significant difference between Tamil and English medium students in their competency and total self esteem. But there is significant difference between English and Tamil medium students in their global self esteem, moral and self control, social esteem, family and body and physical appearance.
18. There is no significant difference between joint family and nuclear family students in their competency, moral and self control, social esteem, body and physical appearance and total self esteem. But there is significant difference between joint and nuclear family students in their global self esteem and family.
19. There is significant difference in the academic achievement of higher secondary students in biology with reference to 1. Sex 2. Standard 3. Locality of the school 4. Nativity of the student 5. Medium of the school 6. Status of the family.

Section-III

1. There is no significant difference among boys, girls and coeducation school students in their environmental factors. But there is significant difference among boys, girls and coeducation school students in the dimensions of home environment and school environment.
2. There is no significant difference among boys, girls and coeducation school students in their study habits. But there is significant difference among boys, girls and coeducation school students in the studies at home, reading and note taking, planning of the subject, habit of concentration, preparation for examination, studies at school and total study habits.
3. There is no significant difference among boys, girls and coeducation school students in their self esteem. But there is significant difference among boys, girls and coeducation school students in their competency, global self esteem, social esteem, family, body and physical appearance and total self esteem.
4. There is significant difference among boys school, girls school and coeducation school biology students in their academic achievement.
5. There is no significant difference among government aided and self financing school students in their environmental factors. But there is significant difference among government, aided and self financing school students in their school environment, social environment and total environment.
6. There is no significant difference among government, aided and self financing school students in their study habits. But there is significant difference among government, aided and self financing school students in their studies at home, reading and note taking, habit of

concentration, preparation for examination, general habit and attitudes and total study habits.

7. There is no significant difference among government, aided and self financing school students in their self esteem. But there is significant difference among government, aided and self financing school students in their competency, global self esteem, family, body and physical appearance and total self esteem.
8. There is significant difference among government, aided and self financing school students in their academic achievement.

Section-IV

1. There is no significant association between fathers' education and their children's home environment, school environment, social environment and total environment.
2. There is no significant association between fathers' education and their children's studies at home, reading and note taking, planning of the subject, habit of concentration, preparation for examination, general habit and attitudes and studies at school. But there is significant association between fathers' education and their children's total study habits.
3. There is no significant association between father's education and their children's competency, moral and self control, family, body and physical appearance and total self esteem. But there is significant association between fathers' education and their children's global self esteem and social esteem.
4. There is no significant association between fathers' education and their children's academic achievement
5. There is no significant association between fathers' occupation and their children's home environment, school environment, social environment and total environment.
6. There is no significant association between fathers' occupation and their children's studies at home, habit of concentration, studies at school and total study habits. But there is significant association between fathers' occupation and their children's reading and note taking, planning of the subject, preparation for examination and general habit and attitudes.
7. There is no significant association between fathers' occupations and their children's competency, global self esteem, body and physical appearance and total self esteem. But there is significant association between fathers' occupation and their children's moral and self control, social esteem and family.
8. There is no significant association between fathers' occupation and their children's academic achievement

9. There is no significant association between fathers' income and their children's home environment, social environment and total environment. But there is significant association between fathers' income and their children's school environment.
10. There is no significant association between fathers' income and their children's studies at home, reading and note taking, habit of concentration, preparation for examination, general habit and attitudes, studies at school and total study habits. But there is significant association between fathers' income and their children's planning of the subject.
11. There is no significant association between fathers' income and their children's moral and self control, body and physical appearance and total self esteem. But there is significant association between fathers' income and their children's competency, global self esteem, social esteem and family.
12. There is no significant association between fathers' income and their children's academic achievement
13. There is no significant association between mothers' education and their children's home environment and total environment. But there is significant association between mothers' education and their children's school environment and social environment
14. There is no significant association between mothers' education and their children's studies at home, reading and note taking, planning of the subject, habit of concentration, general habit and attitudes, studies at school and total study habits. But there is significant association between mothers' education and their children's preparation for examination.
15. There is no significant association between mothers' education and their children's competency and total self esteem. But there is significant association between mothers' education and their children's global self esteem, moral and self control, social esteem, family and body and physical appearance.
16. There is no significant association between mothers' education and their children's academic achievement.
17. There is no significant association between mothers' occupation and their children's school environment, social environment and total environment. But there is significant association between mothers' occupation and their children's home environment
18. There is no significant association between mothers' occupations and their children's reading and note taking, planning of the subject, habit of concentration, general habit and attitudes, studies at school and total study habits. But there is significant association between mothers'

occupations and their children's studies at home and preparation for examination.

19. There is no significant association between mothers' occupation and their children's competency, moral and self control, body and physical appearance and total self esteem. But there is significant association between mothers' occupation and their children's global self esteem, social esteem and family.
20. There is no significant association between mothers' occupation and their children's academic achievement.
21. There is no significant association between mothers' income and their children's home environment, school environment, social environment and total environment.
22. There is no significant association between mothers' income and their studies at home, reading and note taking, planning of the subject, habit of concentration, general habit and attitudes and total study habits. But there is significant association between mothers' income and their children's preparation for examination and studies at school.
23. There is no significant association between mothers' income and their children's competency, global and self esteem, body and physical appearance and total self esteem. But there is significant association between mothers' income and their children's moral and self control, social esteem and family.
24. There is no significant association between mothers' income and their children's academic achievement

Section-V

1. There is significant relationship between environmental factors and academic achievement with reference to background variables except girls school, government and aided school.
2. There is significant relationship between home environment and achievement with reference to background variables except rural students, girls school, coeducation school, government school and aided school students.
3. There is significant relationship between school environment and academic achievement with reference to background variables except XI standard students, girls' schools and aided school.
4. There is significant relationship between social environment and academic achievement with reference to background variables except rural, urban, girls, Government and aided school
5. There is significant relationship between study habits and academic achievement with reference to background variables.

6. There is significant relationship between self esteem and academic achievement with reference to background variables.

Interpretations

(a) Discussion on the Percentage Analysis Results

Based on percentage analysis, the value of social environmental factors boys is higher than girls. This may be due to the fact that the boys are more out going than girls. Boys interact with the society more than girls. The percentage score of XI standard students is higher than XII standard students. This may be due to the fact that XII standard students are much more exam oriented hence they have little time to interact with the social environment. The same is true for urban students who have better percentage score than the rural students.

The percentage score for environment with regard to nativity is higher for urban students than for rural students the modern urban life may be creating good family environment. The same score is higher for boys' school than for girls' schools. The percentage score for social environment is higher for government school. This may be due to the fact that, the majority of the poor students is studying in the government school. The percentage score for home environment and social environment are higher for Tamil medium students. It appears that the medium of instruction has an influence over this factor. The percentage score for social environment of students from joint family is higher than that of students from nuclear family, this means that joint family promotes social environment.

The percentage scores for study habits among girls are higher than boys. This may be due to fact that girls are far more systematic. The percentage score of XI standard students is higher than XII standard students. This may be due to the fact that XI students are involved not only in the exams but other school related activities also. In the same way the urban school students' score is higher than that of rural students in study habit. This may be due to the fact that the urban school students are given more coaching and practice. The percentage score of urban students with regard to study habits is higher than that of rural students. Urban students get more guidance with regard to the study habit. The study habits score for girls is higher than that of boys as girls are far more committed than boys in the studies. The percentage score for study habits is higher for aided school. This may be due to special classes conducted by aided schools, special efforts by management and also efficient teachers. The same score for Tamil medium student is higher than for English medium students. This shows the medium of instruction has a role to play with regard to study habits.

The percentage score for self esteem of girls is higher. It appears that girls view themselves better than their male counterparts. The same score for XI standard students is higher than XII standard students. The academic pressure on XII standard students has a bearing on the self esteem. The percentage score for self esteem is higher among urban school students. Urban school students have more exposure and experience which contribute the self esteem. The same is true with regard to nativity as urban school students have better percentage score in self esteem.

Students of co-education institution have better percentage score of self esteem. The interaction and competition between boys and girls may have promoted self esteem. The government school students have higher self esteem than aided and private school students. This may be due to the fact that more freedom is given with respect to the dimensions of the self esteem. The percentage of self esteem score of English medium students on selected dimensions are higher as students of English medium might have view themselves better than Tamil medium students. The percentage score of self esteem among students from nuclear families is higher than that of students from joint family. More independence and freedom- appear to promote self esteem

Female students have high level of achievement in biology than the male students. Male students may have a lot of out world distractions like outing, chatting, and mass media like TV, movies and internet. Normally, female students remain at home most of the time after the school is over and they put serious efforts in their studies. This may in turn result in their higher achievement in biology. The achievement score is high for XII standard students. This may be due to the fact that the pressure against future life is more. Rural schools are much better than urban schools. This may be due to the development of the modernization. The same is true for rural students who have better percentage score than the urban students. The achievement score is high for girls' school student. It is because of the special coaching given to girls. English medium students have better achievement than Tamil medium students. This may be due to the fact that good discipline and good environment in the English medium schools. The same is true for joint family students who have better percentage score than the nuclear family students.

(b) Discussion on the "t" test Analysis Results

There is significant difference between XI standard and XII standard students in their home environment, school environment. In this XI standard students home environment is high. This may be due to the fact that there is no need of getting high marks in the public examination; syllabus is not heavy for XI standard and also less periodical test than XII standard students. Parent may expect high marks in XII standard not in XI standard. XI standard examination does not decide the higher studies of the students. So disturbance in home environment, like T.V, music, guest and other family functions do not disturb their studies. Regarding XII standard, school environment is high. This may be due to the fact that XII standard students in anticipation of school results there is an important of school facilities like classroom laboratories, library etc. The qualified school teachers take personal care for the students.

There is significant difference between rural and urban students in their home environment, school environment. Urban students' home environment is found better. This may be due to the fact that educated parents, facilities like internet, reference books, news papers in home, sound economic condition, exposure of current development in education and job opportunity. Rural students' school environment is found high. This may be due to the fact that the school location is calm with large laboratories and playground in a natural atmosphere.

There is significant difference between Tamil medium and English medium in their social environment and total environment. English medium students are better than Tamil medium students. This may be due to the fact that command over the English language enhances their leadership qualities to improve their communication and interaction towards society. There is a significant difference between nuclear family and joint family students in their home environment, school environment, social environment and total environment. This may be due to the fact that minimum members in the family, parents care, less problems, facilities, confident and more communicative.

There is significant difference between boys and girls students in their habit of concentration, general habit and attitude. In habit of concentration, girls are better than boys. This may be due to the fact that girls are naturally studious and they have less deviation in the society. In the dimensions, general habit and attitude, boys are better than girls. This may be due to the fact that self interest, motivation and interact freely with the society.

There is significant difference between XI standard and XII standard students in their studies at home and reading and note taking. This may be due to the fact that XII standard students are aspiring for high marks in the public examination and ensuring higher studies and the bright career. There is significant difference between rural school and urban school in their studies at home, reading and note taking, habit of concentration, general habit and attitude and total study habits. Rural school is better than urban school in the dimension of studies at home, reading and note taking general habit and attitude. This may be due to the fact that spacious school calm atmosphere, less noise pollution and tendency of the rural population. In habit of concentration, urban schools are better than rural schools. This may be due to the awareness of study habits.

There is significant difference between rural students and urban student in their preparation for examination, general habit and attitudes. This may be due to the fact that awareness of study habit and studying in competition school. There is significant difference between Tamil medium and English medium students in their studies at home, reading and note taking, preparation for examination and total study habit. This may be due to the fact that the master over the English language, confidence and awareness of study habits, self motivation curiosity and interest because of the non availability of proper guidance and counseling to them from their close surroundings. There is significant difference between nuclear family and joint family students in their studies at home and reading and note taking. This may be due to the fact that individual care taken by parents and sound economic background.

There is significant difference between boys and girls in their global self esteem, moral and self control, social esteem, family, body and physical appearance and total self esteem. Girls are better than boys in the self esteem. This may be due to the fact that the girls are very much exposed to the culture, and family background. There is significant difference between XI standard and XII standard students in their global self esteem, family, body and physical appearance. XII standard students are better than XI standard students. This may be due to the fact that recognition from the family relatives and peer groups, environment of encouragement and appreciation, transition period in terms of physical factors with respect to the dimension. There is significant difference between rural school and urban schools students in their global self esteem, social esteem, family, body and physical appearance. The urban school students are better than rural school students. This may be due to the development of urbanization and enough facilities.

There is significant difference between rural and urban students in their competency, global self esteem, moral and self control, social esteem, body and physical appearance. Rural students are better than urban students in the dimensions competency and global self esteem. This may be due to various bad practices and habits which are not prevalent among rural students as compared to those of modern urban society, which might have promoted them to have better self esteem.

The urban students are better than rural students in the dimensions moral and self control, social esteem, body and physical appearance. This may be due to the fact that the facilities and opportunities provided in urban school promoted their self esteem. There is significant difference between English medium and Tamil Medium students in their global self esteem, moral and self control, social esteem, family, body and physical appearance. This may be due to the fact that English language plays a vital role and it's easy to help in the higher studies, good discipline and good environment and wealthy family background. There is significant difference between nuclear and joint family students in their global self esteem, family. This may be due to the small size of the family and low expenses.

(c) Discussion on the "F" test Analysis Results

There is significant difference among boys, girls and coeducation school in their home environment and school environment. Girls school are better than boys school and coeducation school. This may be due to the fact that female students are involved in limited activity, their interactions with friends and immediate environment around them are less than in the case of the males.

There is significant difference among boys, girls and coeducation schools in their studies at home, reading and note taking, planning of the subject, habit of concentration, preparation for examination, studies at school and total study habits. Girls school are better than boys and coeducation school. This may be due to the fact that female students have obtained higher scores than male students; female students may spend more time in home, tuition-classes and act as per the tips given by parents and elders as a support for their study.

There is significant difference among boys, girls and coeducation school students in their competency, global self esteem, social esteem, family, body and physical appearance and total self esteem. Boys school competency is better than girls and co-education school. This may be due to the fact that male students are actively involved in co-curricular activities. Male students have wider knowledge about the external worlds with the help of chatting, roaming, magazine, films, newspapers etc. Girls schools are better than boys school and coeducation school in the dimension of global self esteem, social esteem, family, body and physical appearance and total self esteem. This may be due to the fact that competitive and ego centered attitudes exhibited by these schools. This may also be due to their longing to come forward in the society.

There is significant difference among boys, girls and coeducation schools students in their achievement. Girls school are better than boys and coeducation schools. This may be due to the fact that girls are more responsible, devoted to their work and systematic than boys. Girls give importance to rote memory for learning, the understanding and grasping capacity also very high compared with boys. Girls have daily learned their subjects and the boys only concentrate during the exam days in depth manner recognize the main theme of the subject.

There is significant difference among government, aided and self financing school in their school environment, social environment, and total environment. Aided schools are better than government and self financing schools. This may be due to the fact that aided schools are getting more financial assistance from well wishers and utilize them better than government and self financing school.

There is significant difference among government, aided and self financing school students in their studies at home, reading and note taking, habit of concentration, preparation for examination, general habits and attitudes and total study habits. Self financing school students are better than government and aided school students. This may be due to the fact that strict and well discipline, quality teaching and coaching imparted by majority of the self financing schools.

There is significant difference among government aided and self financing school students in their competency, global self esteem, family, body and physical appearance and total self esteem. Aided school students are better than government, self financing school students. This may be due to the fact that more concentration is given respect to the above dimension.

There is significant difference among government, aided and self financing school students in their academic achievement. Self financing school students are better than government and self financing school. This may be due to the special classes conducted by self financing schools special efforts taken by management and also by efficient teachers. Due to the competition among the local schools best results are achieved

(d) Discussion on the Chi-Square Analysis Results

There is significant association between mother's education and their children's school environment and social environment. This may be due the fact that the mother's impart knowledge and the educational background very helpful to their children. The same is true with regard to mother's occupation and their children's home environment.

The chi-square analysis result shows that there is significant association between educational qualification of parents and their study habits of their children. The study habits involved the student and their educational qualification. The school level, college level and professional level parents are highly motivated to studying their children in the same. Because the world is highly competitive now a days. The students recognize the situation of rapid change in scientific worlds. The recent technologies are changing their attitude towards their learning in biology. This shows that the educated parents are very helpful to their children in getting high score in their academic performance.

There is significant association between fathers' and mothers' education and their children's self esteem. It shows that the fathers' education and mothers' education influence the study skills. This may be due to the fact that the parents impart knowledge and so the educational background helps to shine in the self esteem of higher secondary biology students.

The parents' occupation is an important factor of their children's study habits in biology. The parents know the present day situation and so they give the advice to their young ones. It is very useful to them. There is significant association between parent's occupation and their children's self esteem of higher secondary biology students. Government employees' children's are having high self esteem than the children's of private job, self-employed, daily wages, and house wife. The government employees make their living condition better, and can give special care to their children's for the health and other things.

The parents' monthly income is depending upon their children's studies in biology. The parents are helping their kids favorably. The laboratory equipments like dissection box and other things are bought by the students with the help of their parents in adequate manner. So their achievement is very high.

(e) Discussion on the Correlation Analysis Results

It is found out that there is no significant relationship between total environmental factors and academic achievement in girls school, government and aided school. Generally there is significant relationship between total environmental factors and academic achievement. It is because of the proper guidance and motivation provided at surrounding places.

There is no significant relationship between home environment and academic achievement in rural student, girls' school, coeducation school, government and aided school. Generally there is significant relationship between home environment and academic achievement. This may be due to availability of pleasant atmosphere at home.

There is no significant relationship between school environment and academic achievement in XI standard, girls' school and aided school. Generally there is significant relationship between school environment and academic achievement. This may be due to the reason that the present investigation school environments do not influence the academic achievement of the higher secondary students, because the higher secondary students do not pledge their concentration on such things and they shoulder the responsibility of scoring good marks in the examination. For this, they work hard and develop the positive perception on school environment.

There is no significant relationship between social environment and academic achievement in rural, urban, girls, government and aided school. Generally there is significant relationship between social environment and academic achievement. This may be due to public education and awareness programmes to promote positive perception. But there is significant relationship between study habits, self esteem and academic achievement with reference to background variables. It shows that these variables do not have impact over the establishment of relationship between those traits.

Recommendations and Educational Implications of the Study

Based on the findings of the present study, the following recommendations are made to maximize achievement in biology.

Influence of environmental factors on academic achievement is home environments, school environment, laboratory situation, faculty relationship, peer group environment and social environment. The study is made in terms of the variables such as gender, standard, locality of the school, nativity of the student, nature of the school, type of management, medium of the institution, status of the family, parents educational qualification, parents occupation and parents monthly income. Biology is an important subject which has a great future for students. So the government can take the necessary steps to over come the problem of studying biology and achievement at the higher secondary level.

- Parents should provide congenial atmosphere for the student to study well at home.
- Seminars should be arranged for higher secondary students focusing attention on varied dimensions of school environment. During the seminars question hours should be allotted for the students in order to clarify their doubts regarding the school environment and its impact.
- Provision of better school environment is in the hands of the government, private bodies as well as the public. Hence a joint venture can be undertaken for improving the school environment.
- Good school environment would be a significant factor. It is not provided to the students of higher secondary schools. Hence, the management of every educational institution should provide a conducive school as well as classroom environment, which may fulfill the basic needs of a healthy organizational climate.
- Achievement motivation can be enhanced in the students through rewards, praises, setting models by teachers and creating pleasant school environment.
- Teacher should encourage feelings of cohesiveness among students through effective communication. This beneficial cohesive feeling can be induced by arranging tours and trips and by taking them to the places where people are in need of external help. Students can be taken to various sports where natural calamities cause dander to common public and can be made to help those sufferers. This sort of experience will give sense of sensitivity and their knowledge to recognize their social environment.
- The biology teacher should give the assignment and to draw the internal structure of animal parts and floral diagrams regularly and check their work also. This will help their way of presentation, expression and also enhance their achievements.
- The syllabus system is the main barrier for teaching and learning biology, because the CBSE system is totally different from State Board syllabus. So the State Board syllabus must be updated.

- The government should provide fund for schools in an adequate manner to buy the aids. And the regular staff should be appointed for teaching biology in all schools.
- Teacher's behaviour must be conducive and clear cut friendly manner for the students.
- Guidance and counseling may be given to the students about various good study habits and their importance in their academic career in the higher secondary level.
- The students may be made available with various literatures on study habits.
- The mode of examinations to test the aural, oral and communicative skills of students, just being introduced by the directorate of government examinations with due credit at the final and concluding examination at the higher secondary stage thereby enabling them to develop good study habits.
- A "How to study" summer course of 30-45 days may be imparted to the interested students and those who have undergone this course may be given due preference in joining the desired group at the high secondary stage itself.
- Group discussions may be arranged by the teachers then and there to enable them active high.
- The low achievers may be induced to participate in co-curricular activities of their interest in the view of helping them develop good study habits.
- The various elements which are acting as hurdles or barriers in developing good study habits may be identified and not be allowed to exert their impact in this regard.
- The students themselves may be made to realize the importance of good study habits in their academic career.
- The students should plan a proper time schedule. The time schedule may be followed strictly which in due course, becomes routine in the minds of the students. While preparing a time schedule by the students, priority may be given according to the need of the programme.
- Spaced studying can be encouraged instead of un-spaced studying. This may improve one's memory-power and help in avoiding studying. This may improve one's memory-power and help in avoiding day dreaming due to continuous studying.
- Alternative types of work while studying should not be given by their family members.

- The financial situation of the students has a negative impact on the students' academic achievements. Poor performance may be due to the fact that their needs are not satisfied. These types of children could be financial aided by way of scholarship, loans and concessions, which could serve as motivating factor to do better in their studies.

For the improvement of global self-esteem students should be helped to set realistic goals for themselves and write down steps to work towards those goals. Students must not allow past experiences to determine their lives. They should be trained to take time regularly to be alone and enjoy their own company. Hobbies, individual sports, crafts and reading are examples of ways to be alone. They must be trained to become creative and have their own ideas. They should be asked about their other activities.

To improve the moral and self-control level of students, they must be taught to identify their strengths and weaknesses. It is better to remember that no one is perfect and they don't have to be perfect either. They must be helped not to over-react when they make a mistake. They should be made to accept that they are only human being and learn from the mistakes. They must be taught to trust their own feelings and intuitions but at the same time they must be taught to have control over their behaviour. When they show breach of moral ethics, they should be allowed to suffer the consequences of their behaviour.

It seems that changes in the culture lead to changes in self-esteem. The social-esteem of students can be improved by helping them to make friends easily and also to show enthusiasm for new activities. They should be trained to be co-operative. Relationships with friends help to form their self-esteem, as do experiences with work and career. Therefore they should always look for friends with high self-esteem for their positive attitude would influence others to be more positive. The students must be advised to avoid people who make them unhappy. Also a student must avoid being judgmental. If a lot of students' interactions with others are criticisms, put-downs, complaints, or judgments, it may be keeping others away. For some people, a judgmental attitude comes from low self-esteem which they try to overcome by criticizing others. Hence the student should be trained to work on viewing others more positively.

Self-esteem develops and changes over the course of one's life. Therefore as regards family esteem, experiences and relationships with family members from birth until the present are strong influences. Hence they must be patient with the weaknesses and faults of others. They must be taught not to put any one down. Each student must be counseled about the responsibility they hold in the family

To improve the esteem level concerning the phenomenon of body and physical appearance the students must be trained to be optimistic. In her book, Negaholics, psychologist Cherie Carter Scott offers this advice "Think

Positive". The students must take time to realize the positive aspects in them. Self-esteem is based on the thoughts and feelings the students have about themselves. These can be positive or negative. High self-esteem is reflected by positive thoughts such as "I'm smart, attractive and interesting". These thoughts can help them feel effective, capable and lovable. Low self-esteem is reflected by negative thoughts such as "I'm ugly, stupid and boring". These thoughts can make them feel worthless, unlovable and incompetent. People with high self-esteem accept and like themselves.

"Think of what you have rather than what you lack. Of the things you have, select the best and then reflect how eagerly you would have sought them if you did not have them".

—Marcus Aurelius, 31 BC

Suggestions for Further Research

Here in this present study the investigator has executed the studies with the environmental factors, study habit and self esteem influencing academic achievement of higher secondary biology students. Even then, in order to make the educational process still better, the investigator requests the future investigations to precede their research process in the following directions.

1. This study covers only Kanyakumari, Thoothukudi and Tirunelveli district in Tamil Nadu state. A similar study may also be conducted in other districts of Tamil Nadu.
2. A comparative study on the academic achievement of school and college students could be undertaken.
3. Academic achievement in relation to psychological aspect of the subjects could be studied.
4. A comparative study of academic achievement of technical and non-technical subjects could be undertaken.
5. Similar study may be undertaken in other subjects such as Mathematics, Physics, Chemistry, Social science and languages.
6. Longitudinal study of academic achievement may be undertaken from high school to higher secondary schools level.
7. A study of academic achievement in relation to intelligence and other social variables may be taken up.
8. A comparative study on the academic achievement of professional and other college students may be done.
9. The investigator had made the study of only the students of XI and XII standard, the study can be extended to different classes of all types of schools, including ICSE CBSE and Anglo Indian schools at different levels such as higher secondary, arts and science and professional college.

10. A similar study can be undertaken with different categories of students physically and mentally challenged and the impact of the problems they face in life and their effect on their academic achievement.

Conclusion

Now a day, one has to live in the scientific world. The biological research leads to the nano technology and found the human genome also. So our government should provide the facilities to the schools and encourage the students for risk taking, allows for co-operation, acceptance of the individual, and improve their reasoning ability. Above all, the suggestions for nurturing relationships or sharing authority with students should not be misinterpreted as mandates for teachers to change their personalities. Instead, teachers will shape the learning environment to their students in order to promote the intellectual growth and well-being of all members. The teachers may find the resources helpful in creating and sustaining a learning community.

Higher secondary education plays a very significant role in every individual life since after this education all decisions are made for the future. Students need proper guidance for the management of their time and efforts for better prospects. The study habits individually cultivated by them are likely to determine the level of their success. High self-esteem quickens the work, while low self-esteem slowed down the work leads to low motivation, and inhibits the capacity of human beings to care for themselves, Hence a growing number of people in society no longer have sufficient energy power or means of self reliance (mentally or physically) and have to rely on state provision. So, there is lack of self respect and a lack of respect for others. It leads to discrimination and poverty.

In addition to routine class room academic activities, all faculty students should be encouraged to explore themselves in order to gain self esteem. The teachers, parents and the society should encourage students to entrance their self esteem.

Abdul Kalam A.P.J had expressed that the youth had to develop aspiration and aspiration leads to achievement. This research, in this regard will help the students to lead a better achievement.

Bibliography

BOOKS

Agarwal, P. (2007), *"Modern Educational Research"*, Dominant Publishers and Distributors, New Delhi.

Aggarwal, J.C. (1966), *"Educational Research, an Introduction"*, Arya Book Depot, New Delhi.

Aggarwal, Y.P. (1990), *"Statistical Methods"*. Sterling Publishers Pvt. Ltd., New Delhi.

Best, J.W., Khan, J.V. (1995), *"Research in education* (7th ed.)". N.J. Prentice – Hall.

Bhatia, R.L. and Ahuja, B.N (1993), *"Modern Indian education and in its problems"*. Surjeet Publications.

Carter, V. Good (1973), *"Dictionary of education, 3rd edition"*. McGraw Hill Book Company, USA, P.6.

Chandra Rajendra, S.S. Sharma, K. (2004), *" Principles of Education"*. Atlantic Publishers & Distributors, B -2, Vishal Enclave Opp. Rajouri Garden, New Delhi 110 027.

Chaube, S.P and Chaube, A. (1999), *"Foundation of education"*. vikas publishing House Pvt., Ltd, New Delhi.

Chauhan, C.P.S. (1997), *"Modern Indian Education Policies, Progress, and Problems"*. Kannishka Publishers, Distributors, New Delhi.

Chauhan,S.S (2000), *"Advanced Educational Psychology"*. Vikas Publishing House Pvt. Ltd. New Delhi.

Coleman, (1965), "Advanced Educational Psychology". New Delhi, Vikas.

Coopersmith, S. (1967), *"The Antecedents of Self-esteem". San Francisco"*,N.H Freeman Publishers.

Coopersmith, S. (1967), Manual for Self-Esteem Inventory, *"Educational Research in Class Rooms and Schools"*. London; Harper and Row Publishers, University of Bradfond.

Cornall, G. Francis (1960), *"Sampling methods, Encyclopedia of Educational Research"*. Macmillan Company, New York.

Corsini, Raymond. I (1987), *"Concise Encyclopedia of Psychology"*. John Wiley and Sons. New York.

Das R.C. (1985), *"Science Teaching in Schools"*. Sterling Publishers, Private Limited, New Dehi-110020.

Dash B.N. (1985), *"Teaching of Science"*. Dominant publishers and distributors New Delhi-110002.

David Moshman John, A. Glover Roger, H. Bruning, (1987), *"Developmental Psychology- A topical Approach Little"*. Brown and Company, Boston.

Dustoor Homai, P. E. Dustoor, P. (1964), *"A time to think"*. Mac Millian and Co limited, Calcutta.

Edmonson, J.B., Joseph roemer and Francis L. Bacon (1953), *"The Administration of the Modern Secondary School"*. Fourth Edition, the Macmillan Company, USA.

Elizabeth, B. Hurlock, (1994), *"Developmental Psychology: A Lifespan Approach"*. McGraw Hill Publishing Company Ltd., New Delhi.

Franklin Lakes, N.J. Sharma Prabha Shashi, (1997), *"Basic Principles of Education"*. Kannishka Publishers, Distributors, New Delhi.

Frantine, J. (1972), *"Study Guide to Psychology Today-An Introduction"*. CRM Books, Delmar, California.

Gadde Bhuvaneswara Lakshmi, Digumatri Bhaskara Rao (2004), *"Methods of teaching life sciences"*. Discovery publishing house, New Delhi-110002.

Gerrett Hentry, E. (1981), *"Statistics in Psychology and Education"*. Valils Feffer and Simons Ltd., Bombay.

Good, C.V (1994), "Dictionary of Education". New York, McGraw Hill Book Company Inc., NY.

Gupta, S.K. (1994), *"Applied Statistics for Educational Research"*. Mittal Publication, New Delhi.

Gurney, P.W. (1988), *"Self-esteem in Children with Special Educational Needs"*. Rout ledge, London.

Heilman, W. Arthur, (1961), *"Principles and Practices of Teaching Reading"*. Charles E. Merrill Publishing Company, Sydney.

Henry Clay Lindgram, (1974), *"An Introduction to social Psychology"*. Wiley Eastern Private Limited, New Delhi.

Horney, K. (1937), The Neurotic Personality of our Time, New York: Norton.

Hughes, A.G. (1990), *"Learning and Teaching"*. Somali Publications, New Delhi.

Hurlock, B (1994), *"Developmental Psychology: A Lifespan Approach"*. McGraw Hill Publishing Company Ltd., New Delhi.

Hyde, J. Krajnik, M and Skuldt-Nierderberger, K. (1991), *"An-drogyny across the life span: A replication and longitudinal follow-up. Developmental psychology"*, 27,516-519. (Chaps16, 18)

Jamuar, K.K. (1974), *"Learning and Teaching"*. Sonali Publications, New Delhi.

Jamuar, K.K. (1974), *"Study Habits of College students"*.Indian International Publications, Allahabad.

John W. Best and James V. Khan, (1995), *"Research in Education"*. prentice Hall of India, New Delhi.

Johri, P.K. (2006), *"Educational Psychology"*. SBS Publishers and Distributors Pvt. Ltd, New Delhi.

Judd, William, C. Reavis and Charles, H. (1942), "The Teacher and Educational Administration". Houghton Mifflin company USA.

Kothari, C.R (1998), *"Research Methodology –Methods and Techniques"*. Vishwa Parkashan, New Delhi.

Kothari, C.R. (1980), *"Research Methodology: Methods and Techniques"*. Vishwa Prakasham, New Delhi.

Kothari, C.R. (1990), *"Research Methodology Methods and Techniques (2nd edition)"*. Wiley Eastern Limited, New Delhi.

Lawrence. D (1987), *"Enhancing Self-esteem in the Classroom"*. Paul Chapman Publishers Pvt. Ltd, London.

Le E.Bourne, Jr. Bruce R. Ekstrand, (1985); *"Psychology its Principles and Meanings"*. Holt, Rinehart and Winston New York.

Lokesh Koul (1990), *"Methodology of Education Research"*. Vikas publishing Pvt. Ltd., New Delhi.

Louis Cohen and Lawrence Manion (1989), *"Research Methods in education"*. Routledge, New York.

Macmillan. J.H and Schumachers. S (1984) *"Research in Education, A Conceptual Introduction"*. Little Brown, Boston.

Manchala C. (1997), *"Achievement of B.Ed Students"*, Discovery Publishing House, New Delhi.

Mangal S. K. (1999), *"Educational Psychology"*. Prakash Brothers, Ludhiana.

Mangal, S. K. (2000), *"Advanced Educational Psychology"*. Prentice Hall of India Private Limited, New Delhi.

Mangal, S.K. (2004), *"Teaching of Life Science"*. Arya book Dept, New Delhi-110005.

Muriet James, (1971), *"Born to Win"*. Addison Wesley Publishing Company, Inc Philippines.

Narayana Rao, S. (1990), *"Educational Psychology"*. Willey Easter Ltd., New Delhi.

Norman Vincent Peale, (1990), *"How to be your best foundation for Christian living"*. Pawling, New York.

Norman Vincent Peale, (1994), *"Treasury of Courage and Confidence"*. Orient paper backs, New Delhi.

Nurang, C.L. (1991), *"Modern Indian Education and its Problems"*. Vinod Publications, Ludhiana.

Pathak, R.P (2008), *"Methodology of Educational Research"*. Atlantic Publishers and Distributors, Pvt., Ltd., New Delhi.

Pigat, Jean., (1952), "Origin of Intelligence". New York, International University Press.

Radhakrishnan, S. (1956), "Occasional Speeches and Writing". October 1982. First Series.

Ramakrishnaiah, D. Digumarti Bhaskara Rao, (1998), *"Job Satisfaction of College Teachers"*. Discovery Publishing House, New Delhi.

Rao, V.K (2003), "Quality education". APH Publishing Corporation 5 Ausari road darya ganj, New Delhi.

Sharma, N.K. (1996), Statistical Techniques, Mangal Deep Publications, Jaipur.

Sharma, R.C. (2002), Modern Science Teaching, Dhanpat Rai Publishing company, Pvt. Ltd., New Delhi.

Taylor, L.S (1956) The Psychology of Human Differences (2nd ed.) Appleton Century Croft, New York. 123-129.

Weiner, B (1972) "Theories of Motivation". Chicago Rand McNally.

William Wiersma, (1986), Research Methods in Education, Jeffrey John and Bacon, London.

William, C. Morse and Max Wingo, G. (1968), Psychology and Teaching, D.B. Taraporewaba sons and Co. Pvt. Ltd., Delhi.

Yadav, K. (1993), *"Teaching of Life Sciences"*. Anomal publication Pvt. Ltd. New Delhi-110002.

JOURNALS

Abid Hussain Ch, (2006), Effect of Guidance Services on Study Attitudes, Study Habits and Academic Achievement of Secondary School Students Bulletin of Education & Research June 2006, Vol. 28, No. 1, pp. 35-45

Amrit Rai (2008), Self-Esteem and the Level of Aspiration of High School Students in Srilankan Refuge camps. P-22, Research and Reflections on Eduction, A Quarterly Journal, vol: 06, Apr – June

Amruth G. Kumar (2005), "Emotional Balance of Secondary School Students in Relation to their Home Environment", Edutracks, Vol.4, No.7, March 2005, Pp.31-32.

Arati, C. and Rathna Prabha C. (2004), Influence of family Environment on Emotion Competence of Adolescents", Journal of community Guidancee and Research vol.21, No. 2, 2004, pp.215-17.

Armstrong, Shelley; Oomen-Early, Jody, (2009), "Social Connectedness, Self-Esteem and Depression symptomlogy Among Collegiate Athletes Verses Non Athletes." *Journal of Educational Psychology,* vol.57, (5), p.521-526.

Arockiadoss, .S (2005) Study Habits and Academic Performance of the College Students. Indian Educational Abstract ISSN: 0972-5652 Vol. 5 No. 1 & 2 January and July 2005.

Atkinson, R.C., & Shiffrin R.M (1968), Human Memory: A proposed System and its control. In K.W Spence & J.T Spence(Eds). The Psychology of Learning and Motivation (Vol.2 pp89-105) New York; Academic Press (T)

Attri, Kanchan, (2001), A study on Educational "Administration and Management". The Rajasthan Board Journal of Education, vol.40 (1), 2001, pp. 49-52

Basantia M.Jaga and Mukhopadhyaya D.(2001), "Effect of Environmental factors on Achievement", Educational Review, volo.44, No.11, November, 2001, p.201.

Bosacki, Sandra; Dane, Andrew; Marini, Zopito, (2007), Peer Relationships and Internalizing Problems in Adolescents; Mediating Role of Self-Esteem, Emotionals, Behavioural Difficulties, V12, n4, P261-282 Dec

Byrne, B. (1990), Self concept and Academic achievement: Investigating their Importance as Discriminators of Academic Track Membership in High School. Canadian Journal of Education, 15 (2)

Callaway, R. (1979), Teachers Beliefs Concerning Values and the Functions and Purposes of Schooling, Eric Document Reproduction Service No. ED 177 110.

Carell, IB. (1943) "The Factorial Reprehensive of Mental Ability and Academic Achievement". Educational psychology, Meerut, 3: 307-332

Cislo, Andrew M. (2008), Ethnic Identity and Self-Esteem: Contrasting and Nicaraguan young Adults, Hispanic Journal of Behavioral Sciences, V 30, n2, P230-250,

Dillip Kumar Giri, (2006), "Leadership behaviour of the Heads of the Secondary Schools in Relation to the Attitude of Teachers". P-35, Edutracks (April 2006), Vol-5; No.8, Neelkamal Publications Pvt., Ltd., Hydrabad, India.

Distefano hristine; Moti, Robert . W, (2009), "Self-esteem and Methods Effects Associated with Negatively Worded items Investigating Factorial Invariance by Sex." *Journal of Educational Psychology,* vol.16, P134-146

Eagly,A.H, Karau, S.J&Makhigani M.G (1995), Gender and the Effectiveness of Leaders; A meta-analysis Psychological Bulletin 117,125-145 (11)

Erickson Sarah J; Hahn Smith, Anne; Smith Jane Eellen, (2009), "How Weight Atomicity Body Esteem, Body Dissatisfaction and Disordered Eating Attitudes or Behaviors Contribute to Global and Dimensional Self-Esteem in Pre Adolescent Girls". *Journal of General Psychology,* Vol.30, p129-139.

Farmer, H & Bohn M. (1970), Home-Career Conflict Reduction and the Level of Career Interest in Women. Journal of Counseling Psychology, 17,228-232 (11)

Francis A. Adesoji Segun M. Olatunbosun (2008), Student, Teacher And School Environment Factors As determinants Of Achievement In Senior Secondary school Chemistry In Oyo State, Nigeria. *Uluslararasý Sosyal Ara_týrmalar Dergisi*The Journal Of International Social Research *Volume 1/2 Winter 2008*

Geslat, V.K. (1997), " A Study of the Effect of Study Habits on Educational Achievement of the Students of Secondary schools, The Progress of Education, Pune Vidyarthi Griha prakashan, Vol. LXXI, No.6, January

Goel, S.P. (2004), Effect of Gender, Home and Environment on Educational Aspiration", Journal of community Guidance and Research Vol.21, No.1, 2004, Pp 77-78.

Hamacheck, D. (1995), Self concept and School Achievement : Interaction Dynamics and a too for Assessing the Self Concept Component, Journal of counseling and Development 73(4).

Impett, Emily A; Sorsoli, Lynn; Schooler, Deborah; Henson; James M; Tolman; Deborah L , (2008), Girls Relationship authenticity and Self-Esteem across Adolescence, Developmental Psychology, V44, n3, P722-733,

Kim, Young-II, (2003) The Effects of Assertiveness Training on Enhancing the Social Skills of Adolescents with Visual Impairments, Journal of Visual Impairment Blindness, V97, n5, P285 –297.

Kumaran, D. and kamala, S. (2001), variables affecting academic performance of successful and unsuccessful learners in science subjects: A Disseminate study. Journal of Perspective in education, 17(4)

Lane, Kathleen Lynn, Pierson, Melinda R., Givner, Christine. C, (2003), Teacher Expectations of Student Behavior; Which Skills Do Elementary and Secondary Teacher Deem, Education and Treatment of Children, V26, n4, P413-430.

Lee, Jennifer Wen-Shya (2008), The effect of Ethnic Identity and Bilingual Confidence on Chinese Youth's Self-Esteem, Alberta Journal of Educational Research, V 54, n1, P83-96.

Meers, K.P. and Prathapan P. (2008) Classroom learning Environment and Self Esteem as Correlates of Achievement in Social Studies. Journal of educational Research and Extension, Vol.45 (4): 39-50

Moffett, Aaron; Alexander, Melissa G. F. Dummer, Gail .M, (2006), Teaching Social Skills and Assertiveness to Students with Disabilities". Teaching Elementary Physical Education, V17, n6, P43-47.

Molia, Manganalal . S, (2000), "Home Environment of Rural and Urban Students of Secondary School," Journal of Psychometry, vol.13(1+2) pp.7-11.

Nalini H.K.,H.S. Ganesha Bhatta, (2009), Study Habit and Students and Students Achievement in Relation to Some Influencing Factors Edutracks vol.9 no.2

Neelkamal Publications Pvt., Ltd., Hydrabad, India.

Nygard, R. (1982), Achievement Motives and Individual Differences in Situational Specificity of behaviour. Journal Personality and Social Psychology) 43,319-327 (11).

Ogyz-Duan, Nagihan; Tezer, Esin, (2009), "Wellness and Self-Esteem among Turkish University Students." *Journal of Educational Research,* vol.31, p32-44.

Patel, M.R. (1997), "Study Habits of Pupils and its Impact upon their Academic Achievement," The progress of Education, Pune Vidyarthi Griha Prakashan, Vol. LXXI, No. 6.

Patel, Minakshi . K, (2000), Perceived Family Environment in Relation to Economic Status of Family". Journal of the Indian Academy of Applied Psychology, vol.26 (192), pp.109-114.

Poyrazli, Senel; Arbona, Consuelo; Nora, Amaury; McPherson, Robert; Pisecco, Stewart, (2002), Relation between Assertiveness, Academic Self-Efficacy, and Psychosocial Adjustment among International Graduate Students, Journal of College student Development, V43, n5, P632-642.

Priyadharshini, S.K. Velayudhan, A. (2008), Prosocial Behaviour and Self-Esteem of Day Scholars and Hostel Students. Journal of community Guidance & Research vol.25 No. 3pp. 272-283.

Raj, P. (2004), Relation of Self-Esteem with Behavioural Problems and School Performance of Children. A Behaviour Modifications Approach (2004), Indian Educational Abstracts Vol M-2, Puran Chand Professor and Head Publication Department.

Reese, Elaine; Bird, Amy; Tripp, Gail, (2007), Children's Self-Esteem and Moral Self: Links to Parent-Child Conservations Regarding Emotion, Social Development, V16, n3, P460-478.

Ryan, Ellen Bouchard,; Anas, Ann P; Mays, Hether, (2008), Assertiveness by Older Adults with Visual Impairment; Context Matters, Educational Gerontology, V34, n6, P503-519.

Sanz de Acedo Lizarraga, M. Lusia; Ugarte, M. Doloers; Cardelle-Elawar, Maria; Iriarte, M. Dolers; Sanz de Acedo Baquedano,M.Teresa, (2003) Enhancement of Self-Regulation, Assertiveness, and Empathy, Learning and Instruction, V13, n4, P423-439.

Sarita Saini (2005), "Family Environment and Academic Achievement of Adolescent Children of Working and Non Working Mothers". Half-Yearly Journal of Educational Research, Indian Educational Review Volume: 41 No: 2 July 2005.

Segal and Daniel, (2005), Relationship of Assertiveness, Depression, and Social Among Older Nursing Home Residents, Behaviour Modification, V29 n4, P689-695. **Shen, April Chiung- Tao.,** (2009), "Self-Esteem of Young Adults Experiencing Inter personal Violence and Child Physical Mat treatment" vol.24, p770-794.

Amutha ranjini, G. and Sivakumar, D. (2008), Classroom Environment and Academic Achievement in Biology of XI Standard Students in Thoothukudi District. New Horizons in Educational Research vol.1 no.1.

Steinfield, Charles; Ellision, Nicole B; Lampe, Cliff , (2008), Social Capital, Self-Esteem, and Use of Online Social Networks Sites: A Longitudinal Analysis, Journal of Applied Developmental Psychology, V 29, n6, P 434-445.

Surila Agarwala, Meenakshi Verma and **Satya Singh** (2008), Self-Ssteem among Orphan Children: A Behavior Modification Approach. Journal of Community Guidance & Research 2008 Vol. 25 No. 3 PP. 362-370.

Susai Rajendran, P. Sumathi, A. Rosaly, J. Wilson sahayaraj, (2009), Are study habits gender biased? Edutracks vol.8 no.9.

Swinson and **Jeremy,** (2008), The Self-Esteem of Pupils in Schools for Pupils with Social, Emotional and Behavioral Difficulties: Myth and Reality, British Journal of Special Education, V35, 43, P 165-172.

Szymanski, Dawn M; Gupta and **Arpana,** (2009), "The Relationship between Multiple Internationalized Oppressions and African American Lesbian, Gay, Bisexual and Questioning Person's Self-Esteem and Psychological Distress." *Journal of social Behaviour and personality,* vol.56, p-110-118.

T ***M.I.V. Nagaraju K. Sumalatha, V. and Govinda Reddy*** *(2003),* The Educational Review Academic Achievements of Senior Intermediate Students in Relation to Certain factors. *Vol. 46. No. 2 Feb, Bangalore.*

Thilagavathi T. (2008), A study on Academic Achievement of Adolescents in Relation to their Self-Esteem, P-17, Research and Reflections on Eduction, A Quarterly Journal,Palayakkotai.

Umana-Taylor, Adriana J. Vargas-Chanes, Delfino ; Garcia, Cristal D; Gonzales-Backen, Meldina, (2008), A Longitudinal Examination of Latino Adolescents' Ethnic Identity, Coping with Discrimination, and Self-Esteem, Journal of Early Adolescene; V28 n1, P16-50

WanZer,Melissa Bekelja; Mccroskey, James.C, (1998), Teacher Socio-Communicative Style as a Correlate of Student Affect toward Teacher and Course Material, Communication Education ,V4,n1,p 43-52.

Wissink, Inge B., Dekovic, Maja; Yagmur, Sengul; Stams, Geert Jan; de HAnn, Mariette, (2008), Ethnic Identity, Externalizing Problem Behaviour and the Mediating Role of Self-Esteem among Dutch, Turkish Dutch and Morocan-Dutch Adolescents, Journal of Adoescne, V31, P 223-240.

DISSERTATION ABSTRACTS

1. Dissertation Abstracts International Vol. 60 no. 11 May 2000.
2. Dissertation Abstracts International Vol. 61 no.9 March 2001
3. Dissertation Abstracts International Vol. 62 No. 2 August 2001
5. Dissertation Abstracts International Vol.62 no.10 April 2002
6. Dissertation Abstracts International Vol.62 No.12 June 2002
7. Dissertation Abstracts International Vol. 63 no.7 January 2003
8. Dissertation abstracts International Vol. 64 No: 2, August 2003.
9. Dissertation Abstracts International Vol.64 No.5 November 2003
10. Dissertation Abstracts International Vol.64 No.8 February 2004
11. Dissertation Abstracts International Vol. 65 no.3 September 2004
12. Dissertation Abstract International Vol. 65, no. 10 April 2005.
13. Dissertation Abstracts International Vol.66 no.6 December 2005.
14. Dissertation Abstracts International Vol.66 no.8 February 2006
15. Dissertation Abstracts International Vol.66 No.11May 2006
16. Dissertation Abstracts International Vol.67 no. 12 June 2007
17. Dissertation Abstract International Vol. 68 no.1 July 2007.
18. Dissertation Abstracts International Vol.68 No.5 November 2007
19. Dissertation abstracts International Vol.68 no.7 January'08.
20. Dissertation Abstracts International Vol.68 No.11 May 2008
21. Dissertation Abstracts International Vol.68, no.12 June 2008
22. Dissertation Abstracts International Vol.69, no;1, July 2008.
23. Dissertation Abstracts International Vol.69 No.2 August 2008

UNPUBLISHED DISSERTATION

Amutha Ranjini, G. and Sivakumar, D. (2007) Class room Environment and Academic Achievement in Biology of XI Standard in Thoothukudi District in Unpublished M.Ed Dissertation, Manonmanium Sundaranar University, Tirunelveli.

Bronfenbrenner, (1979), Impact of Environmental Factors on Academic Achievement of Higher Secondary Biology Students in Tirunelveli Educational District in Subaramanian, S. (2009) Unpublished M.Ed Dissertation Tamilnadu Teacher Education University, Chennai.

Jaganathan, *(1986), A Perception of Class room Environment among Higher Secondary Biology Students in Cuddalore District in Sivakumar, D.(2005)* Unpublished M.Ed. Dissertation, IASE, Madras University, Chennai.

Jain,*(1965), A Study of the Influence of Pupils Family Environment on their Academic Achievement in Science IX Standard in Kopperundevi, N.(2006) Unpublished M.phil Dissertation, Annamalai University, Chidambaram.*

Mohanty *(1991), A Study of Mental Health of B.Ed Students of Cuddalore District in Relation to their Self-Esteem in Adaikalam, (2006) Unpublished M.phil Dissertation Annamalai University, Chidambaram*

Patel, (1997), Study Habit and Achievement of IX Standard Students in Namakkal District in Moorthy, A.(2008) Unpublished M.Ed Dissertation Manonmanium Sundaranar University, Tirunelveli.

Reedy, M.N, (1977), Age and Sex Differences in Personal Needs and the Nature of Love. Unpublished Doctoral Thesis University of Southern California.

Ron Fry, (2000), Factors Influencing Scholastic Achievement of the Dalit Students in Southern (dt) Andhra Pradesh in Sagayaraj S.J (2006) Unpublished Doctoral Thesis, Manonmanium Sundaranar University Tirunelveli

Rosari, Gnandevan, R. *(2006)* A Study on Social Intelligence and Family Environment of College Students. Unpublished M.phil Dissertation Annamalai University, Chidambaram.

Stanley, (1978), A Critical Study of the Influence of Socio–Economic Status on Academic Achievement of Higher Secondary Students in Rural and Urban Areas of Kanpur in Misra, M. (1986) Unpublished Doctoral Thesis, Kanpur University.

Suresh Bhatnagar (1990) A Study of Achievement in Science Related to Scientific Aptitude and Scientific Attitude in High School Students in Cuddalore District in Sivakumar, D. (2007) *Unpublished M.phil Dissertation, Annamalai University, Chidambaram.*

Thilagavathi, Andal, M. (1995), A Study of Academic Achievement of Adolescents in Relation to their Cognitive Style Locus of Control, Self-Esteem and Mental Health Unpublished Doctoral Thesis, Annamalai University, Chidambaram.

Vasanthi Vinoliya, A.D and **Sivakumar, D** (2009), Influence of Self-Esteem on Academic Achievement of Higher Secondary Students Tuticorin District. Unpublished M.Ed. Dissertation Tamilnadu Teacher Education University, Chennai.

REPORTS

Chief Educational Office, (2008), List of the Higher Secondary Schools, Kanyakumari District.

Chief Educational Office, (2008), List of the Higher Secondary Schools, Tirunelveli District.

Chief Educational Office, (2008), List of the Higher Secondary Schools, Tuticorin District.

Government of India, (1966), Report of the Education Commission (1964-66), Ministry of Education, New Delhi.

WEBSITES

www.Edgate
www.Edword
www.Indina.edu.cfs
www.Moped .com
www.yahoo.com
www.Google.com
www.eric.ed.gov.in
www.apa.org
www.wikipedia.com
www.chssc.salford.ac.uk.

Index

ENTERPRISE RESOURCE PLANNING PROJECT